Contents

		Page
	Acknowledgements	9
1.	Introduction	13
2.	Sources	16
3.	Growing up in Denbigh	25
4.	The March to War	40
5.	Enlisting	48
6.	Training for the Cavalry	61
7.	To France with 3rd Dragoon Guards	71
8.	On the Home Front	85
9.	Officer Training	93
10.	To France with 2RWF	111
11.	Advance to Victory	123
12.	The Final Battle	137
13.	News of Cyril's death reaches Home	144
14.	Back at Home	151
15.	Epilogue	160

Appendices

I	Breakdown of Cyril's wartime service	163
II	Transcripts of various letters referred to in the text	165
III	Composite extract from War Diaries	187

Bibliography   245

Maps

		Page
1.	Britain and the Western Front	15
2.	Cyril and the Cavalry	73
3.	Cyril and 2RWF	113
4.	Cyril and 2RWF: The Hundred Days Advance	125

List of Photographs

		Page
	Frontispiece: Cyril Keepfer	11
1.	Denbigh, 1903	24
2.	Neustadt im Schwarzwald	27
3.	Cyril's father and the family shop	27
4.	Cyril and siblings, 1907	28
5.	County School Examination results, 1907	35
6.	Denbigh County School football XI, 1910–1911	36
7.	Cyril as a young man in London	36
8.	Cyril and his family	38
9.	Cyril astride a horse at the Canterbury barracks	65
10.	Cyril in the dress uniform of a trooper in 3rd Dragoon Guards	67
11.	Cyril as a trooper in 3rd Dragoon Guards	67
12.	Cyril and John, 1915	68
13.	The 'Boll' postcard	90
14.	Cyril and his Sunday School friend, Tom Gee, 1915	103
15.	Cyril at home on leave, 1917	104
16.	Cyril at Romford—I	104
17.	Cyril at Romford—II	104
18.	Cyril and Ivor Watkins, 1917	105
19.	Cyril's officer's watch	105
20.	Cyril's binoculars	105
21.	Newly commissioned 2nd Lieut. Cyril Keepfer	106

22.	Christmas Card sent home by Cyril, 1917	116
23.	The last known photograph of Cyril	130
24.	Cyril's 38 (Welsh) Division shoulder patch	136
25.	Cyril's grave at Englefontaine	143
26.	Cyril's grave at the Montay-Neuvilly War Cemetery	156
27.	Memorial Shrine to the Denbigh War Dead	157
28.	Denbigh War Memorial	158
29.	Cyril's mother's grave, St Marcella's, Denbigh	161
30.	L'Anneau de la Mémoire	244
31.	Enlarged panel of the L'Anneau de la Mémoire	244

Acknowledgements

I wish to acknowledge the support and encouragement given to me by my mother and my sister, Pauline, who encouraged me to write this account of Cyril's life; the late Major Mike Peacock who read, and commented upon, earlier drafts of this book from the perspective of the military history of the First World War —his comments were invaluable to me as a non-military person; R. M. (Bobi) Owen who gave valuable comments upon Denbigh at the time and read an early draft of this book; the staff at the National Archives at Kew, who made available to me numerous record files; the Museum of the Royal Welch Fusiliers at Bodelwyddan, who searched several of their records on my behalf; and Dr. Paul Evans of Denbigh High School who looked through that school's archival records for references to Cyril. Dr. Colin Newbury and Jacqueline Newbury assisted me with the translation of curé Flament's letters to Cyril's father; and my nephews, Adam Field and Samuel Keepfer Field, and R. M. Owen who assisted with the translation of Welsh texts into English. I must also thank Daniella and Francis Keepfer for making available to me certain letters and photographs concerning Cyril. Alison Davies of The Mapping Company provided the maps that are included in this book. Finally, my thanks are also due to Alister Williams of Bridge Books for not only guiding me through the publication process but also providing interpretative comment on certain aspects and suggesting additional sources to consult.

I must also thank my partner, Shi Dazhi, for his unfailing support as I wrote this book and for his taking the time to proof-read the final draft. Of course, I alone am responsible for any errors or inaccuracies in the final version.

Christopher Keepfer Roberts,
August 2017

Formal photograph of Cyril retained, and framed, by the family in his memory. The back was inscribed "Dear Cyril, killed 4th Nov 1918" and used to hang in his family home, Derwenfa. The same photograph was also used in various memorial publications and the War Memorial erected in Denbigh County School.

1. INTRODUCTION

The Nation is currently commemorating the events of the Great War. My mother's elder half-brother served in the British Army for over four years before being killed in one of the final battles of the war. That battle, in turn, evidenced that the British Army had, by the final stages of the war, become a very capable army and one able to execute the most complex of operations. It was a tragedy that Cyril died as negotiations for an Armistice were under way and just seven days before hostilities ceased.

Cyril Keepfer was an ordinary Denbigh boy born and bred. He lived through three tumultuous decades at the close of the nineteenth and the beginning of the twentieth centuries. This book aims to share his experiences with younger generations thereby enabling them to place his short life in the context of those times and the local, national and world influences upon them.

The war was the first time that Britain needed a mass mobilisation of its civilian resources in order to win a war. Cyril was part of this mobilisation, first as an early volunteer for Kitchener's New Armies and then as a junior officer in France. Coming from a very *petit bourgeois* background, he demonstrated the skills to become a competent soldier, a leader of men and an officer in a Regular Army battalion.

In 1887, his grandfather, Wilhelm Keepfer, could proudly display a banner '*Lang Lebe Unsere Gnadige Königen*' above his clockmaker and jeweller's shop on the High Street in Denbigh congratulating Queen Victoria on her Golden Jubilee. Thirty-one years later, as the Great War was ending, Cyril lay dead from friendly fire on the Fields of Flanders. His life, in its own small way, reflects the geo-political changes sweeping through Europe at the time. In foreign relations, Britain was transitioning from 'splendid isolation' with a foreign policy displaying (if not exactly a pro-German line) something of an anti-French and anti-Russian bias through an increasing suspicion of the Kaiser's Germany and its *Weltpolitik* into the *Entente Cordiale* and, finally, a declaration of war on Germany in August 1914.

Domestically, British political and social conditions were also changing with increased trades union militancy, major constitutional changes afoot and the beginnings of the welfare state.

Britain and the Western Front.

2. SOURCES

The First World War is one of the most written about events in history. It is also one upon which there is almost no agreement surrounding the causes or, in many cases, the flow of developments through the war. To date, little has been published purely on the Denbigh boys and men generally who fought in the Great War, although Cliff Kearns' recent work[1] is a partial attempt to remedy this omission. It follows on from Peter Glynn's work which focuses on those Denbigh-ites who served in 4th Battalion of the Royal Welsh Fusiliers (RWF).[2] The material for this book has been sourced from a mixture of primary and secondary sources.

Our direct links with Cyril are a handful of letters written by him to family members whilst he was in the Army. In addition, we have letters written to his father by three fellow soldiers after his death and two letters written by the parish priest at Englefontaine where Cyril fell and was initially buried. The latter two are just the one-sided remains of correspondence between Cyril's father and the parish priest concerning the location of Cyril's grave and the nature of the countryside in which he fell. The longer letters have been transcribed and are set out in Appendix II. Certain staff records relating to Cyril and minutes of board meetings of his employer are also available at the London Metropolitan Archives.

Primary sources also include local newspapers—principally, the *Denbighshire Free Press,* the *North Wales Times* and *Baner ac Amserau*

---

1. Kearns, Cliff, *A Town at War – Denbigh and the Western Front* (Denbigh: Dol Awel Publishing, 2016).
2. Glynn, Peter, *All That We Have We Gave: Denbigh Territorials in the 4th (Denbighshire) Battalion The Royal Welsh Fusiliers* (Denbigh: Gee and Sons Limited, 1999; updated and extended: Kindle Edition, 2017) (Glynn).

Cymru, popularly known as *Y Faner*. While the newspaper reports are broadly accurate, it is clear that the reporters' attention (or that of their informants) to an accurate reporting of detail was often lacking. Thus, the detail of the various newspaper reports should always be treated with a degree of caution.

We are also fortunate to have Cyril's War Office papers[3] amongst the records kept at the National Archives at Kew as over half the War Office's records on individual officers were destroyed during the Blitz in the Second World War. These papers provide us with the key information regarding Cyril's enlistment and service — albeit with some inconsistencies (doubtless the result of confusion from the work pressure at the time) and giving rise to further questions. Frustratingly, in a note on the front cover, the file also suggests that, when it was stored in 1934, it was 'weeded' of 134 pages which were then destroyed. The remaining papers are mainly his Attestation Form on enlistment, his application for a commission and a disproportionate number of papers dealing with the calculation, and settlement of, amounts due on his death and the administration of his effects.

The National Archives also holds the war diaries of units that fought in the war.[4] Cyril served in the 3rd (Prince of Wales's) Dragoon Guards (3DG) and in the 2nd Battalion, Royal Welsh[5] Fusiliers (2RWF). In addition, I have consulted the higher-level war diaries of the brigades and divisions of which 3DG and 2RWF were part. These place the role of the regiment and battalion within a

---

3. WO 339/99563.
4. For those unable to access the National Archives easily, The Naval & Military Press Limited has, in recent years, also published facsimile copies of various war diaries. Ones relevant to Cyril's time with 3DG and 2RWF are listed in the Biblio-graphy.
5. The spelling of 'Welsh' is inconsistent. The old English spelling when the regiment was originally raised was 'Welch.' The regiment was attached to this spelling and stuck steadfastly by it; but, in official records during the First World War, the spelling was always 'Welsh.' For consistency with the official records, I have adhered to the contemporary official spelling. This was changed to 'Welch' only in 1920 by Army Order N°· 56.
6. Detailed citations from the war diaries are not given; but the war diaries were comp-

wider context. We are fortunate to have a complete set of war diaries for 3DG and 2RWF (and their associated brigades and divisions) covering the period of Cyril's service with them. Appendix III is a composite summary of those war diaries that are relevant to units in which Cyril served and the description of his time in France is based upon those war diaries.[6]

Every battalion, brigade and division maintained war diaries on pre-printed flimsy forms. War diaries were meant to be completed on a daily basis and to be a record of the unit concerned's involvement in the field and to record significant happenings affecting the unit. These were variously handwritten or typed[7] up by the relevant adjutant and counter-signed or initialled by the relevant commanding officer. Inevitably, they vary in quality depending upon the person who had the prime responsibility for their maintenance. War diaries were rarely maintained while a unit was at home in Great Britain so we have no equivalent records of Cyril's time at home or during his training —neither his initial cavalry training nor his officer training.

As for secondary sources, I have considered a number of regimental histories of the two regiments in which Cyril served. Both regiments are the subjects of such histories; indeed, the RWF is one of the most written about regiments in the British Army.

During the 1920 and 1930s, many units, from divisions down to regiments and battalions, caused accounts to be written of that unit's service in the Great War. These accounts are based partly upon the unit concerned's war diaries and partly upon personal memories of contributors to the various publications. Regimental histories tend to suffer from two failings that frustrate anyone seeking to write about a particular individual: first, they are

---

leted chronologically so it is easy to find the relevant entries in Appendix III.

7. All were handwritten in the early days of the war; but, as the war progressed, typewriters became available to units—starting with divisions before trickling down to lower units.
8. Munby, Lieut. Col. J. E., *A History of the 38th (Welsh) Division by the G.S.O.s I of the*

'corporate' histories and do not focus on individuals; and secondly, even where they do, they tend to focus on officers—not other ranks. This second failing is due to the fact that other ranks were only exceptionally referred to by individual name in the war diaries. Also, not unnaturally, it is sometimes difficult to see a particular incident or action in its wider context.

Two books which are helpful in placing 2RWF and 38th (Welsh) Division in the Western Front's wider context are: J. E. Munby's *History of the 38th (Welsh) Division*[8] and Depree's *A History of the 38th (Welsh) and 33rd Divisions in the last five weeks of the Great War*.[9] The former is a very short history of 38th (Welsh) Division —its formation and principal operations in France, whilst the latter, as its name implies, covers just the last five weeks of the war. During this period, the two named divisions, which formed V Corps' right wing, continuously 'leap-frogged' each other as part of the British Third Army's final advance as it fought its way through the last German pre-prepared defences and broke out into open countryside. Of particular interest for any study of Cyril is Depree's description of how 2RWF fitted into the greater scheme of this Allied advance and his description of the part played by 2RWF in the Battle of the Sambre —the last set battle of the war— in which Cyril fell.[10]

John Clayton has studied the wider picture of this battle and compared the parts played by, and the relative performance of, the various British units in it.[11] So far as that part of the battle near

---

Division (London: Hugh Rees. Ltd, 1920; reprinted: Uckfield, The Naval & Military Press Limited, 2003) (Munby).

9. Depree, Maj. Gen. H. D., *A History of the 38th (Welsh) and 33rd Divisions in the last five weeks of the Great War* (originally published in the *Journal of the Royal Artillery* over five issues in 1931 and 1932 (Vol LVIII No. 3 pages 332–74 and N°· 4 pages 448–95, and Vol. LIX No. 1 pages 46–69, N°· 2 pages 168–97, and N°· 3 pages 310–36; reprinted as a single volume—Eastbourne: The Naval & Military Press Ltd., 2017) (Depree).
10. ibid, pages 168–97.
11. Clayton, John Derek, 'The Battle of the Sambre, 4 November 1918' (PhD diss, University of Birmingham, 2015) (Clayton).
12. Bickersteth, J. B., *History of the 6th Cavalry Brigade 1914–1918* (London: The Baynard

Englefontaine is concerned, he draws heavily on Depree's work and the relevant units' war diaries. As such, he adds little to the context of Cyril's death, but his evaluation of the fighting effectiveness of the various British units engaged in the battle is of interest.

Much less has been written regarding 3DG than 2RWF. This is, principally, a reflection of the restricted role played by the cavalry on the Western Front after the end of 1914 when trenches stretched from the North Sea to Switzerland.

J. B. Bickersteth wrote the history of 6th Cavalry Brigade in 1920.[12] Then, in the mid 1930s, H. P. Holt wrote a short history of 3DG and the war;[13] but, just 13 pages[14] (out of a total of 124) and 10 pages[15] (out of a total of 112 pages) respectively cover Cyril's time with 3DG. In 1966, L. B. Oatts covered the whole of the First World War in just 47 pages in his regimental history of the 3rd Carabiniers (into which 3DG was amalgamated in 1922).[16] Anglesey's magisterial work on the history of the British cavalry[17] draws, in turn, largely upon Bickersteth and Holt for his description of the role of 3DG and 6th Cavalry Brigade in the war.

Two reasons why the cavalry receives such little focus in histories of the Great War are: first, a view that, after the War's initial phase, the cavalry did 'nothing except look after their horses in the back areas;'[18] and the sheer preponderance of the infantry. The result has been that 'there are few subjects where prejudice had a clearer run

---

Press, 1920) (Bickersteth).
13. Holt, H. P., *The History of the 3rd (Prince of Wales's) Dragoon Guards 1914–1918* (published privately) (Holt).
14. Bickersteth, pages 41–54.
15. Holt, pages 39–48.
16. Oatts, Lewis Balfour, *I Serve: Regimental History of the 3rd Carabiniers (Prince of Wales Dragoon Guards)* (Norwich: 1966) (Oatts); pages 196–240.
17. Anglesey, Marquess of, *A History of the British Cavalry;* Vol. 7, The Curragh Incident and the Western Front 1914, and Vol. 8, The Western Front 1915–1918, Epilogue 1919–1939 (Anglesey, Vol. 8) (London: Leo Cooper 1996 and 1997, respectively).
18. Bickersteth, page ix.
19. Kenyon, David, *Horsemen in No Man's Land: British Cavalry & Trench Warfare 1914–*

than with the mounted arm in the First World War.'[19] This means that the cavalry is omitted from much of the more detailed research that has been conducted into the various fighting arms in the war. Although there has been a re-evaluation of the competence of commanders generally during the last 20 to 30 years, there was no major re-examination of the cavalry until Kenyon and Badsey.[20] More recent works on the cavalry and the First World War have focused on particular aspects of the cavalry in general and not on the role of particular units. It, therefore, requires recourse to a number of works to assess just what Cyril's life in the cavalry might have been like; and there is still little written on the detailed training of the cavalryman —as opposed to the infantryman.

Dudley Ward's *Regimental Records of the Royal Welch Fusiliers Vol. III, 1914 – 1918 France and Flanders* was published first in 1928.[21] It is less of a narrative book; rather, an extraction of records and commentary. As its name implies, it is a record not just of 2RWF but of the whole regiment's participation in the war on the Western Front. Besides drawing heavily on the war diaries, it also reflects various private written accounts of the time. These latter accounts also appear to some extent in other works, particularly *The War The Infantry Knew*. There is, thus, some overlap between this work and subsequent ones. Just under a quarter of the volume covers the period when Cyril was posted to the RWF.[22]

The RWF were, of course, the basis of much of the narrative in Robert Graves's *Goodbye to All That* and a much smaller element of Siegfried Sassoon's *Memoirs of an Infantry Officer*, first published in

---

1918 (Barnsley: Pen & Sword Military, 2011) (*Horsemen*), citing Richard Holmes on page 1.
20. *Horsemen*, page 1. The reference to Badsey is to Badsey, Stephen, *Doctrine and Reform in the British Cavalry, 1880–1918* (Aldershot, Ashgate, 2008).
21. Ward, Dudley, *Regimental Records of the Royal Welch Fusiliers*, Vol. III, 1914–1918, France and Flanders (reprinted Uckfield: The Naval & Military Press Ltd., 2005) (Ward).
22. Pages 361–491.
23. Neither author's service with 2RWF overlapped with Cyril. Robert Graves served

1929 and 1930 respectively.[23] In turn, they were the trigger for James Dunn's great work, *The War The Infantry Knew*,[24] which was first published in 1938 and written as a counter-point to the pictures painted by Graves and Sassoon. Dunn portrayed what he saw as the real story of life in 2RWF. His work, based, in part, upon the battalion's official war diaries but also, substantially, upon his own recollections as the battalion's medical officer and the memories of over 50 others (of all ranks) who had served in the battalion, is now the standard reference work and starting point for anyone considering 2RWF and the First World War. Dunn follows 2RWF on a day by day basis but his real bonus is the 'colour' that he gives to life in the battalion, his comments upon morale and discipline (which were not always of the highest), officers' views of their superiors and his descriptions of the countryside in which the battalion fought —items that cannot be expected to be found in the war diaries. Pages 406 to 565 (out of a total of 583 pages) cover Cyril's time with 2RWF.

A more idiosyncratic and individual narrative of the battalion's service through the war is Frank Richards's *Old Soldiers Never Die* published in response to Sassoon's work. In it, Richards, a reservist re-called to the Colours on the outbreak of the war, describes life in the battalion from an ordinary soldier's perspective. Pages 242–312 cover the period during which Cyril served with 2RWF, with pages 309–12 covering the battle in which Cyril fell.

More recently, David Langley used the battalion's war diaries, *The War The Infantry Knew* and other War Office papers in the National Archives concerning individual officers to consider the

---

in 2RWF from September to November 1915, when he transferred to 1st Battalion RWF, and temporarily for short periods in July 1916 and January and February 1917. Siegfried Sassoon served with 2RWF for just over a month in the Spring of 1917, from 13 March to 16 April.

24. Dunn, J. C., *The War The Infantry Knew 1914–1919; a Chronicle of Service in France and Belgium* (reprinted: London: Jane's Publishing Company Limited, 1987) (Dunn).

25. Langley, David, *Duty Done: 2nd Battalion, The Royal Welch Fusiliers in the Great War*

battalion's social make-up.[25] The War Office papers relate only to officers as (apart from medal papers) the War Office rarely retained papers relating to individual other rankers.

In 1989, Michael Glover published *That Astonishing Infantry, The History of the Royal Welch Fusiliers* which was updated by Jonathon Riley in 2008.[26] As its name implies, it covers the whole of the RWF and not just 2RWF. However, for the general reader, it places 2RWF very much in a broader context when describing its role in the war.

In recent years, in connection with the centenary commemorations, a whole slew of books on different aspects of the Great War has come off the production line. It would be impossible to try to list them all, although some are mentioned in the Bibliography. *The British Army and the First World War*[27] is a particularly good general overview of the war as a whole and synthesis of recent more detailed works on particular aspects of the war. Of particular interest to Welsh readers is Robin Barlow's *Wales and World War One*[28] which seeks to re-examine some of the existing general assumptions about Wales and the Great War.

Although not of direct relevance to Cyril, a book of local interest to Denbigh-ites is Capt. Ellis's history of the 4th (Denbighshire) Battalion of the RWF,[29] of which the original D Company (when that battalion was still constituted on the basis of eight companies) was designated the Denbigh Company as it recruited largely from that town. Ellis provides a very vivid picture of aspects of the war with which Cyril would have been all too familiar: from initial

---

(Caernarfon: The Trustees, The Royal Welch Fusiliers Museum, 2001) (*Duty Done*).

26. Glover, Michael and Riley, Jonathon, *'That Astonishing Infantry': The History of the Royal Welch Fusiliers 1689–2006* (Barnsley: Pen & Sword Military, 2006) (Glover and Riley).

27. Beckett, Ian, Brown, Timothy and Connell, Mark, *The British Army and the First World War* (Cambridge: Cambridge University Press, 2017) (*The British Army*).

28. Barlow, Robin, *Wales and World War One* (Llandysul: Gomer Press, 2014) (Barlow).

29. Ellis, Capt. C., *The 4th (Denbighshire) Battalion Royal Welsh Fusiliers in the Great War* (Wrexham: Woodall, Minshall, Thomas and Co., Ltd., Principality Press, 1926) (Ellis).

mobilisation and training in camp, through route marches to and from the front line, daily life in the trenches, digging parties and the chaos of battle.

Finally, I have relied upon family lore for one or two aspects. Although it is often incorrect as a matter of detail when reference is made to the other sources, it usually has a resonance in those other sources.

1. Denbigh, 1903.
The card shows the High Street and an oblique view of the family shop—the third building from the right with a clock face on the wall. Addressed to Cyril at his Nain's in Cyffylliog, the card was franked at 2.00pm at Denbigh on 6 August 1903—a Thursday

3. GROWING UP IN DENBIGH

Cyril Keepfer grew up in Denbigh in the last part of the nineteenth century in a Germano-Welsh family. His grandfather, Wilhelm Keepfer was what, today, we would call an 'economic migrant.' In 1853,[1] Wilhelm Keepfer, then aged 17, came over with his father (John, or Johann) from the small town of Neustadt in the Black Forest (or Schwarzwald) in the Breisgau region of the then independent Grand Duchy of Baden[2] to settle in Denbigh where they established a clockmaker and jeweller's shop, first in Panton Hall before moving to High Street. They were part of a number of German immigrants —all clockmakers, watchmakers and jewellers — who settled in North Wales and the greater Liverpool area around this time.[3]

1. Copies of old invoices issued by the jewellers shop variously state its establishment date as 1850 and 1852. We can be fairly certain that Wilhelm came to the UK in 1853 because a clock-maker, Wilhelm Küpfer from Baden, is recorded on the List of Alien Arrivals as having arrived at Dover on the *Chemin de Fer Belge* ferry from Ostend on 17 March 1853. Those lists record eight Küpfers from Germany (sic — even though it did not then exist as a country) and Switzerland as having entered the UK between 1840 and 1860. Three references can be discarded as clearly not relating to either Wilhelm or his father; but two of the other references to a Küpfer arriving on 28 July and 1 October 1851 from Ostend, again on a *Chemin de Fer Belge* ferry, and from Calais on the *Garland* respectively could well be references to Wilhelm or his father. The three lists providing even this information were all completed to different degrees of completeness so it may well be that either not all lists of aliens landing at Channel ports were completed or, if completed, not all were retained.
2. Baden was an independent member state of the German Confederation that had been established by the Congress of Vienna in 1815. In 1871, Baden (along with the other remaining independent German states) became part of the Prussian dominated Second German Empire.
3. For a fuller discussion of clock and watch-makers in Denbigh and the wider Vale of Clwyd area in the nineteenth century, see Parker, Paul, *Clockmaking in the Vale*

Wilhelm quickly adapted to his new home; he became fluent in both English and Welsh; and participated fully in Denbigh life: serving for several years as a private in the Denbighshire Rifle Volunteers;[4] on the local School Board for nine years from 1886; and, as a councillor and alderman, on the Town Council for a total of twelve years from 1886 to 1895 and 1898 to 1901, respectively. Despite adapting to his adopted homeland, Wilhelm retained his links with other members of this German immigrant community. He married Elizabeth Booz —the daughter of fellow German settlers from Hesse— in 1864, and maintained close friendships with other German settlers in North Wales and the Liverpool area. He also regularly employed German apprentices in his Denbigh shop —the most noted of whom, Jakob Bauer (anglicised as Jacob Bower), gave his name to Bower's Villas off Lenton Pool in Denbigh, where he lived in Cynhassedd.

From around the time they arrived in Denbigh, Wilhelm and his father anglicised their German surname of Küpfer as Keepfer, but both usages are regularly found in local records and newspapers until around 1870 when Wilhelm appears to have adopted Keepfer solely and we find no further references to Küpfer. It is unclear just what precipitated this change: it may be that, with his marriage in 1864 and the birth of four children in the late 1860s, he simply accepted the fact that he would not be returning to his native land —although the absence of any records for his father after around

---

of Clwyd (Denbigh: published privately, 1993); pages 51–61 have an extensive commentary on Wilhelm Keepfer. Iorweth Peate's *Clock and Watch Makers in Wales* (Cardiff: National Museum of Wales, 1975) also refers to Johann and Wilhelm Keepfer.

4. He was listed —as a private— as one of the original members of the Denbighshire Rifle Volunteers when the corps was first founded in 1859; article recounting the 50th anniversary of the corps' founding, 3 July 1909, *Denbighshire Free Press* (FP). Wilhelm was also recorded as being a member of the corps at a festive dinner held jointly with the Ruthin corps in 1866; 24 November 1866, *Carnarvon & Denbigh Herald and North & South Wales Independent*. A brief description of the Denbighshire Rifle Volunteers is contained in Westlake, Ray, *Tracing the Rifle Volunteers: A Guide for Military and Family Historians* (Barnsley: Pen & Sword Books Limited, 2010), pages 57 and 58.

2. Neustadt im Schwarzwald.

3. Cyril's father and the family shop.

4. *Cyril and siblings, 1907.*
L–R: *Josephine Diamond (so named because she was born in 1897, the year of Queen Victoria's Diamond Jubilee. She was known within the family as Josie), Cyril and Phyllis who is holding John. (We can date this to shortly after John's birth on 21 April 1907; around the time that Cyril passed his scholarship examination for the County School.)*

1855 suggests that his father may well have returned to Germany. It may also be connected with the formation of the Prussian dominated Second German Empire in 1871 upon which, as a Roman Catholic south German, Wilhelm may not have looked with favour. He would not have been the only German to have viewed the Prussian aggrandisement with alarm and distaste —although his family photograph album contained photographs of Prince Otto von Bismarck and Count Helmuth von Moltke,[5] the two key creators of the Second German Empire.

Wilhelm was clearly proud of his German heritage and background. Hence, his banner celebrating Queen Victoria's Golden Jubilee which, he was keen to explain to the local newspaper, the *Denbighshire Free Press*, meant 'God Save our Gracious Queen.'[6] In the 1890s, he went back to Germany on a visit to his homeland[7] and he named his final home in Denbigh in Broomhill Lane as Schwarzwald Cottage in memory of his birthplace.

Despite living all his adult life in Denbigh, Wilhelm appears not to have become naturalised[8] and he classified himself as a German national in the 1911 Census.[9] This is less surprising in the nineteenth century than it would be today as that was a time when migrants

---

5. Usually referred to as 'the Elder Moltke' to distinguish him from his nephew ('the Younger Moltke') who was Chief of the German General Staff at the outbreak of the Great War.
6. 25 June 1887, *FP*. Strictly, of course, the translation is 'Long Live our Gracious Queen.'
7. But, as evidence for the incompleteness of the lists of aliens arriving at British ports, there is no record of his return from Germany after this trip.
8. At least there is no record of any application for, or grant of, letters of naturalisation or denizenship in the National Archives for Wilhelm. A letter writer to *The North Wales Times* (*NWT*), 17 April 1897, also stated that he was 'a German by nationality.'
9. The 1911 census was the first census to require individuals to state their nationality —doubtless as a result of the passing of the Aliens Act 1905, which was designed to restrict the entry of alien criminals and paupers into the country— but in earlier censuses the enumerator had added the initials 'FS' or 'NBS' (Foreign Subject or Non British Subject) against his place of birth. So, it appears that some account was being taken even before 1911 of an individual's nationality.

and foreign travellers did not need passports to cross frontiers[10] or to settle in other countries. But, this fact was held against him when he was proposed as candidate for the Denbigh mayoralty in 1894.[11] Of course, all Wilhelm's children and grandchildren were British subjects by virtue of having been born in Britain.

Cyril, born William Robert Cyril,[12] was born on 20 October 1894, the son of William (or Willie) Leopold and Elizabeth (or Lizzie) Keepfer. William Leopold was the second child, and only son, of Wilhelm. He was born in 1868 and christened Wilhelm Leopold but, from very early on, his name was anglicised as William Leopold and he grew up speaking English and Welsh. His entry in the 1911 Census also shows that he claimed to speak German. This would be unsurprising given that both his parents were native Germans, although there is no evidence that he used these language skills[13] and the 1901 census records him as just speaking English and Welsh. He was educated at Mount St Mary, a Jesuit boarding school in Derbyshire.

In 1892, William married Elizabeth Lloyd from Cyffylliog. The marriage was what would, at that time, have been regarded as a

10. Although passports had been required by Britain from time to time prior to (and, then, during) the Napoleonic Wars, their need was dropped for most of the nineteenth century until re-introduced during the Great War when passports came to be used pretty much as they are today.
11. 17 November 1894, FP.
12. Presumably, he was named William after his father and paternal grandfather; Robert after J. R. (Robert) Owen who was a friend of both his parents and his grandfather and whose general grocery shop, Star Shop, on High Street was next door but one to the Keepfers' jewellers shop and who was to live next door to the Keepfers at Haulfryn; but I have been unable to determine why he was named Cyril.
13. In the 1911 Census, his sister, Sister Mary Josephine at St Clare's Convent, Pantasaph stated she (like all the other sisters there) spoke only English. Given that there is no consistency on the subject of languages spoken between the different census records for both Cyril's father and grandfather, one must assume that either this question was somewhat haphazardly answered by respondents generally or the answers were filtered by the enumerators. In short, we should not rely totally upon the census records as to an individual's linguistic abilities.

'mixed marriage' in that William Leopold was a member of one of the few Roman Catholic families in Denbigh while Elizabeth was a Calvinistic Methodist and a member of Capel Mawr.[14] It is clear that both families reached a compromise on the subject of religion as the marriage took place in a Registry Office and it was agreed (contrary to what would have been Roman Catholic teaching and practice at the time) that the issue of the marriage would all be brought up attending Capel Mawr. Today, the majority of people in this country think little of religious differences; but, at that time, it was no small matter —especially in Wales. Cyril would have grown up only too well aware of the suspicion and distrust of, and intolerance for, Roman Catholics by many in Denbigh and the wider community —particularly amongst non-conformists, who formed the majority of the town's population. His grandfather, Wilhelm, had fought long and hard on the Town Council in 1888/9 against Thomas Gee, one of Wales's leading Non-conformists, to have part of the new municipal cemetery on Ystrad Road dedicated to the use of Roman Catholics. Despite the law allowing this being quite clear, Gee — who was all for Non-conformists' rights— opposed any concession to Roman Catholicism.[15] Then, just after Cyril was born, Wilhelm had been denied the mayoralty of the borough on two essential grounds: his religion and his German nationality.[16]

14. The principal centre for Calvinistic Methodist (or Presbyterian) worship in Denbigh, Capel Mawr was the largest Non-conformist chapel in Denbigh and was a well-known congregation throughout North Wales.
15. The debates in the Town Council were extensively covered in the *Denbighshire Free Press* at the time. Wilhelm's contribution to the Roman Catholic cause was noted in the Register of Deaths of St Joseph's (the Roman Catholic parish church in Denbigh) with a handwritten note affixed to that Register in the appropriate place:
'Memo October 6th, 1889
The portion of the new cemetery which was secured to us through the efforts of Mr Wm. Keepfer was solemnly blessed according to the form prescribed in the Roman Ritual on Sunday 6th October 1889, in virtue of faculties received by me from the Bishop for this ceremony.
J. Smallwood, S.J.'
16. The voting was 8:7 against Wilhelm's nomination as Mayor. The Town Council appears

Another cultural difference between Cyril's parents background was politics. His mother came from a Liberal background and was active in the Denbigh Women's Liberal Association[17] while his paternal grandfather was a strong Tory. My sense has always been that his father was also a Tory; but, probably, not as involved in the cause as his grandfather. Cyril's father, having seen how Wilhelm had been treated in Town Council politics, stayed clear of local and national politics throughout his life.

Cyril was born at home in Derwen House, 6 Beacons Hill,[18] where his parents lived before 1904 when the family moved to Derwenfa,[19] one of two semi-detached houses (the other being Haulfryn) built at the top of Bryn Dedwydd by his parents and J. R. Owen. Cyril's mother was related through marriage to the Owens, who also had Cyffylliog roots.[20]

Cyril's sisters, Phyllis and Josephine, were born in 1893 and 1897 respectively. A younger brother, John, was born in 1907. From around 1890, Cyril's father took principal charge of running the family shop. The business provided the family with an adequate *petit bourgeois* standard of living. His parents were both very much part of the Denbigh community; his father as a member of the Reading and Recreation Rooms Committee and of the Denbigh Cricket Club and his mother at Capel Mawr.

During his early years, Cyril's name crops up frequently in the

---

    to have split along Anglican and Roman Catholic v. non-conformist lines —which, despite all councilors being nominally Independents, may well also have mirrored a more general Tory-Liberal divide. One opponent argued that Wilhelm Keepfer's 'being a German and being a Roman Catholic must be a very great drawback and inconvenience, to put it in a very moderate way;' 17 November 1894, *FP*.

17. 13 November 1897, *FP*.
18. 26 October 1894, *Llangollen Advertiser Denbighshire Merionethshire and Wales Journal* and 27 October 1894, *FP*. The house, which no longer bears that name, is a couple of doors down from Capel Mawr on the southern side of Beacon's Hill.
19. Presumably, the family chose the name Derwenfa (place of the oak) as it was similar to the name of their former house, Derwen House (Oak House) in Beacons Hill.
20. Her father (John Lloyd)'s second wife (Kitty Griffiths) was Robert Owen's first wife.

local Press in connection with the Sunday School at Capel Mawr, where his mother was a leading member of the ladies section and keenly involved in the Sunday Schools,[21] and winning a number of prizes and awards over the years. He came second in the under 10 category at the annual Competitive Meeting for the Capel Mawr Sunday School in March 1904.[22] Later that year, Cyril and his friend, Thomas Gee (generally known as Tom Gee),[23] were listed as passing and winning awards in the Vale of Clwyd C.M. Scriptural examinations for children under ten years of age.[24] In 1909, he won a prize for a violin solo.[25] The next year, he was listed as fourth in Section IX of the Vale of Clwyd (C.M.) senior Sunday School Examination.[26]

His general education began at the Love Lane School. This was a School Board school unaffiliated to the Anglican schools in the town. School Boards had been set up after the Elementary Education Act 1870 to administer non-denominational (more specifically, non-Anglican doctrine) schools and Board members were directly elected by local ratepayers. When the local, seven-member School Board was first established in Denbigh, the various denominations in Denbigh agreed a carve-up of the seven places on the Board and Cyril's grandfather had been elected —in effect, to represent the Roman Catholic interest. This was a minority interest in Denbigh;[27] the principal division being between Anglicans

---

21. For example, she is listed as an adjudicator for the Prose and Scriptural examinations in 1904; 5 March 1904, *FP*.
22. 5 March 1904, *FP*.
23. Tom Gee was the grandson of the Thomas Gee with whom Cyril's grandfather had battled over the Denbigh Cemetery. The friendships were definitely more on Cyril's mother's —Capel Mawr— side than on his father's side of the family.
24. 25 June 1904, *FP*. His sister, Josephine, won a prize in the under eight category.
25. 13 March 1909, *FP*.
26. 28 May 1910, *FP*.
27. There were just 30 Roman Catholic school pupils in Denbigh at the time; 11 December 1886, *FP*.
28. The Church of England was only dis-established in Wales in 1919 when it became the Church in Wales.

(and the Church of England[28] supported schools) and the Nonconformists.

At that time, children were required to stay at school until the age of twelve[29] and the Love Lane School accommodated children up to that age. The Welsh Intermediate Education Act of 1889 had allowed county councils in Wales to make provision for certain of the older children to attend a local grammar school and Denbighshire County Council had established County Schools at Denbigh and Ruthin. The district's boys went to the Denbigh County School while, until 1938, the girls took the train from Denbigh to the Ruthin County School.

Whereas Cyril's father had had to go away for his secondary schooling, Cyril, in 1907 at the age of twelve, passed the examinations for the Denbigh County School —of which his paternal grandfather had been a governor some years earlier, as a nominee of the Town Council. Cyril came fifth in the list of local boys entering the examinations — the top eight all being from Love Lane School— with a total of 453 marks out of a possible 550 and was awarded one of the two open scholarships for candidates under thirteen to attend the Denbigh County School.[30] Winning a scholarship meant that Cyril would not be required to pay fees to attend the County School. Out of a possible 100 marks, he achieved 85 marks for composition, 94 for geography, 80 for history, 88 for algebra and 106 out of a possible 150 for arithmetic. In his final year

---

29. Elementary Education (School Attendance) Act 1893 as amended in 1899.
30. 13 and 27 July and 17 August 1907, *FP*. Another two scholarships were available for children aged 13 to 14; one for a town candidate and one for a rural candidate. The Governors of Denbigh County School formally resolved to award this scholarship to Cyril at their meeting on 22 July 1907; Minutes of the Board of Governors of Denbigh County School, pages 552–3, currently held by Denbigh High School and made available to the author.

   His sister, Josephine, having won a scholarship (24 July 1909, *FP*), subsequently went to the Ruthin County School for girls while his younger brother, John, later also attended the Denbigh County School. His elder sister, Phyllis, was educated privately at Howell's School in Denbigh.

5. County School Examination results, 1907.
Cyril is the boy with N°· 5 pinned to his chest. Thomas E. Davies, whose letter to Cyril's father is in Appendix II, has N°· 3 pinned to his chest.

6. *Denbigh County School football XI, 1910–11. Cyril played in goal.*

7. *Cyril as a young man in London.*

at Love Lane School, Cyril was one of the prize-winners for having made a full attendance at school during that year.[31]

We have no details of his time at the Denbigh County School save that he was clearly a keen sportsman and kept goal for the school football team in 1910–11. In 1909, at the age of 14, he passed the Junior Certificate[32] in English language, history, arithmetic, mathematics, Latin, geography and drawing.[33]

In 1911, aged 17, he went to London to work as a clerk in the insurance industry. He joined the Law Fire Insurance Society Limited in Chancery Lane as a 'Clerk on Probation' on 12 December of that year.[34] It is probable that Cyril found this job with the assistance of Ted Vaughan who worked in insurance and whose wife, Katie, was Cyril's aunt —his mother's sister.

The company had some 70 employees listed on 1 January 1912, of whom 20 were clerks on probation. Cyril started out in the company's 'Agency' department before moving, in 1912, to its 'Town' (i.e. London orientated) department. His starting salary was £25 per annum which was increased by the usual £10 increment to £35 on 1 January 1913. During that year, he was promoted, although still within the clerks on probation, so that, by 1914, his salary was £50 a year. By then, only one other clerk on probation was paid more than Cyril (£55) and just one the same as him.[35]

Later press reports sow some confusion over the company for which he worked and show why the detail contained in newspaper reports should be treated with caution. The *Denbighshire Free Press*[36] report of his going to France in 1915 suggested that the company was called the London Assurance Company while that newspaper's

---

31. 3 August 1907, *FP*.
32. Broadly, the equivalent of today's GCSEs.
33. 18 September 1909, *FP*.
34. See the company's Salaries Ledger at the London Metropolitan Archives (LMA), reference: CLC/B/192/MS/15018 Salaries 1883–1914, pages dealing with 1912–1914.
35. ibid.
36. 9 October 1915, *FP*.

8. Cyril and his family.
L–R: Cyril's father, William Leopold, Cyril, John, Josie, Phyllis, his mother, Elizabeth. (We have no date for this but, as it is clearly a 'family' photograph, it is likely to have been taken when Cyril was either working in, or about to go off to, London, and before he had enlisted. So, we can date it as being between 1911 and 1914.)

obituary of him[37] suggested that it was the Lancashire Fire Assurance Society. Both of these companies were later subsumed within what is now the Aviva insurance group[38] whereas the Law Fire Insurance Society Limited's business was subsumed within what is now the Royal & Sun Alliance insurance group.

On 7 September 1914, just one month after the start of the Great War, Cyril enlisted in London.

It is important to realise that, unlike the Second World War, enlistment at the beginning of the Great War was entirely voluntary. This was the British way: unlike the continental powers, Britain had never had a conscript army. But, when it became clear that there was no other means of supplying the manpower required by the British Army on the Western Front, conscription was introduced at

---

37. 16 November 1918, *FP*.
38. See www.heritage.aviva.com/our-history/companies.

the beginning of 1916.[39] At first, men who were unmarried as at 1 November 1915 and were aged from 18 to 40 (inclusive) were liable to be called up. This initial exemption of married men was due partly to compassion and partly to financial motivations —HM Treasury was leery of the potential cost of the war pensions that might need to be paid to war widows!

It rapidly became clear that the numbers that would be produced by this first Act would be insufficient to meet the Army's desperate need for men so a second Act[40] was passed in May 1916 to extend liability for conscription to all men (single or not) aged 18 to 40 (inclusive). Initially (and controversially), conscription did not extend to Ireland; but, a third Act,[41] passed on 18 April 1918, extended conscription to Ireland,[42] the Isle of Man and the Channel Islands and raised the upper limit to 50 with a provision that the upper age could be extended to 55. Thus, even Cyril's father was only just outside its ambit and, had the war continued, would almost have certainly been caught if the extension provision had been implemented.

---

39. Military Service Act 1916 passed on 27 January 1916.
40. Military Service Act 1916 (Session 2).
41. Military Service Act 1918.
42. Despite the Act, conscription was never implemented in Ireland.

4. THE MARCH TO WAR

Britain declared war on Germany at 11.00 pm on 4 August 1914. What led to Britain becoming embroiled in this war and how did earlier milestones on the march to war tie in with Cyril's earlier life?

The reasons for the First World War—and even Britain's entry into it—are complex and multi-faceted; but, nonetheless, it is easy to see how the world changed even during Cyril's childhood. In 1890, when Cyril's parents married, the world was at peace; but 1894, the year of Cyril's birth, saw the beginnings of the alliance system which many argue tipped Europe into the maelstrom of the First World War.

The new German Empire—and Bismarck who had forged the new Empire through 'blood and iron' in three quick wars in the 1860s and 1870 —feared encirclement (*enkreisung*) by the discontented powers surrounding it. Given Germany's position at the centre of the European landmass, this was an inevitable concern. Bismarck had sought to deflect such a possibility: first by an alliance with Austria-Hungary and, then, by giving assurances to Russia, Austria-Hungary's rival for influence in south-east Europe, through the 'Reinsurance Treaty.' Thus, Germany could rest easy on its eastern front and need not fear an isolated France, still resentful from its defeat in 1870 and its loss of Alsace-Lorraine. But, in 1890, Germany's new and somewhat unstable ruler, Kaiser Wilhelm II, sacked Bismarck and, in 1892, failed to renew the 'Reinsurance Treaty' when it expired.

In 1894, the unthinkable happened: absolutist czarist Russia signed an alliance with republican France. Thus, in one bound, not only was France freed from isolation but Germany itself was threatened with encirclement and, if it fought either Power, the threat of a war on two fronts.

Initially, Britain, unattached —and largely unloved— in her 'splendid isolation,' had more to worry about the Franco-Russian Alliance than about Germany for sources of conflict abounded with an expansionist Russia and France on the edges of Imperial India in Central Asia and in Africa, respectively.

Nevertheless, even during Cyril's early childhood, the first hints of the clouds of Anglo-German rivalry were beginning to form on the horizon. The Kaiser, envious of the Royal Navy, was making plans for an expanded Imperial Navy and the mood-music was changing. At Victoria's Diamond Jubilee in 1897, with Cyril's British born father now running the family business, there was no repeat of Wilhelm's German language greeting of 1887. The decorative arch over the shop was no different from the other arches in town.[1]

Then, in 1900, just after Cyril had started primary school, the German parliament passed a second Navy Bill that provided for a significant expansion of the German High Seas Fleet. This was 'tantamount to a unilateral German declaration of 'cold war' against Britannia'[2] and led to the Twentieth Century's first arms race. The Navy Bill was passed while Britain was embroiled in the Boer War, a colonial conflict that began in 1899 and escalated to involve over 250,000 British and Imperial troops in South Africa before it ended in 1902. The Boer War proved that Britain's isolation was anything but 'splendid'.

With the growing threat posed by the German Fleet, Britain started to cast around for allies and, in 1902, sealed the first Anglo-Japanese Alliance to provide for Japanese assistance in the defence of British possessions in Asia. This enabled Britain to withdraw ships from the China Station to reinforce the Home Fleet to face Germany across the North Sea.

In 1904, Britain and France brokered the *Entente Cordiale*.

---

1. 26 June 1897, FP.
2. Herwig, Holger H., *'Luxury' Fleet: The Imperial German Navy 1888–1918* (London: George Allen & Unwin, 1980), page 43.

Although this was not a military alliance and aimed merely to settle long-standing colonial disputes between the two Powers, it did signal a rapprochement which only served to heighten German fears of encirclement; fears that were exacerbated in 1907, as Cyril passed his entrance exams to the County School, when Britain and Russia reached an understanding in respect of conflicts and spheres of influence in Central Asia and Persia (modern day Iran).

Meanwhile, Britain had reacted to German naval expansion by launching HMS *Dreadnought* in 1906. This new class of battleship transformed the naval race. Anglo-German tensions continued to mount with German supplementary Naval Bills later that year and in 1908 which triggered a British naval construction response characterised by the popular demand 'We want eight [new Dreadnoughts] and we won't wait.'

For Britain, the Royal Navy was a necessity whereas, in Churchill's famous words, Germany's High Seas Fleet was a 'luxury fleet.' By 1912, Britain had won the naval arms race as Germany could no longer afford to build against Britain and maintain and strengthen her army against the Franco-Russian threat.

The Balkan Wars of 1912–13 brought home to Germany the fact that no fleet could protect it from the huge, and strengthening, Russian and French armies. This led to pressure, within Germany, for a pre-emptive war before Russia, in particular, became too strong to be capable of being defeated. Although Britain engaged in military and naval discussions with France —and to a much lesser extent Russia— Britain studiously avoided any commitments to either of the other Entente Powers in the event of their being engaged in any war.

The immediate events leading to the First World War are well-known: the shooting of Archduke Franz Ferdinand, heir to the Habsburg throne, by Gavrilo Prinčip in Sarajevo on 28 June 1914. This unleashed Austro-Hungarian desires for a short quick war to supress Serbia. In turn, Serbia was supported by Russia which refused to back down in the face of German support for Austria-Hungary. France was tied to Russia by military alliance. Britain had no immediate interest in the conflict; indeed, it had been supportive of Austria-Hungary during the Balkan Wars.

Britain's immediate focus was entirely domestic. It must not be forgotten that the years leading up to the First World War were years of considerable domestic political and economic turmoil in Britain. 1906 had seen the election of a Liberal government by a landslide. When its modernising legislation had been mutilated by wrecking amendments in the House of Lords which then refused to pass Lloyd George's budget in 1909, Britain endured two years of constitutional crisis over the government's attempts to curtail the legislative powers of the House of Lords. As a result of the two General Elections in 1910, the Liberal government lost its majority and became dependent upon the Irish Nationalists' votes to stay in office. The Nationalists' price for this support was Irish Home Rule. By the Summer of 1914, the Irish Home Rule Bill was almost on the statute books; but, civil insurrection was looming in Ulster and the cavalry garrison at the Curragh had mutinied earlier that Easter and had refused to be involved in suppressing the Unionists. Alongside the Irish Home Rule Bill, Welsh disestablishment of the Church of England in Wales was about to reach the statute books. The years 1911–14, when Cyril had been working in London, had also seen numerous strikes by the leading unions —dockworkers and railwaymen. Throughout all this, the Suffragettes were also agitating for the franchise to be extended to women. The United Kingdom was anything but united —economically, socially or politically— in 1914.

It was in this febrile British domestic climate that the war clouds darkened the skies over Europe from 28 June onwards. In 1914, Britain had no united Ministry of Defence: separate departments of state controlled the armed forces. The Admiralty —then under Churchill as First Lord of the Admiralty— was responsible for the Navy while the War Office was responsible for the Army (as distinct from the Indian Army). The War Office did not even have a permanent political head in July 1914 as Seeley, the Secretary of State, had been obliged to resign in the aftermath of the Curragh

Mutiny and Asquith, the Prime Minister, was holding the fort on a temporary basis.

The British Cabinet did not discuss the looming crisis in Europe until the afternoon of Friday 24 July —less than a fortnight before war was declared: it had been concentrating full-time on the Irish Question. When the European situation was discussed, it was clear that the Liberal government was deeply divided between, in simplistic terms, the more pacifist and the imperialist wings of the party —a division that could be traced back to the Boer War and beyond. Ministers belonging to the pacifist wing had been kept in the dark about the naval and military discussions with France over preceding years: these had been kept very much on a 'deniable' basis. The Tory Opposition favoured following through on the *Entente Cordiale*, which Balfour's government had negotiated in 1904, and supporting France. It was certainly unclear what the *casus belli* would be for Britain's entering the looming European conflagration.

As diplomatic telegrams flew between the chancelleries of Europe and the British Cabinet agonised over the course to adopt, the Admiralty took precautionary steps. The Royal Navy had just completed its long-planned annual manoeuvres off the Isle of Wight. Most of the reservists had returned home but the great capital ships were still off Portland[3] and, on 26 July, Churchill secretly ordered the Fleet to remain in being, not to disband and for all reservists still with the Fleet to remain with their vessels. On 27 July, the War Office ordered key reserve officers to report to their army units.

When Austria-Hungary declared war on Serbia in the morning of 28 July, Churchill ordered the Fleet to sail —darkened and at high speed— through the Straits of Dover that night to its wartime stations in the North Sea and at Scapa Flow. On 1 August, he ordered the Fleet to mobilise.

---

3. Palmer, Alan, *The Salient: Ypres, 1914–1918* (London: Constable, 2016) (*Ypres*), page 24.

But still, the question remained: what would Britain do? Initially, the British Press had not been unsympathetic to the Habsburg position. We need to think only of the USA's reaction to the attack on the World Trade Centre to recognise that a Great Power was hardly likely to accept without any reaction the murder of the heir to its throne.

The question was answered by Belgium. Since the reign of Elizabeth I, it had been in Britain's interest to deprive any other major Power (*a fortiori* one with a significant naval capability) of control of the Flanders coast facing Britain.

When the Great Powers recognised Belgian independence by the Treaty of London in 1839, they also recognised, and agreed to guarantee, Belgium's neutrality. During the 1870 Franco-Prussian war, Gladstone had demanded, and obtained, from both Prussia and France renewed undertakings not to interfere with Belgium's independence and neutrality. But, in 1905, with Germany increasingly concerned about a war on two fronts against Russia and France, Alfred von Schlieffen, Chief of the German General Staff, devised a plan, for ever afterwards known as the Schlieffen Plan, to enable Germany to fight, and win, a war on two fronts. In essence, Germany should strike quickly at France by sweeping through Belgium to surround, and defeat, the French army before turning east to face Russia —which, by then, would be alone. Military historians have never reached a conclusion as to whether von Schlieffen's plan could ever have been effective —even without British intervention; but, in ignoring the 1839 Treaty of London, it almost certainly ensured British participation in any European war right from its beginning.

Although Germany had tried several times during the early 1900s and again in 1912 to obtain Britain's neutrality in any Franco-German conflict, divisions over Germany's High Seas Fleet prevented any accommodation. While Germany recognised the strength —nay, dominance— of the Royal Navy, the German General Staff had little regard for either Britain's small army or the wider European diplomatic situation and continued to ignore both the British Army and the Treaty of London for planning purposes.

Despite Sir Edward Grey's attempts to convene a European conference —along the lines of the recent London conferences to settle the Balkan Wars and the early nineteenth century Congresses — the assassination of Franz Ferdinand had ceased to be capable of being localised as an Austro-Hungarian/Serbian conflict as A. J. P. Taylor's famous railway timetables swung into play.

The German advance into Belgium in August 1914 was the immediate *casus belli* that united most of the Liberal government[4] and the country when the King-Emperor declared war —for Britain and the Empire— on Germany on 4 August 1914.[5] It was Bank Holiday weekend and Britain was largely unprepared —although, by then, everyone in the Regular Army had been recalled from leave. Full army mobilisation orders were issued on 5 August to call up the Reserves and the Territorials.

When war came in 1914, Britain, alone among the European Great Powers, maintained an entirely voluntary —and professional — army. It numbered just some 250,000 men with a further 350,000 former soldiers in the Reserve who were liable to be recalled to fill the establishment quotas of their regiments. In addition, the Territorial Army had an establishment figure of another 250,000 men but it was nearly 70,000 men below its establishment figure— and many were not committed to serving overseas. Apart from recalling the Reserve and calling out the Territorial Army, Britain had no contingency plans in place for any substantial increase in military numbers in the event of such a major European conflagration.

Of course, Britain's army was principally for Imperial defence and control and, at any one time, about a third of the Regular Army was on garrison duty in India and elsewhere within the Empire. Britain's numbers paled into insignificance against the German, Austro-Hungarian, French and Russian armies at approximately

---

4. Just two Cabinet ministers resigned in protest.
5. Britain only declared war on Austria-Hungary on 12 August —and then principally due to pressure from Russia to do so.

4.5 million, 3 million, 4 million, and 6 million men respectively.

The Royal Navy was Britain's front line of defence and, since 1889,[6] Britain had striven to maintain a naval 'two-power' standard in ships.[7] In August 1914, many in Britain expected Britain to follow its 'traditional' way of warfare for the last three centuries. Put simply, this involved Britain using the Royal Navy to command the seas, to continue to trade, to provide gold and wealth to continental allies who would supply the men and do most of the fighting[8] while the Royal Navy allowed Britain to seize Germany's colonial possessions and attack the Central Powers at peripheral points.

Lord Kitchener, appointed Secretary of State for War on 5 August 1914, did not share the popular belief that the war would be over by Christmas and planned for a long campaign. He called immediately for 100,000 volunteers to join the army and, on 7 August, the government sought Parliamentary sanction for a new army of some 500,000 men.

---

6. Naval Defence Act 1889.
7. That is Britain aimed to maintain the Royal Navy at a size equal to at least the sum of the next two largest navies in the world.
8. This may have been the perception of how Britain had acted, but the reality had never been quite so clear-cut.

5. ENLISTING

Cyril's enlistment application is in his War Office records. There are inconsistencies even within these records. For instance, there is a statement that he 'joined at Newport on 7 September 1914' as a private and was posted to the Dragoons of the Line and sent to the West Reserve Depot.

However, Cyril's enlistment attestation form suggests that, on 7 September, he went to Hampstead Heath in north London to enlist. This is far more likely as Cyril was then lodging with a Mrs Simpson in Calabria Road, Highbury—just down the road from Hampstead Heath. He enlisted for a short service term of three years (or the duration of the war—whichever was the longer). His medical history record, which is among his papers, confirms that he enlisted and was examined at Hampstead on 7 September.

Cyril's enlistment was, technically, into the Regular Army.[1] His enlistment Attestation form recorded details of his being born in Denbigh and gave his county as North Wales —as opposed to Denbighshire. This may have been simple ignorance (or, possibly, arrogance) on the part of the English recruiting sergeant who completed the form.

Cyril described himself as an insurance clerk. He answered 'No' to the standard questions asking whether he was an apprentice, whether he was married, whether he had ever been imprisoned, and whether he had previously served in (or been rejected for service by) the Royal Navy or the Army. Apprentices were contract-

---

1. Regular enlistment was usually for seven years full time with the Colours and five years in the Army Reserve but, in August 1914, Kitchener introduced the short service enlistment term.

ually bound to their masters for the term of their apprenticeship and could not enlist voluntarily without their consent.

He also confirmed that he had never resided in his own freeholder's house for three years or more or had occupied a house or land with a yearly value of £10 for more than a year. The purpose of this question was clearly to determine whether or not Cyril was entitled to vote. We must remember that, in 1914, the franchise was restricted to men aged 21 and over and, even then, only to landholders or householders. In practice, just over half the nation's male population was entitled to vote. No woman had the right to vote. Thus, unlike today, Cyril was enlisting to fight in a war where he had no say in electing any government.

Then, he confirmed that he was willing to be vaccinated, was telling the whole truth and was willing to enlist for general service. Enlistment for general service indicated that he was prepared to serve abroad. Other forms of service restricted a person's commitment to serving only at home within Great Britain.[2]

He answered 'Yes' to being a Wesleyan —as opposed to a Presbyterian. Having attended Capel Mawr in his youth, one would have expected him to have indicated that he was a Presbyterian. Was this, again, just a simplistic decision on the part of the recruiting sergeant or had Cyril changed his denomination affiliation in London? At that time, people would certainly have known the theological differences between Presbyterians and Wesleyans[3] so one must wonder why he described himself here as a Wesleyan. It may be that, on coming to London, he worshipped at a Wesleyan chapel —the great Wesleyan chapel at City Road[4]

---

2. Gradually, these more restricted forms of service were changed (and the restrictions removed) as the war progressed to meet the exigencies of the demand for manpower at the Front. By 1917, there was no practical difference between service in the Regular Army, the Territorials, the Reserve and the New Armies.
3. See Edwards, Huw, *City Mission, The Story of London's Welsh Chapels* (Talybont: Y Lolfa, 2015), pages 307–8 for a brief description of the distinction.
4. ibid.

would not have been that far from his lodgings in Highbury; but, equally, the Holloway Presbyterian chapel would not have been far away either. All this is, however, speculation: we simply do not know.

It may, of course, have been the result of the influence of other people who he met in London. We know he was very close to a Miss B. M. Hayes who lived in Liberia Road —just off Calabria Road. He only disclosed this friendship to his parents in October 1915 just before he was posted to France.[5]

As part of the enlistment process, Cyril was medically examined and confirmed fit for general service in Dragoons of the Line. The records show that he was 5' 8½' (174 cms) tall, weighed 141 lbs (64kg), had a chest measurement of 36½' (92.5 cm), was in good physical condition and had a sallow complexion with hazel coloured eyes—6/6 eyesight in both eyes—and black hair. The records also noted that he had 'Two scars just below the left knee cap.'

At that time, there was still a rigid adherence to the minimum physical requirements for those applying for full service enlistment; namely, a man had to be aged between 18 and 35, weigh at least 110 lbs (50 kg) and be at least 5' 3'(160 cm) tall with a chest measurement of at least 32' (81 cm).[6] One reason for the poor volunteering figures in the war's early months was that many potential volunteers —particularly urban volunteers— did not meet these requirements and, so, were rejected. It would only be later, as manpower shortages loomed, that these requirements were reduced again and again. For instance, in September 1914, at one recruiting meeting in London, 150 men volunteered but only fifteen passed the preliminary medical inspection; the rest were sent home.[7]

---

5. Letter from Cyril to his parents, 4 October 1915; see Appendix II.
6. Barlow, pages 25–6.
7. White, Jerry, *Zeppelin Nights: London in the First World War* (Vintage: London, 2015) (*Zeppelin Nights*), page 34.

The formality of voluntary enlistment as opposed to conscripted service meant that, upon Cyril's signing the attestation form,[8] he was cautioned and sworn before a Justice of the Peace. Once enlisted, he would have been paid the King's Shilling (5p).[9] In 1914, the eighteenth century practice of paying recruiting bonuses to the recruiting parties still continued. A recruiting sergeant would receive two shillings and six pence (half-a-crown, or 12.5p) for each recruit into a cavalry regiment.[10]

The next step was for a recruit to be issued with a railway warrant and ordered to report to the permanent depot of the regiment that he had joined.[11]

On 9 September, Cyril was designated Private 7253 and posted to the Reserve in 3rd Reserve Regiment of Cavalry. The records are consistent that he enlisted, and was paid from, 7 September,[12] so the date 9 September must be a reference to the date he arrived at the training depot in Canterbury, Kent. Since the mid 1880s, other ranks were given an identifying number by their regiments. These numbers were allocated sequentially to soldiers as they joined the regiment

Two immediate questions spring to mind: One, why did Cyril enlist when he did? Second, why the cavalry? We have no idea why Cyril enlisted in September 1914, and we can only postulate. Although his father had no military links whatsoever, his grandfather, Wilhelm, had not only been a member of the local Denbighshire Rifle Volunteers for a number of years but had also done

---

8. The form was certainly completed by a different hand from the signature.
9. Simkins, Peter, *Kitchener's Army: The Raising of the New Armies 1914–1916* (Manchester: Manchester University Press, 1988; reprinted Barnsley: Pen & Sword Military, 2007) (*Kitchener's Army*), page 176.
10. *Kitchener's Army*, page 181. This bonus was later reduced to one shilling (5p) as the recruitment boom had made such bonuses both expensive and unnecessary.
11. *Kitchener's Army*, page 191.
12. On his Application for a Commission, Cyril, gives that date as 6 September 1914; but this may have been simple forgetfulness after two and half years of war as everything else tends towards the 7 September date.

military service back in Baden before coming over to Wales.[13] Thus, it is unlikely that Cyril would have been entirely unaware of soldiering.

On the other hand, Cyril's religious upbringing was Nonconformist and the Welsh chapels were strongly anti-militaristic in the nineteenth century.[14] While too much should not be made of this sentiment, Barlow shows that, contrary to post-war myths of a superior Welsh commitment to the war, Welsh voluntary enlistment was below that in England and Scotland[15] and there was initial scepticism within Wales that the war was their fight.[16] In certain parts, particularly in industrial South Wales, there was considerable resistance to involvement in the war.[17]

Service in the Army before 1914 was generally unpopular; pay and conditions were poor and there was a continuing stigma against military service among the 'respectable' working classes.[18] This was reflected in the poor physical condition of many British troops that had been commented upon in the Boer War —and which had not improved much since then.

Whether his mixed Cymro-German parentage played any psychological part in his enlisting and Cyril enlisted so as to demonstrate his patriotism we will never know. If this were the case, he would not have been alone: there were many people in the Britain of that time with German relations: not least the entire Royal

13. In 1891, there was a discussion in the Denbigh Town Council surrounding soldiers and their morality. Wilhelm denounced those criticising the morality of British soldiers. He said that, as the son of a soldier and one who had done military service in his native land, he must protest against those members of the Council who degraded the character of Welsh soldiers sent to foreign climes and foreign territories to fight for their country; 24 January 1891, *FP*.
14. Barlow, page 22.
15. Barlow, pages 19-22. Wales contributed just 5.83% of its population through voluntary enlistment against 6.04% in England and 6.61% in Scotland.
16. Barlow, pages 2-3.
17. See Adams, Philip, *Not in OUR Name: War dissent in a Welsh town* and *Daring to Defy: Port Talbot's War Resistance, 1914–1918* (Ludlow: published privately by Philip Adams in 2015 and 2016 respectively).
18. Gilbert, Adrian, *Challenge of Battle: The Real Story of the British Army in 1914* (Oxford: Osprey Publishing, 2013) (*Challenge of Battle*), page 26.

Family, including the First Sea Lord. German individuals and German owned property were attacked in the early days of the war: often fuelled by tales of alleged German atrocities in Belgium. It would have been surprising if, on the immediate outbreak of war, Cyril had not received at least some comments on his surname and background. His German connections were certainly no secret for Dunn was to make reference to his 'German name' in his description of Cyril's part in 2RWF's final battle.[19]

Equally, we do not know whether 'peer pressure' of any kind played a part: it was certainly a time when young ladies handed out white feathers to young men with some abandon.

Cyril had lived in London since 1911 and it may be that London life and social values influenced him towards enlisting. London seems to have been quicker than the provinces in responding to Kitchener's call for volunteers. For instance, on 9 August, London produced 1,100 recruits; Wales just 58. On 8 August, a third of all recruits in the country had enlisted at Scotland Yard in London.[20]

By 12 November 1914, the recruitment rate in London was noticeable higher than elsewhere in the country (14.3 % to 10.2%). It is likely that the over-representation of middle-class employment in London was one factor in generating London's higher recruitment rate. The lower middle classes (i.e. Cyril's social class) and above were over-represented among volunteers, especially in London as around 40% of eligibly aged men employed in financial services, commerce and the professions volunteered against just 28% of industrial workers.[21]

Despite patriotic shows of jingoism on the outbreak of war, initial recruitment was slow and Simkins says it would be wrong to say 'the flower of British manhood was merely swept into the army on a tide of national hysteria:'[22] only 8,200 men volunteered

---

19. Dunn, page 564.
20. Barlow, page 25.
21. *Zeppelin Nights*, page 34.

between 4 and 8 August.[23] Momentum picked up with nearly 44,000 volunteering in the week to 15 August, just under 50,000 the following week and 66,000 in the week to 29 August. The weekly total of recruits hit the highest point during the week to 5 September when 175,000 volunteered.[24] Voluntary recruitment in Wales —like England and Scotland— reached its peak in the fortnight to 10 September.[25]

So, Cyril really was at the tail end of this great increase when he enlisted on 7 September as the weekly totals fell rapidly thereafter and were below 5,000 by 18 September and, from 1 October to the end of 1914, hovered between 1,500 and 4,500.[26]

It is traditional to ascribe the sharp rise in recruitment at the end of August to news of the British retreat from Mons filtering back home. On 23 August, the British Expeditionary Force (BEF) in France had its first contact with the advancing German troops at Mons and, the next day, began its steady retreat towards the Amiens–Paris line until 3 September when, implored by Joffre (commander-in-chief of the French armies), it turned south-east and counter-attacked across the Marne. News of the retreat, which appeared in the newspapers on 25 August, made it clear to all that war had been enjoined and things were not going well for the BEF.

Simkins[27] considers the reasons for people joining up. For some, it was a patriotic decision —but even they waited a few weeks before enlisting. For others, a mixture of morality, certainly the events at Mons, sheer economic necessity at a time when a worker might earn 12 shillings (60p) a week for a 65-hour week —against 7 shillings (35p) as a private in the infantry; others to avoid the police and some because their friends were joining up.

---

22. *Kitchener's Army*, page 186.
23. Messenger, Charles, *Call-to-Arms: The British Army 1914–1918* (London: Cassell Military Paperbacks, 2006) (Messenger), page 96.
24. ibid.
25. Barlow, page 26.
26. *Kitchener's Army*, page 169.
27. ibid, pages 169–75.

Why the initial delay? Some of the volunteers were married. Some held a good job and either needed to obtain their employer's permission to enlist or sought assurances that they would have a job to return to —one must not forget that employees in those days had an ever present concern about unemployment— and employers became more public spirited with the retreat from Mons.[28] Others may well have wished at least to consult their family—although we have no evidence that this was a consideration in Cyril's case.

Part of the answer may well be connected with Cyril's employer. On Tuesday 1 September, the board of directors of Law Fire Insurance Society Limited passed a resolution which referred to Kitchener's recent 'Urgent Appeal for Recruits' and resolved that members of staff aged between 19 and 35 and eligible for active military service and who were accepted by the armed services would have their military pay whilst on service supplemented by such sum as would make it up to equal their salaries with the company at that date.[29]

Whereas the board had earlier agreed that staff who were in the Reserve and who had been ordered to re-join their regiments upon the general mobilisation at the end of July would have their army pay made up to their company pay for the duration,[30] the board's decision on 1 September was of general application to the company's employees. The decision could also be taken as a general consent from the employer to anyone who enlisted in response to Kitchener's appeal. Another implication was that employees who joined up would also have a position to which they could return at the war's end.

28. ibid, pages 57 and 65.
29. Board Minutes for the company's board meeting held on 1 September 1914, CLC/B/192/MS15010/039 in the LMA, Board Minutes, 1914–1915, vol N, page 124.
30. Board Minutes for the company's board meeting held on 11 August 1914, ibid.

Thus, Cyril now had both his employer's approval to join up and an assurance that he would suffer no loss of income by doing so. That he enlisted on Monday, 7 September —a normal working day— further suggests that he had cleared his intention to enlist with the company beforehand.

The company was to continue this policy of making up employees' army pay to the level of their previous salary even in the case of men who were conscripted after the Military Service Acts were passed in 1916.[31] However, the company did not allow for any increases in pay —even though prices more than doubled during the course of the war— or include serving men in the award of bonuses. In fact, when resolving to pay staff a 10% bonus on 5 December 1916, the board specifically said that it did not apply to 'officials in H.M. Forces.'[32]

The company clearly expected its employees who had joined up to maintain contact with it. We know that Cyril did[33] and the fact that medal awards to employees on active service were regularly recorded in the board minutes[34] indicates that other employees did likewise.

Before the war, a volunteer could, in theory at least, choose the unit in which he wished to serve. On 21 August 1914, the War Office issued an instruction that a recruiting officer should 'as far as possible' go along with the volunteer's wishes —although, doubtless, some 'guidance' may well have been given.[35] So, why the cavalry?

---

31. Board Minutes for the company's board meeting held on 11 July 1916; CLC/B/192/MS15010/040 in the LMA, Board Minutes Book, 1915–1917, vol. O, page 223.
32. ibid, page 353.
33. In his letter to his parents dated 4 October 1915, he said he was about to write to the company to let them know that he was being posted to France. See Appendix II.
34. E.g. the award of the Military Cross to Lt. C. R. Brown and the Military Medal to E. H. Hickman were noted; Board Minutes for the company's board meetings held on 18 January 1916 and 15 August 1916, respectively; CLC/B/192/MS15010/040 in the LMA, Board Minutes Book, 1915–1917, vol. O, pages 78 and 254.
35. *Kitchener's Army*, page 76.

It is no secret that, in 1914, the reputation of Tommy Atkins (the name given to the average British soldier) was not high and the nineteenth century army was seen as a 'refuge for the destitute, desperate and unemployable.'[36] Robert Graves, in his Introduction to *Old Soldier Sahib*, described the Tommy Atkins of 1914 as being 'known ... for his foul language, his love of drink and prostitutes, his irreligion, his rowdiness and his ignorance ...'[37] Messenger describes the first recruits as 'a pretty rough crowd' before saying that 'The next lot were rather better. They'd had jobs and had given them up ...'[38] This fits in with Cyril's volunteering in September.

Welshmen made up just 1.3% of the Regular Army in 1913 whose ranks 'were overwhelmingly Anglican, and working class.'[39]

Given that Cyril was later to apply for the RWF, one must ask why, as a volunteer in the early days of the war, he did not apply for a Welsh regiment? Besides there being no Wales-linked cavalry regiment, this would not have been an easy option for someone enlisting in London which was well outside the usual recruiting grounds of the three regiments associated with Wales. All three, despite their nominal association with Wales, relied upon English recruits to maintain their establishment strength and had little direct connection with Wales in the early years of the twentieth century.[40] Unlike the London Scottish and the London Irish, there was no Wales related Territorial Army regiment based, and recruiting, in London when the war began.[41] This was to change; but only after Cyril had enlisted.

---

36. Barlow, page 22.
37. Richards, Frank, *Old Soldier Sahib* (reprinted Uckfield: Naval & Military Press Ltd., 2003), Introduction by Robert Graves, page 1.
38. Messenger, page 97.
39. Barlow, page 25.
40. Barlow, pages 22–3.
41. Riley, Jonathon, 'Llewelyn Wyn Griffith and the London Welsh 1914–1918', *Transactions of the Honourable Society of Cymmrodorion*, New series, Volume 21, 2015, page 53.

In a public speech in London on 19 September, in which he evoked memories of Glyndŵr and the Welsh archers at Crécy, David Lloyd George advocated the formation of a Welsh Army Corps; but, the Corps was not launched until a public meeting in Cardiff on 29 September. Just before Lloyd George's speech, 15th Battalion (1st London Welsh) of the RWF was inaugurated on 16 September; but it was not officially recognised until 29 October.[42] So, even putting to one side the issues surrounding the infantry's contemporary reputation, a Welsh regiment would not have been a practical option for Cyril when enlisting in London at the beginning of September.

It would have been easy for Cyril to have followed the masses in London and enlisted in the infantry, so we must assume that he made a positive decision to join a cavalry regiment.

As a boy from a chapel background, he may have had the prejudices of his background against joining the infantry.[43] For an enlisted man, the cavalry may have seemed to offer a more congenial berth—or have conveyed a more exciting and glamorous image. It certainly paid more. As a trooper (or private) in the Cavalry of the Line, he would be paid 1s 2d (6p) per day whereas a private in the infantry earned just 1s (5p) a day—i.e. he earned 20% more in the cavalry than in the infantry;[44] (i.e. between 42% and 36% less than he was then being paid as an insurance clerk.) Although, this made no practical difference for Cyril as his company would make up any loss of his salary in any event.

---

42. ibid, pages 53–4.
43. The reverse was probably true at officer level where it was generally assumed that brighter officer candidates opted for the infantry or more specialised regiments such as the engineers or artillery. The drawback for cavalry officers was the cost of maintaining their horses etc. Winston Churchill's own father complained when Churchill did not pass high enough in the Sandhurst examinations to avoid a cavalry regiment —see Thomson, Malcolm, *Churchill: His Life and Times* (London: Odhams Books Limited, 1965), page 34.
44. War Office Instruction 166 (1914). These pay rates were revised upwards slightly on 13 December 1915.

Of course, one must also ask what an insurance clerk who was a clockmaker's son knew about horses. For the answer we should probably look to Cyffylliog, a small village just outside Ruthin. Cyril's mother came from farming stock and the children used to spend much of their summer holidays in Cyffylliog on the farms of her relatives. It is, therefore, likely that Cyril had learnt the basics of riding as child.

One assumes that the cavalry would look first for recruits who knew the rudiments of horses and riding. Perhaps that is why the recruitment station was on Hampstead Heath —so that potential recruits could be put on a horse and show what they knew. Certainly, in the first few weeks of the war, regiments could be highly selective about who they chose —given the abundance of volunteers.[45] This was certainly true of the infantry regiments (in which there was a degree of elitism as between Regular battalions and newly formed battalions). Given the smaller numbers, this was probably also true of the cavalry. It is noticeable that Cyril joined a Regular cavalry regiment. This suggests that he must have been one of the better volunteers for the cavalry.

Cyril's military career, from enlistment on 7 September 1914 to his death on 4 November 1918, may be divided into five, unequal, parts:

a. Being posted to, and training at Home for, the cavalry from 9 September to 10 October 1915 when he reached 3DG in France (398 days);
b. Service in the Field with 3DG from 10 October 1915 to 25 February 1917 (504 days);
c. Leave, officer training and service at Home with 3RWF from 25 February to 2 October 1917 (225 days);
d. Commissioned service in the Field with 2RWF from 2 October 1917 to 7 August 1918; a period of stasis and trench warfare (309 days); and

---

45. *Kitchener's Army*, page 177.

e. Service with 2RWF during the '100 Day Advance' from 8 August to his death on 4 November 1918 (89 days); the last two months of which he was in command of D Company.

6. TRAINING FOR THE CAVALRY

The Cavalry Depot at Canterbury was the training and reserve depot for 3 Cavalry Reserve. This reserve regiment was one of 17 reserve cavalry regiments formed in August 1914 to train and supply reserves for their associated regiments.[1] In the case of 3 Cavalry Reserve, its three Regular Army regiments were those in 6 Cavalry Brigade; namely: 3rd Dragoon Guards, 6th Dragoon Guards and the Northamptonshire Yeomanry. 6 Cavalry Brigade was, in turn, one of the three brigades in the 3rd Cavalry Division. 3DG remained in this brigade and division throughout the war.

For the next thirteen months, from 9 September to early October 1915, Cyril (along with other volunteers for these regiments) was engaged in training. He was fortunate to be assigned to a regular cavalry training depot for, in the swelling new infantry battalions, recruits paid 'a stiff price for such rapid expansion. On every side there were shortages of accommodation, uniforms, weapons, personal equipment, blankets, bedding and even rations.'[2] For many volunteers it was a rude awakening: the literature on the subject is littered with tales of men arriving at 'training camps' that were often little better than open fields with either few billets or only canvas tents for shelter, and with no clothes or uniform available to them other than the clothes in which they arrived. As a result, lice and vermin were prevalent in these encampments.[3]

Many recruits were raised locally, for it was still a time when local towns or wealthy landowners raised and equipped local

1. *The Long, Long Trail*.
2. *Kitchener's Army*, pages 68–9.
3. Barlow, page 29.

regiments —and paid the associated costs. Large-scale central planning and consistency had not yet arrived on the scene —it was to do so during the course of the war. The rapid increase in the new armies simply overwhelmed such system as there was in place in August 1914.

The Canterbury barracks, as a long-established cavalry depot for a Regular regiment, would have had proper accommodation and training facilities; but, even it and the cavalry were stretched in terms of resources given the need first to supply available horses and stores to those units (Regular, Reserve or Territorial) that were being despatched to France as part of the BEF.

At the beginning, a lack of equipment rendered exercising and training difficult. Harnesses and saddles were issued first to the Regular (and, then, the Territorial) units that formed, or quickly followed, the BEF. This meant that the supply of saddles was deficient thereby impeding the training of cavalry reserves. Two major problems were a shortage of leather of the right quality and too few British businesses capable of making military standard harnesses and saddles. Supplies were imported from India, Canada and the USA.[4] Horses too were in short supply —although, after the Boer War which had taught the importance of having remounts available, the War Office remounts division had fully researched the question of remounts and put plans in place before the outbreak of the war.[5] It started requisitioning and buying up horses in the UK immediately on the outbreak of war —many from the Vale of Clwyd. It was not a good time to requisition horses as harvest-time was just beginning.[6] In London, cabbies were left without a livelihood when their horses were taken.

The literature contains much detail of infantry training but I have found nothing that deals specifically with training for the

---

4. Winton, Graham, *Theirs not to reason why: Horsing the British Army 1875–1925* (Solihull: Helion & Company, 2013) (Winton), page 300.
5. Anglesey vol. 8, page 290.
6. Up to 150,000 horses were requisitioned; Palmer, page 26.

cavalry. Since the Boer War, which had highlighted so many deficiencies in the British Army that a radical overhaul had been needed and implemented, a training syllabus for the infantry had been developed and various Field Service Regulations and army manuals promulgated and published. Then, in August 1914, the Army Council laid down a standard six months training period for infantry recruits. The training day would start with a dawn reveille followed by a march before breakfast.[7] Basic physical fitness, drill and march discipline were important features of basic training. Men were taught how to handle weapons safely.

Cyril's training certainly included lengthy rides, exercises on the beach at Whitstable and operating in wooded areas with cavalry and the care of horses; in April 1915, he was given the care of a chestnut horse recently imported from Argentina.[8]

The Boer War had also taught the importance of horsemanship: in that war, two-thirds of horses died but by 1914 '… the care and management of his mount was one of the key skills of any British cavalryman.'[9] So, in training, cavalrymen would also have been taught how to look after their horses and horsemanship skills. Bickersteth, although probably biased as a former cavalryman, argued that 'the cavalryman was on the whole the best trained all-round soldier.'[10] Cavalrymen were required not only to ride and look after their horses but also to use a sword and a bayonet, throw bombs and have high standards of musketry.

Unlike the Continental cavalry regiments that, at the outbreak of the war, retained their colourful uniforms, the British cavalry had taken to heart the experiences of the Boer War and now wore the same practical khaki-coloured uniforms as the infantry. Each cavalryman was expected to be able to move and fight independently for up to 48 hours. Thus, he and his horse needed to carry

7. *Kitchener's Army*, pages 296–320.
8. Letter from Cyril to his young brother, John; see Appendix II.
9. *Horsemen*, page 17.
10. Bickersteth, page ix.

something like 110lbs (50*kg*) of equipment and rations for themselves.[11]

The standard equipment included a leather bandolier with room for 90 rounds of .303 ammunition for his Short Magazine Lee Enfield rifle which, together with the 10 rounds in the rifle itself, made 100 rounds. In theory, the bandolier should have been slung over one shoulder but accessing its rear four pouches when on horseback was a practical problem and its weight was an even greater issue for the trooper; so, it was usually hung around the horse's neck while the trooper carried a second leather 50-round bandolier slung over a shoulder. On occasion, as necessary, additional basic cloth 50-round bandoliers would also be carried.

Over the cavalryman's other shoulder, would be a haversack, containing his rations, and a felt covered enamel water bottle. On one side of his saddle was his sword and, on the other side, his rifle in a leather bucket. In addition, the cavalryman needed to carry his mess tin, his picketing peg, a water bucket and feedbag for his horse with a ration of oats or corn. Space also needed to be found for a wallet containing his spare socks and underwear, a shaving kit, horse-grooming brushes and equipment and a waterproof groundsheet. Later in the war, troopers were also issued with wire cutters, bayonets, steel helmets and Mills bombs.[12] As and when the weather demanded it, a cavalryman also had to wear (or find space for) his greatcoat.

When cavalrymen were dismounted and went into the front, they did not take their haversack with them but stuffed everything into their greatcoat pockets or rolled their equipment in their greatcoat which they strapped *en bandolere* around their bodies.[13]

A cavalry regiment's wartime establishment was 25 to 30 officers and about 525 other ranks —just over half the size of an infantry battalion. Each cavalry regiment was commanded by a lieutenant-colonel and was formed of three squadrons—each commanded by

11. *Horsemen*, pages 17–21.
12. ibid.
13. ibid.

9. Cyril astride a horse at the Canterbury barracks.

a major or a captain. Each squadron was then sub-divided into four troops. In addition, there would be a small headquarters unit and a machine gun section of two Vickers guns. Three cavalry regiments would form a brigade. In turn, three brigades were formed into a cavalry division. A cavalry division's wartime establishment strength was, thus, about 439 officers and 8,830 men together with 7,350 riding horses and 2,378 draught horses.[14]

Newly enlisted cavalrymen remained at Home in their reserve regiments until their training period was complete when they would be sent to join their linked regiment as casualty replacements.[15] Initially, at Canterbury, Cyril was posted to 4th Troop in C Squadron of 3DG.[16]

3DG traced its regimental history back to 1685 when the Regiment was raised to help suppress the Duke of Monmouth's rebellion. In 1741, the Regiment became a dragoon guards regiment and, in 1765, was named after George, Prince of Wales, later the Prince Regent and George IV. Dragoons were originally mounted infantrymen but, by 1914, the historic distinctions between different types of cavalry[17] remained in the regimental names only: there was no difference in terms of drills or equipment[18] —except that lancers still retained their lances.

When the war broke out, the Regiment was on garrison duty in Egypt guarding the Suez Canal. It sailed from Egypt at the end of September 1914 and landed at Liverpool on 18 October before proceeding to its base at Ludgershall, Wiltshire. It embarked at Southampton for Le Havre on 31 October and moved swiftly to join the remainder of 6 Cavalry Brigade at Ypres where it took part in

---

14. *Challenge of Battle*, Appendix B on pages 269–70.
15. Mallinson, Allan, *1914: Fight the Good Fight, Britain, the Army and the Coming of the First World War* (London: Bantam Press, 2013) (Mallinson), page 83.
16. Letter (undated but probably end May/early June 1915) from Cyril to his parents; see Appendix II.
17. For example: heavy cavalry, light cavalry, Household cavalry, dragoons, light dragoons, hussars and lancers.
18. *Horsemen*, page xi.

10. Cyril in the dress uniform of a trooper in 3rd Dragoon Guards. This photograph was, presumably, taken in 1915 in Canterbury when he had completed his training.

11. Cyril as a trooper in 3rd Dragoon Guards. Here, he is wearing a typical other ranks' service dress with a 50-round ammunition leather bandolier slung over his left shoulder. His puttees are worn in cavalry style — i.e. wound down from the top. He is also wearing spurs. This photograph was, probably, taken in Denbigh in 1915 when he had finished his training and ahead of being posted to France

12. Cyril and John outside Derwenfa, 1915.

the First Battle of Ypres.

We must assume that, once his training was over, Cyril had a period of leave in Denbigh during 1915. During this leave, he took the opportunity to be photographed in uniform — both formally and informally with family members.

It was not until 5 October 1915 that Cyril embarked for France. He landed there on 6 October and was posted to 3DG on 10 October, along with 41 other privates, four NCOs and 34 replacement riding horses.

This move came about suddenly and meant that he had to postpone the 21st birthday celebrations that he and his sister, Phyllis, had been planning. Cyril and the others who were being posted from Canterbury were warned of the move only on Saturday 2 October. So, it was all something of a rush for them to get their things sorted before leaving at 0400 on Tuesday 5 October for Southampton from where they sailed that evening for France. Cyril took with him to France only those items which he considered 'necessaries' and stored the rest of his effects with his old landlady at Calabria Road. He also found time on the Saturday to wire his parents of his impending departure and, the next day, to write to them. Monday 4 October was spent by the men resting and writing letters home. In Cyril's letter written on the Monday, he sought to calm his parents and re-assured his mother that 'no news is good news.'[19]

---

19. Letter from Cyril to his parents, 4 October 1915; see Appendix II.

In this letter, he also mentioned to his parents, for the first time, a Miss B. M. Hayes —as a friend in London 'who probably you will not have heard about' and asked his father, whose name he had given as his next of kin, to telegram her if the family received any news that Cyril had been 'a little damaged in some mix up.'[20]

The news of his embarkation for France, which coincided with a widening of the war in the Balkans as Britain declared war on Bulgaria which had joined the Central Powers, was reported in the *Denbighshire Free Press*:[21]

ANOTHER DENBIGHITE
GONE ON ACTIVE SERVICE
On Tuesday last, Pte. W. R. Cyril Keepfer, son of Mr and Mrs Keepfer, Derwenfa, and High-street, Denbigh, was one of a draft from the 3rd Dragoon Guards, who left Canterbury for the front. Mr Keepfer, previous to enlisting, was engaged with the London Assurance Company, and was promoted during his first year of service—an event unique in the history of the office. In September he enlisted into 3rd Dragoon Guards, and has been with his regiment in Canterbury ever since. He is a fine athlete and on Easter Monday last kept goal for his team in a football match against Whitstable. He is not yet 21 years of age. We wish him every possible success and a safe return.

With the arrival of Cyril's draft and further drafts, the Regiment's strength was up to 26 officers and 651 other ranks by the middle of October. 3DG was then stationed in billets at Raimbert east of the line Lillers–Burbure–Cauchy-à-la Tour. Cyril remained in France with 3DG for the next nearly 17 months — without any home leave— until February 1917 when he transferred

20. ibid.
21. 9 October 1915, FP. An almost identically worded report also appeared in the NWT of the same date. The latter report included the detail that the movement to the Front was via Southampton.

back to England with a view to admission to an officers cadet unit.

Just before Cyril arrived in France as a replacement, 3DG (and the rest of 6 Cavalry Brigade) had been under the command of the First Army and had taken part in the Battle of Loos from 26–8 September 1915 before being withdrawn, on 1 October, to the Raimbert area[22] when 6 Cavalry Brigade marched into billets.

---

22. Holt, page 39.

7. TO FRANCE WITH 3rd DRAGOON GUARDS

It is arguable that 1914 saw the largest mobilisation of cavalrymen in history: France mobilised 45,000 cavalrymen, Russia 80,000, Germany 55,000 and Austria-Hungary 45,000.[1] For the armies that went to war in 1914, horses were the only means of rapid transport across country: motor cars were in their infancy and tanks were yet to be invented. The cavalry had a number of intended roles in battle and acted both as scouts and as rapid deployment forces — defensively and offensively to outflank an enemy.

However, with the establishment of the trench system and the ensuing stultification in fighting, the cavalry's role diminished and, until a war of movement re-commenced, their role was limited to exploiting any breakthrough in the enemy lines (or, in the parlance of the day, a 'gap') achieved after a full frontal infantry assault on the German trenches. The cavalry 'represented the only means by which large scale penetration of an enemy position in depth could be secured and enlarged before the enemy had time to bring up his reserves.'[2]

When war broke out, the BEF had crossed to France and concentrated in the area around Maubeuge and Le Cateau with the French 5th Army on its right. Little had changed in the deployment of massed troops on the European continent since the days of Marlborough and individual armies were still expected to operate and manoeuvre relatively independently; and the BEF was not

---

1. *Horsemen*, page 17.
2. Oatts, page 217.

under the operational control of the French Army.

Whether a concentration as far forward as Maubeuge (as opposed to further back around Amiens —or, even, in the wholly different area of Antwerp) was the most sensible course for the BEF remains disputed territory. When a Cabinet committee met late in the afternoon on 5 August 1914 to consider answers to the most basic of strategic questions (whether a British army should even cross to France, and, if so, where should the BEF concentrate), it was presented with something of a *fait accompli*. A concentration around Maubeuge simply accorded with the pre-war military disposition discussions between Sir Henry Wilson, the British Director of Plans in the War Office, and his French opposite number. It was not a political decision.

Once assembled around Maubeuge, the BEF crossed the Belgian border and advanced northwards to Mons where it hoped to halt the advancing German forces. The cavalry played its traditional role of scouts and providers of mobile units for flank defence both in the advance to Mons and, more importantly, in the retreat from Mons from August to September. Its subsequent role in the BEF's counter-attack to the Marne and the Aisne was disappointing.

After failing to encircle the French Army, the German Army attempted to swing north and then west around the British and French Armies and encircle them further to the north and cut the BEF off from the Channel ports. This resulted in the 'dash to the Coast' with both armies attempting to manoeuvre northwards around the other. This 'dash,' which began on 16 September 1914, culminated in the First Battle of Ypres (November 1914) where, it is traditionally said, Tommy Atkins and the last of the old British Regular Army died in the defence of Ypres and the BEF's communications with the coast. Here, dismounted cavalry —including 3DG— played a significant role.

With the German failure to break through at Ypres, both sides dug opposing trench systems from the English Channel down to the Swiss frontier. At first, the trenches were shallow and screened by only small amounts of barbed wire; but, within a year, they had

Map 2 – Cyril and the Cavalry

developed into strong sophisticated trench lines arrayed in depth. These trenches provided relative safety from bombardment and their concealed machine gun positions proved immune to all but the most accurate high explosive fire.[3]

On the whole, the British had poorer trench positions than the Germans for, in general, the Germans, who, after their initial attack in 1914, were standing on the defensive, could choose the line that they wished to defend—and they chose the higher ground overlooking the British and dug the more sophisticated trenches. As the fighting was on French and Belgian soil, the British were required, for coalition reasons, to defend the maximum area of France and Belgium and could not withdraw to lines they might otherwise have preferred to defend. Thus, the British trenches tended to be dug in lower ground —ground which often had a high water table so resulting in vast amounts of mud.

The cavalry's next potential major engagement was the Battle of Loos in September 1915. This was the BEF's major set-piece attack of 1915 and the largest battle —in terms of numbers of men involved— that the British Army had fought to date. The British, probably, would not have wished to attack at this stage as their troops —largely Territorials and Reservists from Home along with the first newly minted soldiers of Kitchener's New Armies— were still in need of further training; but war-time coalition politics dictated otherwise. There was a need to meet French demands for action to relieve pressure on the French armies and to compensate for recent Russian setbacks on the Eastern Front. Spencer Jones described this as Britain's 'deadly dilemma.' Britain could avoid heavy losses on the Western Front only by not fighting there; but, if the BEF avoided giving battle, this risked Germany's defeat of France or Russia and, by extension, the defeat of Britain herself.[4]

---

3. Jones, Spencer, 'Introduction: The Forgotten Year', in Jones, Spencer, editor, *Courage without Glory: The British Army on the Western Front, 1915* (Solihull: Helion & Company Limited, 2015) (*Courage without Glory*), page xxv.

The BEF troops launched their attack on 25 September and, initially, were successful; but the cavalry had been held too far back to exploit the opportunities that had opened up before the Germans counter-attacked. With this counter-attack, the initial opportunities were lost and the battle came to nought. By the end of October, the battle was over. It had been a disaster that was not easy to explain away—the British had lost too many men; mostly, the early volunteers and 'the better class of artisan, the upper and the lower middle classes' as Lloyd George described them.[5]

The battle also signalled to many the end of the cavalry's role in the war and many histories of the fighting on the Western Front speak little of the cavalry after this date —although the cavalry did play a role in the British advance from August to November 1918, when the more fluid warfare of movement provided the cavalry with greater opportunities to play its traditional role.

One consequence of the BEF's failure at Loos was the replacement of Sir John French by Sir Douglas Haig as Commander-in-Chief of the BEF on 19 December 1915.

The Army Council in November 1915 considered that the cavalry had played a smaller part in the war than had been expected and sought to make savings —in manpower, cost and logistical support— from the cavalry. In late October 1915, the BEF's GHQ began to plan ways for using the cavalry as dismounted troops so as to plug gaps in the front line caused by the manpower shortage.

It was into this situation that Cyril disembarked in France in October 1915 to join 3DG. As, with very few exceptions, war diaries did not mention other ranks by name —only officers received this courtesy— the following description of Cyril's service with 3DG involves an element of guesswork and the making of assumptions;

---

4. Jones, Spencer 'To make war as we must, and not as we should like,' *Courage without Glory*, page 54.
5. Mallinson, Allan, *Too Important for the Generals: Losing and Winning the First World War* (London: Bantam Press, 2016), page 148.

including the assumption that he remained with C Squadron in the Regiment.

From his arrival with 3DG until the beginning of January 1916, Cyril was in billets, first at Raimbert before moving into Winter billets on 17 October. The latter billets were initially in the area of Westrehem, Nedonchelle and Fontaines-les-Herman before, in the middle of November, 3DG transferred westwards to the Offin/Loison district, west of Fruges.

The daily routine of Winter billets was one of frequent digging parties at Sercus and Lynde (both in an area just west of Hazebrouck) and at Ouderdom (near Poperinghe) on either side of the Franco-Belgian border respectively, improving billets, building horse shelters and training. Holt described the men's quarters as 'comfortable' and said the horses were all under cover in barns.[6] Christmas Day 1915 was a holiday.

Elsewhere, the war was not going well. The Entente Powers had, finally, recognised their defeat at Gallipoli and evacuated their positions at Suvla Bay on 20 December and at Cape Helles on 8 January 1916; while, on the Western Front, manpower shortages were increasingly evident.

To address these shortages, GHQ had, on 6 November, directed the formation of a 'Dismounted Division' which should be organised of two cavalry corps suitable for employment either as mobile reserves or to relieve other troops holding a portion of the line as circumstances required. On 27 December 1915, 3 Cavalry Division received orders regarding the immediate formation of this Dismounted Cavalry Division.

The Dismounted Cavalry Division operated from 1 January–15 February 1916 and was formed of three dismounted cavalry brigades (1, 2 and 3 Dismounted Cavalry Brigades). Each dismounted cavalry brigade was, in turn, composed of three dismounted battalions drawn one battalion from each cavalry brigade within a cavalry division. Thus, 3 Cavalry Division contributed three battalions

---

6. Holt, page 39.

that, together, were designated 3 Dismounted Cavalry Brigade.

In turn, each dismounted cavalry battalion was formed of three companies (or squadrons) drawn one company (or squadron) from each of the battalions comprising the related cavalry brigade. Thus, 3 Dismounted Cavalry Brigade was formed of three battalions (6, 7 and 8 Dismounted Cavalry Battalions) plus a Royal Horse Artillery battery. 6 Dismounted Cavalry Battalion was drawn from the regiments forming 6 Cavalry Brigade; namely: 3DG, 1 (Royal) Dragoons and the North Somerset Yeomanry. For administrative purposes each of these companies was designated by their parent regiment so, within the dismounted cavalry divisions, brigades and battalions, the company (or squadron) contributed by 3DG was referred to simply as 3DG.

In addition to a squadron/company of 320 all ranks, 3DG also contributed the battalion headquarters of 55 all ranks to 6 Dismounted Cavalry Battalion; and 3DG's commanding officer, Lt. Col. A. Burt, was placed in command of 6 Dismounted Battalion. 6 Dismounted Cavalry Battalion's strength was noted as being:

	Officers	*Other Ranks*	*Total*
Battalion	33	907	940
Machine Gun section	6	102	108
Total	39	1,009	1,048

3DG also contributed a machine gun detachment of 42 all ranks plus four guns to the Machine Gun detachment from 6 Cavalry Brigade which formed part of the Machine Gun Section of 3 Dismounted Brigade.

There is no definite indication that Cyril was in the company (or squadron) from 3DG which formed part of 6 Dismounted Battalion; but, his obituary in the *Denbighshire Free Press*[7] talks of his having

---

7. 16 November 1918, *FP*.

served in the front line on five occasions when dismounted. If this statement is accurate, then the most likely occasion for this would have been as part of the 3DG Squadron of 6 Dismounted Battalion. Thus, I have taken account of this battalion's war diary in Appendix III and have treated Cyril as part of it for narrative purposes for the period from 1 January to 15 February 1916.

For the period of its existence, the Dismounted Cavalry Division covered a section of the line near Bethune. 3 Dismounted Cavalry Brigade constituted the Division's left brigade and was stationed so that, at any one time, one of its constituent battalions would be in the front lines, a second in the support sector and the third in reserve at Sailly-la-Bourse.

When first deployed, 6 Dismounted Cavalry Battalion was in reserve in billets at Sailly-la-Bourse. It served in the front line trenches on three occasions: 9–15 and 23–7 January, and 2–8 February. When not in the front line, the Battalion was in reserve at Sailly-la-Bourse or in support at Bethune.

Each time at the front, it occupied two trenches known as the Alexander and Crown trenches. There were no major enemy assaults or Allied actions during its time in the front-line trenches, although the war diaries note regular artillery exchanges and sniper activity. Artillery consisted variously of heavy artillery, trench mortars, rifle grenades and aerial torpedos. While holding Crown trench on 12 January, the trench suffered three direct hits by mortar shells but, although three yards of the trench were blown in, no casualties were taken.

Then, on 25 and 26 January, both Crown and Alexander trenches suffered particularly heavy bombardments. Usually, a German bombardment would trigger a British response until the Germans ceased their bombardment. After each bombardment, of course, the trenches needed to be repaired —usually at night.

After a spell in the front line, the Battalion would spend the next day cleaning up and remedying deficiencies before the usual routine of troops in the support and reserve lines: namely, being detailed to fatigue duties. These duties usually consisted of clearing up billets, improving the rear defences and trenches, carrying equipment and supplies to the forward areas, and the inevitable digging parties. Even these background tasks were not free from risk as the war diaries record occasions when German shelling of the support and rear areas caused casualties.

On 11 February, the Battalion entrained at Bethune to return its constituent companies (or squadrons) to their home regiments—in 3DG's case, to Offin/Loison where the Regiment had remained in Winter billets.

The Dismounted Cavalry Division was disbanded on 15 February when it was relieved from the front line. During its time in the trenches, the Division had suffered nearly 1,000 casualties.[8] As a stop-gap remedy to staunch manpower deficiencies, the Division worked; but dismounted cavalry were not really suited or equipped for trench warfare: their kit was cavalry kit and they had poor means of carrying all the equipment that they needed — particularly in winter.[9]

Back with 3DG, Cyril would have resumed the general routine of being in billets at Offin/Loison and training in the neighbourhood. A cavalryman's skills at looking after his horse were important to keep his horse in good condition. It was important to have shelter for the horses from the rain and the horses needed dry, hard standings and approaches to their shelters and watering places and water troughs. All these had to be built and maintained by the troopers. Billetting with horses was an issue. Clearly, they needed to be in the countryside where both open spaces were available and also shelter. This often meant in rural or village areas. It also meant that, as at the Somme, the cavalry could not be kept up near the front line for extended periods merely in the hope of a gap developing.

Life for 3DG was quiet and uninteresting until mid-Summer of 1916. At a higher level, the Cavalry Corps was disbanded as a

---

8. Anglesey vol. 8, page 28.
9. Messenger, page 194.

Corps on 6 April and 3 Cavalry Division became a GHQ reserve formation under the direct command of the BEF's GHQ. Meanwhile, the great Franco-German battle of attrition at Verdun had commenced on 21 February —and was to last until November. In Mesopotamia, Britain suffered a second defeat at the hands of Ottoman forces when the besieged garrison at Kut al Amara surrendered on 29 April. On 31 May and 1 June, the Royal Navy engaged the German High Seas Fleet at Jutland, the only major naval engagement of the war. Although the battle has generated enduring controversy and questions over the Royal Navy's performance, Jutland did not affect the general strategic position or the Royal Navy's command of the sea.

6 Cavalry Brigade next formed a machine gun squadron of a total of 221 men (eight officers and 213 other ranks drawn from throughout the Brigade) on 29 February, but there is nothing to suggest that Cyril was part of this squadron.

In the middle of May, 3DG took part in a week's Divisional training in the St Riquier area before going to a camp at L'Étaples. 6 Cavalry Brigade had established this camp so that the sands at Paris-Plage could be used for drill as there was no suitable ground in the permanent billeting area around Offin and Loison. Oatts described 3DG as 'resting' at Le Touquet[10] while Anglesey described the period from April to 1 July as the cavalry's being 'fatted up'[11] for the planned advance on the Somme. 6 Cavalry Brigade received orders in the middle of June to concentrate in billets by 22 June.

On 24 June, 3DG set out by route march to Bonnay, just east of Corbie. Long marches —particularly in winter but even in summer— could tell on a horse's condition and it was customary for troopers in the British cavalry to lead their horses for at least a quarter of the time rather than, as the French cavalry did, riding them all the time. Of course, a trooper's own weight was nearly

10. Oatts, page 221.
11. Anglesey, vol. 8 page 40.

doubled by all the kit he had to transport; so adding to the horse's burden.[12] This British practice of marching dismounted and leading the horses for a portion of every hour attracted the derision of their French counter-parts, but its benefits were evident in the relative horse-loss rates of the two armies.[13]

As they marched towards Bonnay, Cyril would have heard the softening up bombardment ahead of the Somme offensive.[14] This bombardment began a week before Zero day, or 1 July; but, a worryingly large number of British shells —75% made in America— simply did not explode.[15] In expanding their ammunition supply so rapidly, the British 'had surrendered quality for quantity.'[16]

3DG arrived at Bonnay on a very wet day. Here, 6 Cavalry Brigade were held, as part of 3 Cavalry Division, in reserve to exploit any opportunities that might arise from the forthcoming Somme offensive. 3DG's strength was given as:

	Officers	*O/ Ranks*	*Horses*	*Wagons*
Fighting Troops	23	380	433	
A Echelon[17]	2	71	109	10
B Echelon	2	25	24	5
Total	27	476	566	15

The Regiment was originally ordered to be ready by 0730 on 29 June but this was delayed until 1 July when the Fourth Army was to commence the Somme offensive in the neighbourhood of Albert. So, by 0730 on 1 July, 6 Cavalry Brigade was all formed up at Bonnay and awaiting orders to move. The plan was that, after the

---

12. Winton, pages 316–7.
13. *Horsemen*, page 17.
14. Holt, page 221.
15. Roberts, Andrew, *Elegy: The First Day on the Somme* (London: Head of Zeus Ltd, 2015) (*Elegy*), page 94.
16. *The British Army*, page 287.
17. An echelon is the fighting unit's support or logistics element that is not directly involved in the fighting.

infantry assault had opened up a gap in the Front, 3 Cavalry Division (along with 1 Cavalry Division and 2 Indian Cavalry Division) should advance on Bapaume —10 miles beyond the start line.

But, fifteen minutes later 3DG was ordered to off-saddle and was put on half-an-hour's readiness —which was extended to two hours at 1730 before, at 1900, the Brigade was told that it would not be advancing on the next day. 3DG, remained in bivouac at Bonnay and the readiness time was extended to four hours at 2040 on 2 July. The initial Somme offensive had failed (with 60,000 British casualties —of whom 20,000 were killed) and, on 4 July, 3 Cavalry Division was ordered to move to the Hallencourt area west of Amiens. The next day, 3DG supplied an officer and 58 men for battlefield clearing duties.

The Somme again highlighted the difficulty of using cavalry in the circumstances of general trench warfare. It was difficult to bring up the cavalry to a point sufficiently close to the Front in order to exploit any gap. The terrain immediately behind the trenches was all churned up and virtually impassable to a massed body of men on horses. So, tracks needed to be constructed up to the Front along which the cavalry could be brought. Anglesey describes the task of constructing these tracks as 'gruelling' and one carried out by working parties of cavalry troopers, who usually worked at night and, often, under shell fire.[18] The cavalry could not remain *en masse* for long near the Front as they took up too much space and placed too great a burden on the transport system with their need to bring up forage and water supplies for the horses.[19]

The Somme was something of a disaster for Kitchener's New Armies. It was not Haig's first choice of battleground. Oatts argued that 'the Somme front was probably the least favourable for an offensive, for there the enemy trenches were particularly strong and

---

18. Anglesey vol. 8, page 42.
19. ibid, page 45

completely overlooked those of the British along the waterlogged ground below them'[20] —but Joffre had persuaded Haig to attack here, in part to relieve pressure on French forces.

By 8 July, it was clear that there would be no cavalry advance and 6 Cavalry Brigade was ordered to move further back from the Hallencourt area to bivouacs in the Corbie area and further back again to La Neuville on 20 July. During this period, 3DG provided several dismounted working parties to work on salvage and burying duties on the battlefield; and to dig and improve trenches in the Contalmaison and Hametz areas, just east of Albert.

At the beginning of August, 6 Cavalry Brigade moved back further westwards from La Neuville to the Fruges area where it returned to permanent billets. 3DG was again billeted at Loison and spent the rest of August in a daily routine of training and the provision of occasional working parties to work on laying cables in the Bouzincourt area, just west of Albert.

This routine continued until the middle of September when 6 Cavalry Brigade was again brought up to Bonnay in the hope that it could be pushed through a gap to be created by an infantry offensive in the Battle of Flers. The battle commenced at dawn on 15 September; but, although the infantry managed to move the front line forward, there was —again— no opportunity for a cavalry advance.[21] So, on 17 September, the Brigade marched back —bivouacking each night— to the Bealcourt/Beauvoir/Wavans area (south-east of L'Etaples and Le Touquet) where it arrived on 24 September and went into billets. This return march must have been particularly unpleasant for the war diaries noted the days as being very wet.

3DG remained in this area until the end of February 1917; first at Maintenay, then at Campigneulles-les-Grandes from 22 October to 6 November when 3DG moved to Berck Sands (Berck Plage)

---

20. Oatts, page 221.
21. This battle saw the first use of tanks.

until 1 December when it returned to Campigneuilles-les-Grandes until 20 December when it exchanged billets there for others at Airon-St.Vaast.

Small dismounted working parties were detached from 3DG from 2 October until 11 November to work near Bouzincourt. Otherwise, the war diaries suggest a daily diet of general routine and training —from 16 December, described as 'Winter Training'— and the occasional inspection parade. The only high-points being that Christmas Day was again a holiday and, on 3 January 1917, a 'cinematograph entertainment' was recorded as having been given in the evening.

On 7 December 1916, David Lloyd George became Prime Minister with the aim of revitalising Britain's war effort.

8. ON THE HOME FRONT

At home, business life in Denbigh continued much as it had before; but, gradually, the war's impact was felt in the town with an increased military presence, the accommodation of Belgian refugees locally and the establishment of a prisoner of war camp at Dyffryn Aled.[1]

Cyril's family played their part in supporting the general war effort: his father was reported to have given a guinea (£1.05) to the National Relief Fund in October 1914;[2] and his mother was reported on several occasions as having raised collections for the troops,[3] Belgian refugees[4] and/or given items for the soldiers and the wounded. In December 1915, his mother was one of the ladies of the town who joined the Mayoress (Mrs Robert Owen) and her campaign to sell picture postcards to augment the National Fund in aid of comforts for the Welsh troops: his mother and younger brother having collected from Park Street and Mellings Lane in Denbigh. In September 1917, his mother was mentioned as having given magazines to the Red Cross Hospital at Ystrad Isaf.[5]

Cyril's mother was not in the best of health during the war and, in 1918, was to suffer a stroke. In the summer of 1915, she spent two weeks or so down near Cyril in Canterbury —partly for her health

---

1. Morris, E. T., *Denbigh Diary: Notes From the Town* (Kindle edition, 2017) provides a description of life in Denbigh during the war's first year.
2. 31 October 1914, *FP*.
3. His mother and Mrs. J. R. Owen, between them, raised 4/6 (22.5p) in the first week of October and 13/- (65p) in three successive weeks for the Queen's Work for Women Fund and Voluntary Aid Organisation; 3, 24 and 31 October and 7 November 1914, *FP*.
4. 7 November 1914, *FP*.
5. 8 September 1917, *FP*.

and, partly, to see him. He wrote of his intention to aim for weekend leave whilst she was down there.[6]

No doubt because of their local birth, upbringing and Welsh-speaking character, Cyril's family back home in Denbigh were well-known locally and do not seem to have suffered from the anti-German feelings and actions that were aroused within Britain during the war. However, it cannot have been totally easy.

Somewhat surprisingly —and, no doubt by 1914, embarrassingly so— his father has given his own nationality as German in the 1911 Census, the first census in which the question of an individual's was specifically asked. It would appear to have been a conscious decision as every other member of the family's nationality was given as British. It is unclear why Cyril's father would have given this answer as, in the eyes of British law, he was a British subject by virtue of his birth here. Of course, German law would have regarded him as being a German subject —as German law looked to patrilineal descent to determine the question of nationality.[7] It may be that, he —or the enumerator— did not appreciate the question or the niceties of the point and simply looked to the fact that he was born to two German subjects.

At this distance in time, we must wonder whether his father realised that, by giving this answer in the 1911 census, he lay himself open to being included in a confidential and unofficial 'aliens register' which the police compiled after 1911. This register was compiled from a variety of police records, intelligence reports and census returns. Of course, the census returns were not intended to be used for this purpose!

German civilian nationals in Britain had their movements

---

6. Letter (undated but probably end May/early June 1915) from Cyril to his parents; see Appendix II.
7. Britain, at that time, followed the *ius soli* principle whereas Germany (like most of continental Europe apart from France) followed the *ius sanguinis* principle to determine nationality.

restricted during the war and many were interned.[8] The Aliens (Restriction) Act, rushed through Parliament on 5 August 1914, required all enemy aliens to register with the local police.[9] In Denbigh, a notice was put up at the police station requiring German nationals to register —or face a fine of up to £100 or up to six months in prison.[10] That Act placed the onus upon the individual concerned of proving whether or not he was an alien or a British subject. Proving the latter would have been easy and straightforward for Cyril's father as he was born in Denbigh. Despite the entry in the 1911 Census, there is no evidence to suggest that Cyril's father was ever treated as anything other than British by the authorities; but, by now, almost all records regarding aliens and registration with the police have been destroyed so it is impossible to say whether or not the point was ever pursued.

However, others whom Cyril would have known from childhood would have been affected. Jakob Bauer, who was a shop assistant in the family shop, was a German national and his movements and property would have been restricted. After the war had ended, Bauer's property was subject to control by the Clearing Office (Enemy Debts).[11] It is also likely that other members of the German

8. For a discussion of German subjects and the registration of enemy aliens in Britain during the war see Bird, John Clement, 'Control of Enemy Alien Civilians in Great Britain 1914–1918,' (PhD diss, University of London, 1981) (Bird); Swan, Jonathan, Aliens (Restriction) Act 1914 in *Criminal Law & Justice Weekly*, Vol. 180, 13 August 2016; and Swan, Jonathan, *Law and War: Magistrates in The Great War* (Barnsley: Pen & Sword Military, 2017), chapter 6 'The Enemy Within', pages 90–110.
9. *Zeppelin Nights*, page 70. Over 50,000 German nationals registered, mostly in London. By October 1915, over 32,000 German nationals had been interned; ibid, page 78.
10. Glynn, Kindle edition, Loc 188 out of 993.
11. When Jakob Bauer and his wife both died in 1924, Cyril's father, who was their executor, needed to apply to the Clearing Office (Enemy Debts) for permission to deal with their estates. See Endorsements on their Grants of Probate—in the author's possession. See Charteris, A. H., 'The Constitution and Organisation of the Clearing Office (Enemy Debts)' in the *Journal of Comparative Legislation and International Law*, Vol. 3, No.1 (1921) pages 31–9, for a discussion of the operation of this body.

diaspora in North Wales and particularly the Liverpool area, with its port and shipping facilities, with whom the family had maintained contact would have had their movements restricted or been interned. Cyril was perhaps fortunate that his paternal grandfather, Wilhelm, had died in 1912 for Wilhelm had remained a German subject and, had he still been alive when the war began, he too would have been liable to internment.

While many German families and businesses in Britain anglicised their names or changed them completely during the war, Wilhelm's British born widow —his second wife and Cyril's step-grandmother— who continued to live in Wilhelm's cottage, in Broomhill Lane at the back of the shop, did not change the cottage's name from Schwarzwald Cottage.

After the RMS *Lusitania* was torpedoed off Cobh (then, Queenstown) on 7 May 1915, anti-German riots broke out in several towns and cities in Britain and many German related businesses were attacked.[12] In Rhyl, on Friday and Saturday evenings 21 and 22 May, soldiers from the nearby Kinmel Bay camp rioted and attacked a German-owned business. Although not directly linked to the RMS *Lusitania's* sinking, this riot nonetheless demonstrates that not even North Wales was immune from attacks on German subjects and German associated businesses. Family oral accounts describe how Cyril's father was forced to call upon the police to protect the family shop on the High Street from soldiers stationed in Denbigh intent on smashing up the shop because of its German sounding name.

London, of course, was, from May 1915, subject to bombing raids by Zeppelin airships and Gotha planes.[13] At one stage during the war, Cyril must have been in London just after some such raids for he writes home that: 'The Johns[14] were very scared over the

12. White talks of a 'frenzy of violence' falling upon German nationals; *Zeppelin Nights*, page 76.
13. See *Zeppelin Nights*.
14. They must have been family friends living in London but I am not able otherwise to identify them.

Zepp. They have an anti-aircraft gun near there & it rather shook them up' before going on to ask his father: 'Please send me 10/- (50p) this week Dad.' It is unclear just when this letter[15] was written but it must have been after May 1915 when the first Zeppelin raids occurred. Cyril continued:

> Am writing this letter up in the room and some of the boys are amusing themselves by making stump speeches & they are most distracting!

before concluding:

> Well I must conclude now—*Nos dewch*.[16]
> With my best love to you all
> Your loving son,
> Cyril

People at home had to put up with not just the occasional bombing raid but, as the war went on, food shortages and increasing inflation, as prices more than doubled over the war's course. Ian Kershaw suggests that most people back home simply wanted to block out of their imaginations what the men at the Front were enduring. He writes that many soldiers returned to France with the sense that those at Home had no understanding of what they were going through.[17]

A more interesting —and somewhat mysterious, if not even potentially problematic— incident for Cyril's family occurred in August 1918. Among various family papers is a postcard from the village of Boll in the Black Forest region of Germany and, presumably received by Cyril's father in August 1918! All we have

---

15. Copy of just pages 3 and 4 in the author's possession, supplied by Cyril's sister, Josephine's, daughter.
16. Night comes.
17. Kershaw, Ian, *To Hell and Back: Europe 1914–1949* (London: Penguin Random House, 2016) (Kershaw).

13. The 'Boll' postcard.

Towards the top of the photograph, just left of centre, one can make out a cross with a line down to a window on the top floor of the house below. The significance of this window is not explained in the message—but, presumably, was intended to indicate just where the 'son' was staying.

is this postcard —and no explanation whatsoever. It was addressed to 'Herrn Küpfer, Uhrmacher, Denbigh, England' and goes on to say:[18]

Boll 10.8.18

We are comfortably together with your son.
Happy that there is still some German blood in Wales. Your son at any rate feels well looked after.
Warm greetings from the Black Forest.

Rud. Hugel.

18. For the German text, see Appendix II.

One thing is clear: the message is not literally true in that there were no unaccounted for Denbigh male Keepfers. Cyril was in France with 2RWF at the time; his brother, John, was still at Love Lane School and there were no other male Keepfers in Denbigh at the time apart from Cyril's father —his grandfather having died in 1912. The only other known male in the family in Britain was a young cousin of Cyril's living in Litherland.

So, the postcard is either a coded message of some kind or is simply a piece of German mischief making.

The note on the card has the feel of being written by someone who does not actually know the recipient—but knows of the recipient. It is also couched in a friendly tone.

Boll is a small village in the Black Forest (or *Schwarzwald*) about twelve miles south west of Neustadt from whence the Keepfers had come originally; so, it is possible that there was some connection, way back, between the Keepfer family and the Hugel family in Boll. How would the card have come to Denbigh? The postcard is unstamped and unfranked. It must, therefore, have come in an envelope, which no longer exists. Boll is no more than fifteen miles north of Switzerland, so it would have been possible for an envelope containing the postcard to have been posted from Switzerland to Britain. The most likely alternative is that it would have been sent via neutral Holland, which is how many communications passed between Britain and Germany and where several sets of inter-governmental discussions (including as regards the exchange of civilians trapped in the enemy country at the war's start) were held during the war. In either case, one must assume that censors in Britain would have examined the correspondence.

If it is some form of coded message, it presumably relates to an individual whom the Keepfers knew and who had been interned previously and then repatriated to Germany. Some 50,000 plus German subjects were trapped in Britain following the declaration of war and discussions and efforts went on throughout the war regarding their possible repatriation —and exchange for Britons similarly trapped in Germany. However, arrangements for large-scale repatriation were only agreed in principle towards the end of 1917 and only formalised in July 1918 and no transfers, via Holland, started before October 1918.[19] Thus, it would need to have been in the nature of a special 'one off' repatriation.

Certainly, Cyril's grandfather had maintained links with the German diaspora in and around North Wales and Liverpool but it is unclear of the extent to which Cyril's father maintained these links —or would have felt close enough to anyone so as to take some form of a protective interest in a youngster (or anyone else) who was trapped in Britain following the declaration of war in 1914. There is no family lore on the matter.

Which leads one to the alternative view that this was simply mischief making on Germany's part. Certainly, the family name could have been obtained easily from several of the gazetteers that had published regularly in other British trade directories in the years leading up to the war. For instance, Wilson's international Trade Directory of Wales in 1885 advertises Keepfer (albeit not Küpfer) of Denbigh as a 'Watchmaker' (or *Horloger* or *Uhrmacher*).

However, if it was a case of German mischief making, why did the family keep the postcard? Surely, the natural instinct would probably have been to destroy any evidence of problematic connections with the enemy state. A century on, all we can say is that the postcard and its background remain a mystery.

---

19. See Bird.

9. OFFICER TRAINING

In 1914, the officer class in the Regular Army —*a fortiori* the cavalry— tended to be gentlemen of independent means; usually public school educated and often from military, clerical or professional families. A major reason for this was the fact that, in many regiments at Home, an officer's pay only partly covered his expected costs —mess bills, uniforms, personal equipment etc.[1] As a result the 'public school ethos [was] firmly entrenched in the officers' outlook.'[2] This was no less true of 2RWF. Both Langley, who provides short potted descriptions of most of the original officers of 2RWF at the outbreak of the war,[3] and Dunn[4] confirm this. Although exceptions did exist, officers nearly all conformed to this stereotype.

The initial replacement officers also came from the same background. Many volunteers with the right connections were simply commissioned at the beginning of the war even if they had little immediate experience —although many had been members of an officer training corps at school or, in a few cases, university. Again, 2RWF was no different. Messenger says that many officer candidates without a public school education were simply refused a commission in the early days —a bias that was more pronounced in southern England than elsewhere. This bias continued until well into 1915 —by which time the supply of suitable candidates had been exhausted so the Army perforce had to be more open.[5]

1. *The British Army*, page 19.
2. *Challenge of Battle*, page 27.
3. *Duty Done*, chapter 4, pages 18–48.
4. Dunn, page xxxvi.
5. Messenger, page 293.

The formal photograph (N⁰· 14) of Cyril and Tom Gee together in their new uniforms evidences this class division. It shows Cyril and his Sunday school friend, Tom Gee, posing for a formal photograph in 1915 —presumably after they had both completed their training and before they went off to war. The state school educated Cyril is a trooper in the cavalry while the private school educated Tom was a commissioned 2nd lieutenant.

As the war dragged on and large numbers of the original officer complement and the volunteers immediately upon the outbreak of hostilities had been killed, the social composition of the officer class began to change. The losses and disasters at the Somme added another impetus to the change. After the Somme, officers tended to be appointed more on grounds of ability rather than what they had done before 1914.[6] Even so, those who held temporary commissions were often referred to, disparagingly, as 'temporary gentlemen' by the more traditional Regular Army officers.

With the expansion of Kitchener's New Armies, the most serious deficiency became a lack of men who could lead and command — not only as officers but also as NCOs. This was to be a continuing issue. Even in 1918, Ellis, in his history of the 4th (Denbighshire) Battalion RWF, wrote that 'the most difficult gaps to fill were those in the commissioned ranks.'[7]

In the summer of 1915, when he was still at Canterbury, there had clearly been earlier correspondence between Cyril and his parents regarding several of his contemporaries who had been promoted while Cyril had not been. He explains that promotion in the new regiments and battalions raised as part of Kitchener's New Army was so quick because they had few experienced non commissioned officers. By contrast, in 3DG, the NCOs were nearly all old soldiers or NCOs who had previously served with the Regiment and who had been recalled in 1914.[8]

---

6. *Elegy*, page 237.
7. Ellis, page 111.
8. Letter (undated but probably late May/early June, 1915) from Cyril to his parents; see Appendix II.

Officer Training

At that time, 400 volunteers had been sought from 3DG to transfer to the infantry, but, Cyril reported, there had been few volunteers —particularly in C Squadron and the men had been paraded a second time when a few further names were taken. He suggested that those volunteering to transfer were allowed their choice of regiment and said that, if he were asked to transfer, he would try for the London Welsh. However, he said he did not 'think some how they would want me to go.' Meanwhile, he was 'interestedly awaiting events.'[9]

As we know, nothing further happened on this subject to Cyril until early 1917.

The comments do, however, suggest a young soldier who was competent at his job and well enough regarded by his fellow soldiers that they would not wish to lose him. They also suggest that Cyril was a considered individual who knew his own mind and who would aim to do things on his own terms —i.e. if he were required to switch to the infantry, then he would aim for a Wales connected regiment. This determination reinforces the belief that his original enlistment in the cavalry was a positive decision on his part and not something into which he had simply drifted.

With the coming of war, the officer cadet training courses for the Regular Army were reduced from 24 and 18 months to six and three months respectively at RMA Woolwich and RMC Sandhurst.[10] Early in the war, the War Office quickly realised how little many newly commissioned officers knew of military matters. Volunteers in the New Armies (as opposed to the Regular Army regiments) were all only given temporary commissions. With the introduction of conscription in early 1916, this rule was extended to all commissions except for graduates from Sandhurst and Woolwich.[11]

Conscription and the high mortality rates amongst junior

---

9. ibid.
10. Messenger, page 289.
11. ibid, page 293.

officers on the Somme placed an additional strain on officer training as there were few individuals left with any prior officer cadet training experience not already in the army. Now, the War Office decreed that nobody could be commissioned unless they had undergone basic training in the ranks or been in an officer training corps at school or university. At the same time, the War Office set about standardising officer training. Officer cadet battalions were established and offered a four and a half months training course.[12] By 1917, some 10,000 new officers were needed each year — compared with a total officer complement of just 13,000 in 1914— and there were 21 officer cadet battalions and each regiment was required to suggest candidates, who needed to be aged 18½ or over, for officer training.

3 Cavalry Division's adjutant noted on 22 December 1916 that GHQ and the War Office had raised the question of the supply of candidates for temporary commissions in the infantry. The Division was ordered to despatch 12 candidates per week up to the end of February 1917 (i.e. an average of 1.25 candidates per week from each regiment in the Division) and the Adjutant ordered that lists of candidates be prepared. During the Winter of 1916/1917, the Army's manpower demands were such that the cavalry reserve was reduced from 15,000 men to below 3,000 and many cavalry recruits were diverted to the Infantry.

It seems that there was no standardised selection process and the decision on who was recommended was down to an individual unit's commanding officer.[13] Most candidates for commissions were NCOs; indeed, there was a general rule that candidates should at least hold the rank of corporal.[14] Thus, we may wonder why Cyril was chosen given that, at least so far as all the records show, he had not been promoted to even the most junior non-commissioned post within 3DG. The most likely explanation is that such promotions

12. ibid, page 314.
13. *The British Army,* page 69.
14. Messenger, page 327.

involved an element of 'dead men's shoes' and, as the cavalry were rarely in battle after he joined 3DG, there simply were no NCO vacancies for him —particularly if, as he had suggested, the Regiment had a number of old-timers as NCOs. Alternatively, as Messenger suggested, regiments may have been reluctant to release experienced NCOs.

To circumvent the general rule that only NCOs could be proposed, it was not unknown for privates to be temporarily promoted to the rank of acting (unpaid) corporal before their names were submitted;[15] but it is not known whether this ruse was adopted in Cyril's case. Of course, Cyril had had a secondary school education to beyond Junior Certificate standard. In any event, he was selected. In his obituary, it is stated that he was one of only six candidates from his Regiment selected for officer training.[16]

Cyril applied formally for a commission on 17 February 1917 but we may assume that things had been pre-arranged and that the application was something of a formality as it was immediately approved by his regimental colonel, Lt.-Col. A. Burt, and, on 20 February, by 6 Cavalry Brigade's commanding officer, Brig. Gen. A. E. W. Harman. Both officers signed to say that they had interviewed him and considered him to be a suitable candidate for officer training.

In his application (which was on a standard printed form — Form MT.393A.), Cyril confirmed that he had made no previous application, he was a British subject by birth, his father was British and that he was of pure European descent,[17] and he provided his father's name and address.[18] The form's standard question as to whether he was able to ride had been crossed out by hand and

---

15. ibid.
16. This must refer to the period up to when Cyril left 3DG as he would not have known the position after he left that regiment.
17. The British Army —as distinct from the Indian Army— would not grant commissions to anyone not of European descent at that time. See Messenger, page 322, for a discussion on the point.
18. Derwenfa, Denbigh, North Wales.

'School at which educated' substituted for it: to which Cyril answered: Denbigh County School. Presumably the original question was deemed redundant in the case of an applicant from a cavalry regiment.

Two Certificates of Character needed to be obtained and he gave the names of Robert Owen, of Star Shop, 45 High Street, Denbigh and the Rev'd E(van) Jones of Brynhyfryd, Denbigh (the Minister at Capel Mawr, 1893–1920) as his referees. His Certificate of Education was to be obtained from D. H. Davies at the Denbigh County School. He was again medically examined and passed fit, by 3DG's medical officer, for military service with 6/6 vision on 17 February 1917.

His application was for a temporary commission in the Regular Army. By this time, all commissions in the Regular Army were meant to be temporary commissions except for those awarded to candidates proceeding from Sandhurst and Woolwich.

An applicant was allowed to state his preference for where he wished to serve and in which unit. Cyril applied for the infantry. The infantry had the greatest demand for new officers and many cavalry officers were already transferring to infantry regiments because of the lack of action.[19] So, it is inconceivable that any application for a commission in the cavalry would have succeeded.

Cyril expressed a wish to serve with the RWF. This would have been the logical choice as he had been born within the Regiment's North Wales recruiting area. However, in his records, a different hand has crossed out his choice of unit in blue crayon and substituted 2 Royal West Kents. The dating and reasoning for this substitution are unclear —not least because the bulk of 2 Royal West Kents had surrendered at Kut al Amara in April the previous year and the remainder were still serving with the Indian Army in Mesopotamia at that time.

On 24 February 1917, Cyril was issued with a railway warrant

19. Messenger, page 194.

to Tidworth[20] and ordered to report to the officer commanding the depot of 6 Cavalry Reserve Regiment at Tidworth.[21] He left France on 25 February and arrived in England on 26 February. Here, he was listed as having been posted as a private to the Cavalry Reserve Regiment of Dragoons on 26 February.[22]

Before starting his officer training, he was allowed home leave. The precise dates of this furlough are unclear because the note in his file giving his address whilst on furlough as Derwenfa is undated. But, the *Baner ac Amserau Cymru* reported, on 10 March 1917, that he was at home on leave:[23]

ADREF O FAES Y RHYFEL
Y mae y Private Cyril Keepfer, mab hynaf Mr a Mrs Keepfer, Derwenfa, wedi dyfod adref am ychydig seibiant o Ffrainc.

The *Denbighshire Free Press* had, the week before, suggested he was in London:[24]

HOME ON LEAVE
Lieut. Keepfer, son of Mr and Mrs Keepfer, High-street, Denbigh, who joined the army immediately on the outbreak of the war and who has for 18 months been out in France through the thick of the fighting without being at home, has now a much needed rest granted him, and is over in London.

20. One of the many garrison towns in Wiltshire.
21. In early 1917, 3rd Reserve Regiment of Cavalry, in which Cyril had done his original training and which was the Home service (or reserve) regiment of 3DG, had been merged into the newly formed 6th Reserve Regiment of Cavalry based at Tidworth; hence the rail warrant to Tidworth.
22. Slightly different from these dates, his Casualty Form – Active Service notes 18 February as the date on which he went to England as a candidate for a Temporary Commission in the Infantry.
23. 10 March 1917, *Baner ac Amserau Cymru* (*Y Faner*): 'Home from the Field of Battle. Private Cyril Keepfer, elder son of Mr & Mrs Keepfer, Derwenfa has come home for a short leave from France.'
24. 3 March 1917, *FP*.

The newspaper then somewhat jumped the gun as regards his promotion and reported that he had been commissioned as a lieutenant[25] when, in fact, he had merely been selected for an Officers' Training Course —at the end of which he could only expect to be commissioned as a second lieutenant:

> His many friends at home will be delighted to hear that he has received his commission as Lieutenant, which speaks highly of his efficiency as a soldier and of his bravery and good work as a soldier of his King and country.

While Cyril was at home, Czar Nicholas II abdicated on 15 March paving the way for the eventual November Revolution and Russia's withdrawal from the war.

Cyril reported to the Artists' Rifles 15 Officer Cadet Battalion at the Romford training camp on 7 April —the day after the United States of America entered the war as an 'associated power' on the Allied side. Until Cyril had completed, and passed, the course at Romford, he remained, on paper, a cavalryman and he was formally posted to the Scottish Cavalry Depot on 29 June under the authority of a letter N°· BM 28 from the War Office dated 22 June.

As we can see from his posed photograph, Cyril continued to wear his cavalry other ranks' service dress while at Romford. He wears an other ranks' belt as opposed to his trooper's bandolier; presumably, this was partly to ensure a similarity of dress with the other cadets and partly a question of practical comfort. The only indication that he was an officer cadet was the white band around his cap.

The officer training courses were demanding and about a sixth of all candidates failed the course.[26] Had he not passed the course, Cyril would have been returned to the cavalry. These courses each lasted four-and-a-half months and there were usually 400 candidates

---

25. ibid.
26. Messenger, page 327.

on each course —although, in May 1917, this number was increased to 600 where the unit could cope. The officer cadet battalions were responsible for almost all the officer commissions granted in the second half of the war and nearly half of all the nearly 223,000 commissions in total awarded during the war.[27]

It appears that Cyril completed the training course by the end of July[28] for he was discharged from the cavalry to a commission as a 2nd lieutenant and posted to Third Battalion of the RWF (3RWF) on 31 July 1917 by order of the War Office dated 24 August.[29] On the same day, the War Office wrote to 3RWF's commanding officer confirming that the appointment of 2nd Lieutenant William Robert Cyril Keepfer in the Special Reserve of Officers (3RWF) had been approved and that the necessary formal notifications would appear in the *London Gazette*[30] in due course. The formal notice appeared in the *London Gazette* on 28 August. Cyril was just under 23 years of age when he was commissioned.

As a 2nd lieutenant, Cyril's pay increased considerably from that of a trooper. A 2nd lieutenant's pay was 7/6 (37.5p) a day (or just over £136 per annum) in 1914 and increased slightly in December 1915.[31] This is nearly ten times what he was paid on enlistment as a trooper in 3DG. Thus, as from when he was commissioned, he would no longer have had his army pay supplemented by his former employer. Even so, his income would have increased nearly threefold.

When he was killed in 1918, he was being paid 10/6 (52.5p) per day. There is nothing in his records that I have been able to trace to

27. ibid, page 333.
28. According to a note in his War Office record. This does, of course, suggest that the course did not last the theoretical standard four and a half months.
29. War Office to commanding officer Scottish Cavalry Depot, 24 August 1917, 43/y.o./118/M.52.
30. The British Government's official publication of formal appointments and events.
31. I have been unable to trace details of the pay increases awarded during the war to reflect inflation. Despite inflation causing retail prices to more than double over the war's course, army pay did not keep pace.

suggest whether this merely reflected a second lieutenant's pay or took account of the extra pay and allowances to which he was entitled as a result of being D Company commander. This scale of pay distinction between officers and privates continued in the British Army until at least the Second World War. Of course, as an officer, Cyril, unlike an ordinary soldier, would have been obliged to purchase his own uniform and camp kit from a military outfitter; but he would, probably, also have had better accommodation — albeit still in billets or encampments when not in the trenches; a batman to take care of him; and better food in the officer's mess, although, when serving out of the line, he would have been obliged to settle mess bills for his food and drink. As a junior officer, he would have carried a total of 61lbs (28 kg) of equipment and clothes on a march —about the same as a private.

By the Summer of 1917, 'gentlemen officers had become a very rare thing.'[32] A War Office survey of demobilised officers at the end of the war showed that almost 60% of officers came from what could be viewed as being middle-class occupations: 'commercial and clerical', 'students and teachers' and 'professional men.' Of the balance, a significant number were lower-middle or working class.[33] At best, Cyril's *petit bourgeois* background and junior clerical position would have been lower middle class. Again, 2RWF was no exception. Langley recognised this new strain of officers in 2RWF as 'the grammar school boy' and mentions Cyril as a represent-ative of this new breed.[34] This change in the social composition and character of the officer cadre reflected the fact that, as the war progressed, the British Army became, largely, a civilian —non-professional— force.

3RWF was not a service battalion within the RWF but merely a training and holding battalion for all ranks awaiting posting to another battalion within the Regiment. From 3RWF, Cyril was

32. Messenger, page 331.
33. ibid, page 333.
34. *Duty Done*, page 88.

14. Cyril and his Sunday School friend, Tom Gee, 1915.
Tom is in the uniform of a second lieutenant RWF.

15. Cyril at home on leave, 1917.
L–R: Josie, Cyril, Phyllis and John. Cyril is wearing an officer cadet's tailored pattern service uniform with infantry-style puttees, but without any unit badges or insignia of rank and an other ranks' leather belt.

16. Cyril as an officer cadet at Romford, May 1917.
He is wearing the same uniform as above but with a white-banded cadet's cap.

17. Cyril at Romford, 1917.
A picture taken during a quiet period during his officer's training course.

18. Cyril and Ivor Watkins, 1917.
This was probably taken on the same leave as photograph N⁰· 15. It would have been taken either in the garden at Derwenfa or at Bryn, Phyllis and Sydney Watkins' house in Bull Lane.

19. Cyril's officer's watch.
The watch, now in the possession of his half-sister, Yvonne, still keeps perfect time.

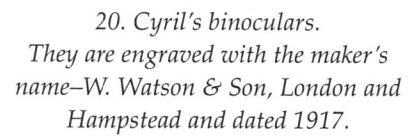

20. Cyril's binoculars.
They are engraved with the maker's name—W. Watson & Son, London and Hampstead and dated 1917.

Overleaf:
21. Newly-commissioned 2nd Lieut Cyril Keepfer.
As the studios where this photograph was taken were at Lime Street, Liverpool, we may assume that this was taken while Cyril was posted to 3RWF in Litherland some time in August or September 1917.

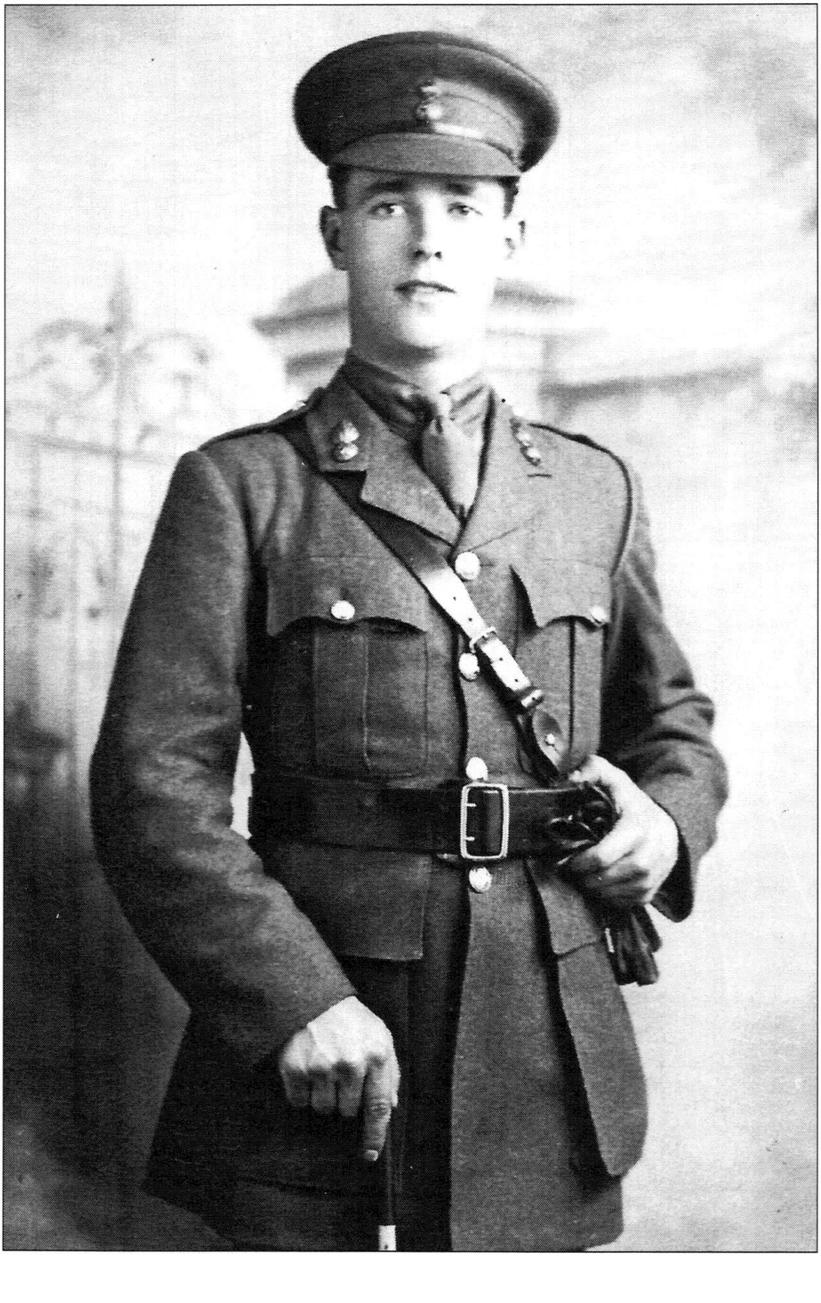

posted to 2RWF. This was a Regular Army battalion: i.e. one that existed in 1914 as part of the Regular Army and not one that had been raised as part of Kitchener's recruiting drive for his New Armies —which resulted in over 20 additional battalions of the RWF being formed.[35]

The process by which Cyril ended up in 2RWF is unclear. Despite his stated preference for the RWF on his application for a commission, Cyril would have had, at the end of the day, little say in the regiment to which he was posted; but, once within a regiment, that regiment would decide on the battalion to which he was posted and it would have been a RWF decision that he was posted to 2RWF. This posting may have been the result of his having passed out highly in his officers' training course. Although, this is mere supposition, it gels with the gut feeling of a number of army officers to whom I have spoken. Certainly, throughout the war, Regular Army officers made all the key decisions —including as to personnel— and they looked beyond the war in terms of careers and a regiment's reputation; and posting potentially good junior officers to a regular battalion would have been important to this end.

Cyril was a Welsh speaker in a battalion that, according to Dunn, was just 10% Welsh speaking in 1914. By 1918, Welsh speakers accounted for half the Battalion.[36] The change in the Battalion's linguistic composition is explicable by the fact that, in 1914, it, like the other nominally Welsh regiments, recruited heavily from England —particularly, the Birmingham area— to make up numbers. However, by 1915, Robert Graves commented that as much Welsh as English was spoken in the Battalion.[37] By 1918, just over 40% of 2RWF's casualties had been born in Wales.[38]

35. See James, E.A., *British Regiments: 1914–1918* (Heathfield: Naval & Military Press Ltd., 1998), pages 66–8.
36. Dunn page xxxvi. See also Barlow, chapter 8, for a discussion on the 'Welshness' of 2RWF.
37. Dunn page 103.
38. Barlow, chapter 8.

The RWF had been founded as the 23rd Regiment of Foot under William III in 1689 to oppose James II and earned the accolade 'Royal' during the War of the Spanish Succession (1701–14). Originally, the RWF was a regiment with just one battalion but 2RWF, in its most recent incarnation, had existed since 1858.[39] By 1914, the RWF comprised three battalions: 1RWF and 2RWF were Regular Army battalions while 3RWF was the reserve battalion co-located with the Regiment's headquarters in Wrexham.

In May 1915, 3RWF moved from Wrexham to Litherland, just outside Liverpool, coincidentally for Cyril, the place where one of his aunts —his father's sister, Winifred Jones— lived as a housewife with her family.

A fully established battalion was divided into four rifle companies, each of about 200 to 220 men and six officers, a headquarters company and a small machine gun section with two Maxim guns. By 1918, the two machine guns had gone but, overall, each battalion's weaponry had been increased to 36 Lewis guns, eight trench mortars and 16 or so rifle bombers.[40] The four companies were named A, B, C and D and each company was divided into four platoons which were again sub-divided into four sections each. On paper, a battalion would be commanded by a lieutenant-colonel (with an average age in 1917 of 28 and, in theory at least, a maximum upper age of 35), each company by a major or a captain, each platoon by a lieutenant or 2nd lieutenant and each section by an NCO. In practice, battalions were seldom up to full strength and officers and NCOs often acted in roles superior to their substantive rank.

Three battalions would be formed together into a brigade and

---

39. A second battalion had also existed for short periods from 1756–58 and 1804–14 during the Seven Years War and the Napoleonic War respectively.
40. McCarthy, Chris, 'Queen of the Battlefield: The Development of Command, Organisation and Tactics in the British Infantry Battalion during the Great War' (pages 173–93) in Sheffield, Gary and Todman, Dan, editors *Command and Control on the Western Front: The British Army's Experience 1914–1918* (Staplehurst: Spellmount Limited, 2007) (*Command and Control*), page 188.

three brigades into an infantry division. Each division would have a supporting unit of engineers, signallers, field ambulances, transport and a cavalry squadron. Two divisions would form a corps.

At the outbreak of the war, 2RWF, which had just returned home from India, had an establishment strength of 30 officers and 977 men. The Battalion transferred quickly to France as part of the BEF; but, although it had peripheral roles in the Retreat from Mons and the counter-advance on the Marne, it was not heavily engaged in the fighting of either. It spent much of 1915 holding trenches before being involved in the Battle of Loos. Its next major engagement was at the Somme where it was engaged in heavy fighting and was instrumental in capturing High Wood on 22 July. However, this success came at a murderous cost: '706 all ranks went into High Wood; less than a hundred came out unwounded.'[41]

The Battalion spent much of the next twelve months recovering, re-equipping and absorbing replacements.

Until then, 1917 had seen the Central Powers concentrate on taking advantage of the Russian collapse in the East while standing on the defensive in the West where, in March, German troops had yielded up more of the Somme battlefield than the Entente Powers had captured in any of the previous fighting when they withdrew behind the Hindenburg Line (or *Siegfriedstellung*). This was the brainchild of Crown Prince Rupprecht of Bavaria and one of the war's great engineering feats. The move, named the *Alberich Bewegung* (or Alberich Manouevre) was designed to free up many divisions for the east by shortening the German defensive line which withdrew, behind a scorched earth policy, to carefully selected, designed and built defensive positions.

In April, the French had launched the Nivelle offensive on the Aisne which failed so disastrously that it severely dented French morale and several mutinies broke out in the French army.

The British, meanwhile, had launched their big campaign of that

---

41. Glover and Riley, page 135.

year in Flanders. The whole campaign was controversial—at the time and subsequently. Haig's aim, when the campaign started, was to achieve a decisive breakthrough and push through Flanders and eliminate the U-boat bases on the Belgian coast; but, as before, there was no breakthrough. Writing with hindsight, Ward claimed that all the campaign achieved was to smash 'the manhood of the Empire —that is to say, there was neither quantity nor quality to draw on thereafter.'[42] As the British 'became glued in the Flemish mud,'[43] the campaign degenerated into a series of smaller battles, now known generally as the Third Battle of Ypres, where the British sought to push back a German salient around the town of Ypres.

Lloyd George and senior politicians in London had been doubtful about the campaign from the beginning —and became the more opposed as casualties mounted. So much so that it was alleged that, at the end of the year, they withheld new troops from the front in an attempt to exert greater control over the generals.[44] This policy caused significant manpower and planning difficulties for the BEF.

Even so, Haig had just over two million men under his command in France at the beginning of October 1917 when Cyril joined 2RWF in France as yet another replacement junior officer.

---

42. Ward, page 381.
43. Kershaw, page 56.
44. There were disputes at the time (and have been since) as to whether Lloyd George exacerbated the shortage of men on the Western France by strangling the reinforcement system at the end of 1917 as part of his ongoing dispute with the Army's high command over its strategy on the Western Front.

10. TO FRANCE WITH 2 RWF

Cyril left 3RWF and Britain at the beginning of October 1917 when he embarked for France to join 2RWF which was then part of 19 Brigade and the 33 Division in V Corps which, in turn, was part of the British Third Army. He was posted to D Company of 2RWF. Initially, he would have been a platoon officer but, in September 1918, became D Company's commander.

With two other junior officers, Cyril joined the Battalion at Blaringhem billets on 2 October just after it had come out of the Battle of Polygon Wood, one of the many battles within the envelope of the Third Battle of Ypres, and was practising for an inspection parade the next day by Haig. The inspection parade — including Cyril— passed off successfully and, after the parade, 2RWF's officers were lectured on the recent operations.

The next move by the British was to attempt to capture the town of Paschendaele to the north east of Ypres. The front line around Ypres had hardly changed since the Second Battle of Ypres in April and May 1915: the British held the city while the Germans held the ridges to the south and east of the city. The Third Battle of Ypres was fought from July to November 1917 for control of these ridges.

The German forces avoided being forced into a general withdrawal due to a combination of factors: unusually wet weather hampered the British attacks, particularly active resistance on the part of the German Fourth Army, and the need, late in the day, to divert British troops from northern France to Italy following the Central Powers' breakthrough at Caporetto which threatened to become an all-out eruption into the Veneto. The British campaign did, however, succeed in relieving pressure on French forces further south and preventing the Germans from capitalising on their having repulsed the Nivelle offensive.

The heavy rain and the churned up mud on the ground made life very difficult for all the troops but, eventually, the high ridges surrounding Ypres were captured and Paschendaele itself was finally taken by the Canadians on 10 November so bringing to an end the Third Battle of Ypres. At the end of this battle, which has been described as 'the most harrowing victory in British military history,'[1] the British had pushed the German trenches back some five miles over a period of five months. Both sides were exhausted and the sector reverted to a period of stasis in trenches where 'the wet winter weather made it difficult to do anything more than survive.'[2] To the south-east, the Battle of Cambrai, fought on 20 November, saw the first successful British use of massed tanks.

The use of troops in the Third Battle of Ypres was very different from the constant stream of minor attacks that had been a feature of the Somme fighting. The British Command had learnt that, once troops had been used in an attack, they should be withdrawn as soon as possible for a rest.[3] Thus, the usual practice was for the Battalion to move up from the reserve areas into the support trenches for two or three days before taking over front line trenches which they would hold for three or four days before being withdrawn to the back areas.

From 5 October 1917 to 9 January 1918, Cyril spent about 30 days in the trenches (front line and support) in the Messines/Paschendaele area split over four spells of about a week each.[4] Apart from a few days in early January 1918, 2RWF was away from the Front for the whole of December 1917 and January 1918. During 2RWF's time out of the front line in January 1918, Cyril was reported as having been at home on leave but no further details are available.[5]

---

1. *Ypres*, page 167.
2. Rawson, page 1.
3. *Command and Control*, page 183.
4. 8–14 October, 30 October–7 November, 20–30 November, and 4 January–9 January.
5. 26 January 1918, *FP*.

Map 3 – Cyril and 2RWF

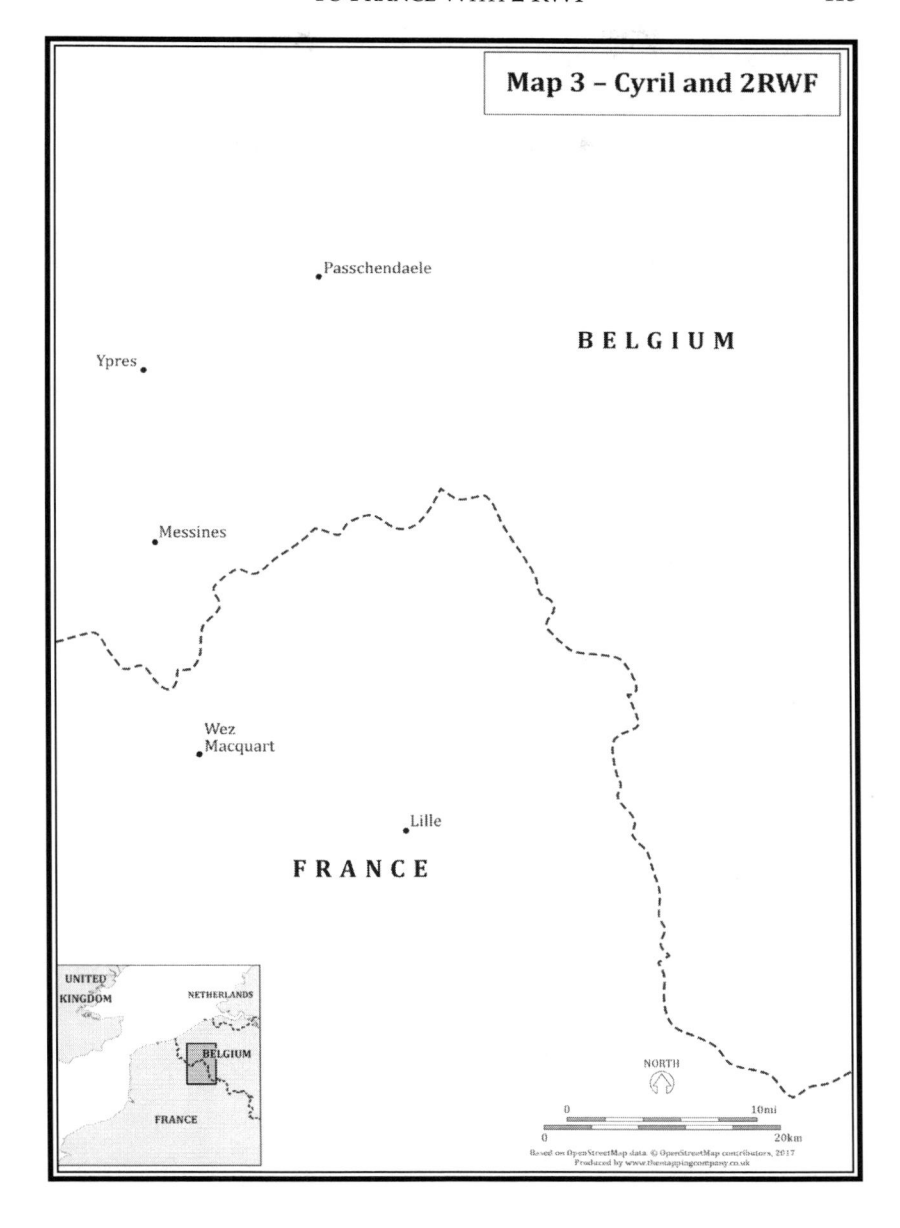

The Battalion's time in the front line varied from periods of total inactivity to being subjected to active enemy artillery. When this caused damage to the trenches, they had to be repaired quickly — usually at night.

Reliefs were always undertaken under cover of darkness. Usually, reliefs went smoothly but casualties could be suffered if the relief was spotted and enemy shelling disrupted the relief. Moves close to the front were done on foot. The wet, muddy conditions could make such moves difficult and Dunn paints a somewhat poetic account of one march with men slipping from greasy single-file duckboards into water-logged shell-holes.[6] Behind the support trenches, troop movements were easier and troops were often bussed or moved about on light railways or the main railways; only occasionally marching from one location to another.

Whenever the Battalion came out of the front line it followed a fairly standard routine —not dissimilar to that mentioned earlier in relation to the Dismounted Cavalry Division:

a. on the first day, resting and clearing up and checking equipment. Everyone's clothes would be put through a disinfecting machine;
b. bathing —baths were usually allotted to a battalion once every seven days;
c. attending church parade on Sundays. The Army provided many Anglican services, half as many Roman Catholic services and just a few Wesleyan services;
d. training. This varied —depending upon the space and conditions available. Where a camp had no facilities for training, the time would be spent in close order drill. Further back in the rear, wider grounds made more extensive training exercises possible. The Battalion also had the occasional gas exercise when everyone would pass through a gas hut;

---

6. Dunn, page 407.

e. providing the inevitable working parties. Working parties included days spent carry supplies and timber from the rear areas up to the front line; working on the trench lines — repairing them or digging new ones or supply cuts; working on local roads and railways. Working parties were not free from danger and there are accounts of the Battalion's working parties being heavily gas shelled and being forced to work for several hours in respirators. Breaks from working parties could come, as on 16 January 1918, because floods prevented any useful work. Attendance at church services was also another reason for a break from a working party.

Away from the front line, the soldiers were usually housed in billets although, in support, it was not unusual to bivouac. When the Battalion spent two days in a bivouac camp around the White Chateau in the middle of November, tents needed to be struck at 0700 daily as the camp was within range of German long-range artillery. Billets varied both in condition and quality and from scattered lodgings in local houses to specially constructed encampments such as the huts at Bulford Camp, near Ypres, which Dunn described as 'comfortable.'[7]

Christmas Day 1917 and New Year's Day 1918 were holidays; although quite how much of a party was had on New Year's Day must be questionable for at least 40 % of D Company were reported to have preferred coffee to beer.[8] There was a Church Parade on Sunday, 30 December while, on Monday 31, baths were allotted to 2RWF. On this occasion, the Battalion's officers were lectured on training and platoon work while the other ranks were at their baths.

During the fighting around Ypres at the end of November, Cyril was commanding another Denbigh boy, Private Evan James Davies of Panton Villas —a couple of hundred yards down the road from

---

7. Dunn, page 412.
8. Dunn, page 429. Coffee drinkers were 25% in two other companies and 30% in the fourth.

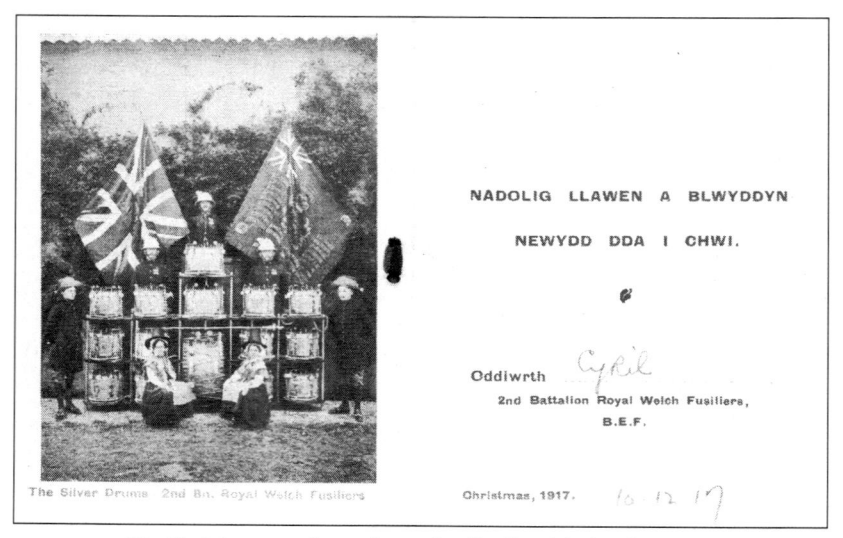

22. *Christmas card sent home by Cyril to his family, 1917.*

Cyril's home at Derwenfa —when Davies was wounded. The Denbighshire Free Press reported the incident and how Cyril had written to Davies's parents to say how lucky Davies was: the only one of six in a shell hole to survive. Davies was injured in his right hand, and his left arm; also in his left ear so as to affect his hearing. Davies reported to his parents that Cyril was 'very popular with the men in the battalion.'[9]

When Cyril returned to France after his home leave in January 1918, 2RWF was about to switch sectors as part of a wholesale restructuring of army divisions from a twelve to a nine battalion structure. In consequence, brigades were themselves reduced from four to three battalions. This restructuring was forced upon the army because of continuing manpower shortage problems. In the ensuing reshuffle, 2RWF was transferred within V Corps from 19 Brigade and 33 Division to 115 Brigade in the 38 (Welsh) Division. Dunn suggests that the decision to move 2RWF to 115 Brigade

---

9. 29 December 1917, *FP*.

reflected the need to strengthen a weak brigade in another division.[10]

The 38 (Welsh) Division was the outcome of Lloyd George's suggestion back in September 1914 to create a Welsh Army Corps of two divisions. The initial plan had been to raise such a corps from recruits in Wales. By the end of 1914, 10,000 recruits had enlisted in units that were intended to form this corps. They were brought together as the 38 Division but, in October 1915 before additional units could be raised and united in a single corps, the Army Council decided that further recruitment in Wales should concentrate on building up reserves rather than the creation of new units. Given the BEF's experience in 1914, it was expected that the New Army units would suffer heavy casualties when they arrived in France and it was necessary to have a supply of ready reserves to maintain units at the Front up to establishment strength. The Army Council's decision marked the 'death knell of the Welsh Army Corps.'[11] All that remained of Lloyd George's idea for a distinct Welsh Army Corps was 38 (Welsh) Division, a division that now consisted principally of units recruited mainly in Wales.

At 1315 on 4 February, 2RWF commenced a three day march to Robermetz (a village just west of Lille) where it was to join 38 (Welsh) Division. The movement orders went into detail of how each company was to march 100 yards apart from each other company and 500 yards were to separate the Battalion and its transport with a 25-yard gap between each group of six vehicles. Four lorries carrying blankets were to accompany the Battalion to its final destination. 33 Division was responsible for sending the Battalion's rations up to 6 February to Thiennes, its last overnight stop.

At Robermetz, 2RWF was met by massed bands and drums of 115 Brigade and 38 (Welsh) Division's acting AAQMG (Assistant Adjutant and Quarter-Master General). Thus, the Battalion became part of 115 Brigade and 38 (Welsh) Division. The Robermetz billets

10. Dunn, page xli.
11. Messenger, page 100.

were described as 'very good' and the next five days were spent in bathing, church parades, working parties and inspections before a return to front line duties.

Back Home, the Representation of the People Act, 1918 was enacted on 6 February and extended the franchise to all men over 21 (and those who turned 19 while on war service in the war)—and, subject to some minimal property qualifications, women over 30. Thus, Cyril was now enfranchised.

The Battalion remained in the Robermetz area until the end of March and had three spells[12] in the front line of the Wez Macquart Sector. During the first spell, German artillery was very active and shelled D Company —Cyril's company— and, for the first time, enemy aircraft are mentioned overhead his position. This was all part of active enemy engagement of the British forward trenches by mortar, machine guns and aircraft.

When the Battalion was relieved from its first stint in the front line here on 1 March, the officers' mess celebrated St David's Day in a requisitioned hut with a full meal prepared by the mess's cook served on proper plates and with cutlery and glasses borrowed from a nearby café and all washed down with what Dunn seems to have regarded as the customary champagne, Benedictine and Kümmel. Only the port was missing —and even the neighbouring Portuguese division, to whom application had been made, claimed to have none available. Of the 31 officers present, 23 were recorded as having eaten 'leek in the odour of the Goat'[13] —presumably some rite of initiation into the Battalion. On this basis, one must assume that Cyril was amongst the 23 to have enjoyed such leeks.

During the Battalion's second spell in the trenches at Wez Macquart, it suffered considerable enemy shelling—so much so that delivering rations to the Battalion was difficult and its relief was delayed.[14] Early one morning, under cover of a heavy barrage,

---

12. 21 February–1 March, 9–17 March and 25–29 March.
13. Dunn, pages 449–50.
14. Interestingly, the descriptions of the shelling in the war diaries of the Battalion

a large German raiding party of around 300 attempted to capture the left part of the Battalion's position and some 20 German troops succeeded in attacking the post held by D Company but were repulsed and D Company captured a prisoner.

Between its second and third spells in the front line here, one platoon from D Company was kept off the working parties and, for three days, practised for a raid on a German trench. The raid was carried out when the Battalion returned for its third spell in the front line trenches here, but it was something of a non-event as the German trench was found to be unoccupied. The raid must have seemed insignificant for the Battalion's war diary does not record it; the only record is in the Brigade's war diary.

1918 had begun with the continued stasis of trench warfare but, on 21 March, the Germans launched their spring offensive, dubbed *Kaiserschlacht* (the Kaiser's battle), in an attempt to break through British and French lines and knock out both armies before American reinforcements could alter the manpower balance on the Western Front. A desperate last push by the German armies, its initial main thrust was along the Somme —away to the south of 2RWF which took no part in these battles or the associated British retreat to defensive lines east of Amiens. By the end of March, the German advance had ground to a halt around Albert, in front of these defences.

On 30 March, the Battalion and the rest of 115 Brigade undertook a three day transfer, by a mixture of road, rail and route march with nightly billets, from the Wez Macquart sector down to this area where they formed part of the British lines just north-west of Albert. Apart from when it was in reserve camps at Hérissart, a village much closer to the northern edge of Amiens, 2RWF remained in this under five square mile area just north of Albert until the end of July 1918. It is perfectly possible that Cyril had been in this area

and the Brigade diverge with the former suggesting that it was 'relatively light' whilst the latter talked of 'considerable enemy shelling.'

before as 3DG had sent several digging parties to there between August and November 1916.

Initially, working parties and training were the order of the day until mid-April when the Battalion moved into the front at Bouzincourt where it had three spells[15] in the front line. Matters were relatively quiet in the front line —although, during the second spell, an officer and one other rank were captured when they essayed a raiding party on German lines. Ward even suggests that, at the end of April, there was a degree of fraternisation between the Battalion's men and German troops facing them in Aveluy Wood until the British High Command peremptorily ordered a stop to the practice.[16]

As the Battalion was being relieved from its second stretch in the front line, the relief was spotted and was heavily shelled, but no casualties were suffered. Again, at the end of its third spell in the front line, the Germans laid down a heavy barrage on the Brigade's lines and the Battalion's relief came under heavy shelling and gassing, with many cases of gas poisoning being recorded.

After this relief, the Battalion marched to reserve camps southeast of Hérissart where it remained for 11 days. This time involved inspections, church parades, sports competitions and training, including the Battalion's first recorded tactical training with tanks —which, of course, were a relatively new invention.

On 3 June, the Battalion moved to Acheux Wood where tents were pitched before a spell in the front in the Centre Mesnil Sector until 13 June, when it was relieved and moved into bivouacs at Forceville as part of the Divisional Reserve.

Here, the Battalion practised over the next week for a planned raid that started at 0200 on 21 June, a very wet night, when it raided enemy lines north of Aveluy Wood under a protective barrage. As the Battalion was under strength, D Company was divided between

---

15. 20–5 April, 2–8 May and 14–20 May.
16. Ward, page 420.

the other companies but, from Dunn, it would appear that Cyril was not part of the raiding party.[17]

Nothing should be read into Cyril's absence from the raiding party. During 1918, the British manpower shortage was very apparent and most battalions were below strength. Therefore, general Fighting Instructions aimed to preserve a core of trained men in each battalion for the future. To achieve this, battalions usually tried to extract a third of the battalion from the front line or any engagement and to operate on the basis of a platoon strength of 28 —though, even this figure was often hard to find.[18] The extracted men were referred to as the 'Battle Surplus.'

Everything seemed to go wrong with the raid and it was not a success. On the left, the objective was reached but the German trenches were found abandoned and no prisoners or material were captured whereas on the right, the troops were unable to achieve their objective due to heavy mortar fire. The Battalion suffered some 22 killed or wounded.

The war diary states just these bare facts but gives no sense of just how badly the raid's failure was perceived. Dunn described it as 'a thoroughly bad Show from start to finish.'[19] The Division's commanding officer gave the Battalion's officers a dressing down for what he considered to have been a hopelessly executed raid[20] and ordered a series of further raids on nearby German trenches. So, when, following the raid, the Battalion took up a position in support east of Englebelmer, the next five days involved working parties during the day and further raiding parties at night—again with mixed success: either the enemy trenches being empty or the raiding parties were held up by enemy fire. By this stage of the war,

---

17. Dunn, page 488. A full description of the raid is given in pages 488–92 and Dunn says only one of D Company's officers —not Cyril— was attached to another company.
18. Ward, page 420.
19. Dunn, page 490.
20. ibid, pages 491–2.

the Germans were using a more flexible form of defence —with only a limited number of forward posts— so making raids far more problematic affairs.

The Battalion returned to the front line in the Mesnil Right Sector from 28 June to 2 July. During its last night here, D Company repulsed a German raid on one of its posts in Aveluy Wood. The raid held up the scheduled relief —which was not completed until 0415 when the Battalion returned to bivouacs at Forceville.

There followed another week of general training, working parties and more training for a further raid.[21] On 10 July, the Battalion moved into the intermediary trench system at Englebelmer in preparation for this raid. Then, at 2300 on 11 July, all four companies advanced under an accurate artillery and machine gun barrage to raid the village of Hamel, behind German lines. This raid was regarded as being very successful. All objectives were taken along with 19 prisoners and one machine gun. 50 enemy soldiers were killed and 20 enemy dug-outs blown-up. The Battalion lost one officer and two men killed, another 44 wounded and three missing. Unlike the last raid, this raid resulted in congratulations from not only the Divisional commander but also the Corps commander.

After the raid, the Battalion returned to Hérissart where it rested and trained until the end of July apart from a five day spell in support trenches in the middle of the month. On 30 July, the Battalion moved forward to camp near Forceville, just north of Albert. The transfer involved a very hot march during which the regimental goat died of heat stroke.

---

21. ibid, pages 497–502 for a description of the raid and the preparations.

11. ADVANCE TO VICTORY

The last German offensive —Operation Marneschutz-Reims— started on 15 July along a 65-mile front with the aim of capturing Rheims but the Allies had anticipated this attack and, by 17 July, it was over. Nevertheless, the Germans had, during their three-month long Spring offensive, recaptured much of the territory that the British had so painfully —and expensively— taken during the Somme battles two years earlier. The British would now have to fight their way through all too familiar towns and villages in order to recapture the ground. 2RWF's July raid was all part of the beginning of the Allied fight-back.

On 18 July, the French and Americans struck west from a salient near Soissons—way to the west of 2RWF. Then, on 8 August, the British launched their offensive along a 15 mile front on the Somme. As six opposing German divisions disintegrated, the British succeeded in driving the German defences back just over six miles in a single day in what Ludendorff was to describe as the German Army's 'Black Day'.

Throughout August and September, the fighting intensified as the British were continually on the offensive and pushing back the German lines. After nearly four years of static trench warfare, the Army faced the challenge of re-learning how to conduct mobile offensive operations.[1] Following up the German armies was never easy or without cost as advancing troops faced shelling, booby traps, machine-gun and sniper fire besides operating in a dangerous

---

1. *Command and Control*, page 184.

chemical environment.² A typical combat experience in this period involved battalions moving forward to flush out German positions; heavy machine gun fire; confusion; swift enemy counter-attacks; and, finally, the German defenders vanishing like wraiths in the morning across a devastated —and largely depopulated— countryside. The advance would then continue until the next defensive position was reached.³

The Battalion was part of this advance. In the 90 day period from 5 August, when it took up a position in the new front line—former German trenches —in the Bouzincourt Sector (just a mile north of Albert), to 4 November, when it fought its last battle in the Forêt de Mormal, 2RWF spent 33 days in front line trenches and 13 days in battle and advancing against 44 days behind the front. Of these 44 days out of the front line, Cyril spent four days in support trenches, four in camp, seven in bivouacs, 15 in billets and 14 on leave. Overall, the Battalion advanced about 45 miles in a largely east/north-easterly direction from Albert to Englefontaine.

The over-arching strategic plan was for the Franco-American forces to push towards Mézières while the British First, Third and Fourth Armies attacked towards Cambrai thereby threatening vital German railway communications systems running through, and around, Maubeuge. The Third Army was in the centre with the First and Fourth Armies on its left and right respectively. 38 (Welsh) Division and 33 Division formed the right wing of V Corps with 17 Division and 21 Division forming the Corps' left wing. Throughout the forward movement of the 100 Days Advance, movements and reliefs of the various units within V Corps became almost a routine with 38 (Welsh) Division and 33 Division continually 'leap-frogging' through each other as the advance progressed.⁴

Depree describes how one or other of the divisions on the right

---

2. Lloyd, Nick, *Hundred Days: The End of the Great War* (London: Penguin Books, 2013) (*Hundred Days*), page 102.
3. ibid, pages xxiv–xxx.
4. Depree, page 336.

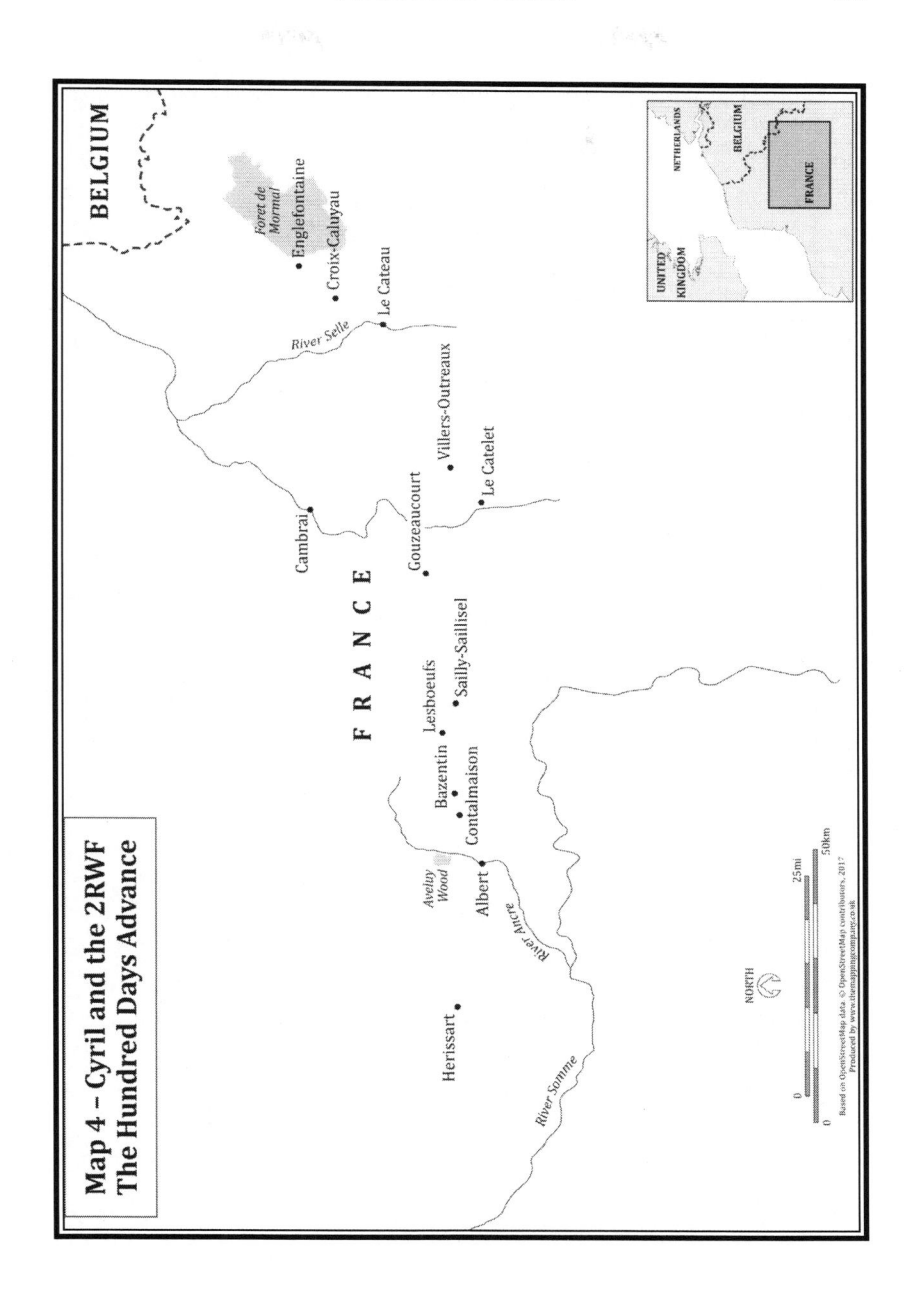

Map 4 – Cyril and the 2RWF
The Hundred Days Advance

(or the left) would carry out an initial assault just so far as a pre-arranged objective whereupon the other division, which had pushed forward in close support, would 'leap-frog' through and continue the assault. The same 'leap-frog' concept applied within each individual formation within the Divisions so that forward movement could be maintained continuously while each unit had its share of rest and recovery time.

In the front at Bouzincourt from 5 to 11 August, 2RWF pushed out forward patrols to reconnoitre potential crossing points over the river Ancre as it flowed south towards Albert. Crossing the river was difficult due to the river's meandering through wide marshes at this point. Dunn records Cyril and some others finding an old boat on the river —but having to return hurriedly when they discovered that the boat leaked.[5]

On 15 August, as news filtered through to the Battalion of a German withdrawal near Serre and Puisieux with indications of a possible withdrawal opposite the 115 Brigade, 2RWF took over the front line of the Welsh Centre Divisional Sector at Martinsart and Aveluy (just north of Albert) and, for the next few days, the Battalion was involved in further reconnaissance of, and preparations for, the river Ancre crossings.

At dawn on 21 August, the British Third Army attacked on a seven-mile front but the Brigade was not involved. At Aveluy, a heavy mist prevailed and 2RWF pushed out patrols across the river Ancre with the aim of establishing crossings but one patrol was held up by rifle fire so further patrols were cancelled. The following morning, during another thick mist, the Battalion pushed out A Company across the river Ancre and established a bridgehead.[6] From now until 6 October, the Battalion's movement was to be almost consistently in a due easterly direction.

On 23 August, 38 (Welsh) Division advanced from west of the

---

5. Dunn, page 505.
6. The Brigade's war diary states it was a company from 17RWF, not 2RWF, as 2RWF could not cross due to an absence of crossing points in its sector.

river Ancre to the outskirts of Morval. As part of this advance, all four companies of 2RWF crossed to the east of the river and continued to move forward until the afternoon of 25 August when the Battalion established a new front line just east of Bazentin-le-Grand and near High Wood, which the Battalion had so expensively captured back in 1916. During the advance, in an operation which Haig described as 'a most brilliant operation —alike in conception and execution' and as being of the highest level of soldierly achievement,[7] the villages of Pozières and Contalmaison had been taken along with 200 prisoners and 17 machine guns. Again, this was another area with which Cyril may have been familiar from earlier digging parties that 3DG had sent to the Contalmaison area during August 1916.

The Battalion continued advancing until 28 August when it reached Lesboeufs (ten miles east of Albert) where it was held up for three days by heavy German shelling. By now, the Battalion's strength was considerably reduced from the numbers that had crossed the Ancre and there were just two officers —both subalterns — per company.[8] Then, on 1 September, the Battalion was 115 Brigade's left assault battalion as it attacked the villages of Sailly and Saillisel (generally referred to as Sailly-Saillisel, and two miles further east from Lesboeufs and eight miles north of Peronne) under a creeping barrage.[9] C and D Companies, in the van, encountered fierce resistance —one party was overwhelmed and 'fought to the last man in a very heroic manner'— but, thanks to support from neighbouring brigades, the Battalion had reached the village's western outskirts by the close of day. However, this success came at the price of the strength of two companies.[10] The advance resumed at 1700 on the next day with the Battalion re-organised

---

7. Munby, Introduction by Earl Haig.
8. Dunn, page 523.
9. ibid, see pages 523–35 for a description of this battle.
10. Glover and Riley, page 159. The Battalion's war diary description of its advance on Sailly-Saillisel is the longest entry during Cyril's time with 2RWF.

into just two companies and, by dawn on 3 September, the enemy had withdrawn from the villages and the Battalion was 500 yards to the east of Sailly-Saillisel.

So great had been the Battalion's losses at Sailly-Saillisel that it was now organised into just a single company of four platoons. It remained in support for the next two days before being relieved to rest for four days and go into bivouacs just south of Lesboeufs on 6 September. It spent these four days re-fitting and re-organising so as to incorporate strong reinforcements of men. It also practised with Lewis guns. On 9 September a concert by a W. W. C. Party (the 'Welsh Wails') was given for the troops of 115 Brigade.

It was now that Cyril would seem to have been given command of D Company. Although his obituary in the *Denbighshire Free Press*[11] states that he had been commanding it for the last three months (i.e. since early August), this does not square with information obtainable from *The War The Infantry Knew*. The latter describes Lt. Charlton as having been in command of D Company until 24 August and the advance on Bazentin-le-Grand, when he was injured by a ricocheting bullet, and 2nd Lt. F. L. C. Jones as in command at Sailly-Saillisel when he was killed in the initial advance.[12] This is, probably, yet another example of either newspaper journalists' lack of detailed attention to the facts or the family, which must have provided the information to the newspaper, adopting a slightly broad-brush approach.

Despite taking over command of D Company, Cyril was not promoted substantively from second lieutenant. A subaltern's promotion was usually simply a question of time and having served for two years. Of course, the Army had no wish to make too many substantive promotions as it would only cause problems at the end of the war and, by this stage, it was very common for men at all levels to be in an acting position one or two ranks higher than their substantive ranks. There is no documentary evidence that he

11. 16 November 1918, FP.
12. Dunn, pages 514, 523 and 526.

was even promoted as an acting full lieutenant to command D Company but the acting position as company commander must have been regularised in some way for Cyril did receive extra pay and allowances for his additional responsibilities. He suggested that the actual rank might come along later —indeed, in a letter to his father, he suggested he should already have been promoted 'but for that old Army bugbear of 'seniority.'"[13]

On 10 September, the Battalion prepared to rejoin battle and, with its transport, moved to east of Lechelle and took over front line trenches near Gouzeaucourt (a village south-east of Cambrai) for the next six days with D Company in left support. These lines had been dug by the British back in 1917 when they had come up against the Hindenburg Line.[14]

The first half of the period was a particularly active one for the Battalion which took some 20 casualties when it was heavily shelled. Later, following a heavy barrage, the Germans counter-attacked the Battalion's front and support lines but —despite penetrating the left trenches— they were beaten off by Lewis gun and rifle fire. Then, enemy aircraft bombed the Battalion. The last three days were relatively quiet and 2RWF was relieved on 16 September and marched five miles to the rear to bivouac north of Equancourt.

Another two day spell in the front line at Gouzeaucourt followed until the Battalion was relieved during the night of 20 September. The relief was a slow one due to a heavy German barrage but the next two weeks were to be spent in the rear. First, the Battalion moved the next day, by route march, to Beaulencourt, a village just south of Bapaume, where it stayed until 27 September when it moved into huts and tents at Sorel-le-Grand for a further week. During this period, the Battalion rested, refitted, bathed, played rugby against 10 South Wales Borderers, paraded and

---

13. Letter from Cyril to his father, 1 November 1918; see Appendix II.
14. Munby, page 62.

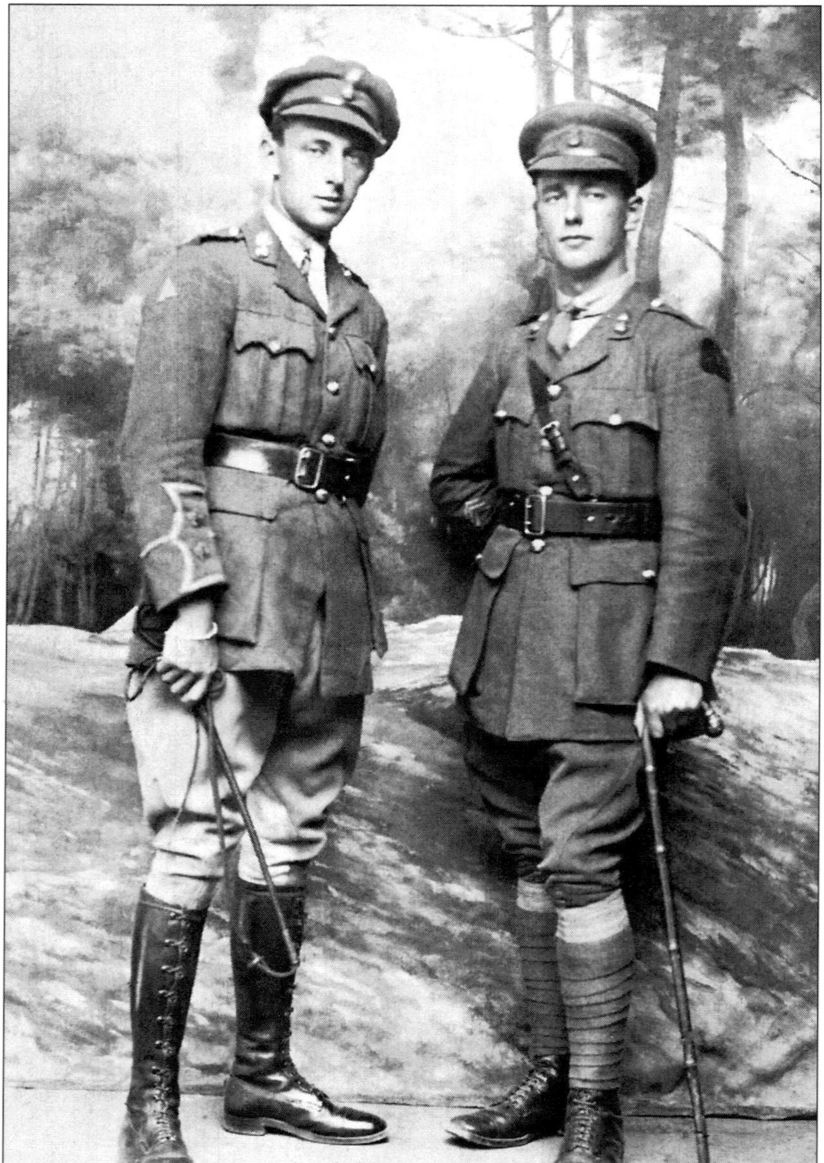

Facing: 23. The last known photograph of Cyril.
This was a posed photograph taken near the Front in September 1918. It is in the form of a postcard—probably locally produced in France given the heading 'Carte Postale' on the reverse where Cyril has scribbled a note (presumably to Josie): 'All the best of everything to my little sister. Your big 'bruvver.' Cyril. BEF. Sept 1918. Write soon.'

It shows Cyril (right) together with a fellow, unknown, officer—a full lieutenant. While this other officer wears his rank on his sleeve, Cyril is dressed in a newish, but much plainer, service dress uniform and he carries a walking stick which is not regular issue. At the top of Cyril's left shoulder is the 38 (Welsh) Division badge—a distinctive red dragon on a black background. There are no rank badges on his sleeves. Early on in the war, most British infantry officers—unlike cavalry officers—adopted plainer uniforms so as not to make themselves such conspicuous targets for German snipers, who targeted officers where they could. Hence, Cyril would have had a single 'pip' on his shoulder epaulettes. He wears the RWF badge on each lapel and on his cap, and RWF buttons on his jacket. He is wearing a Sam Browne belt with a single cross strap and puttees that are wrapped in typical infantry style ending at the top. On his right arm just as it goes behind his back, one can just about make out three chevrons denoting service abroad—one chevron for each year. Given that Cyril went to France in October 1915, one wonders why the third chevron had been added if the photograph was taken in (or before) September 1918 as his scribbled note suggests. Cyril does not wear any wound stripe (a vertical flash worn on the left arm). This would seem to confirm that, to this time, he had not been wounded.

At first glance, the other officer would appear to be a cavalry officer—as he is holding a riding crop, and wearing riding breeches and riding boots. However, closer examination would suggest he is a Territorial officer in one of the RWF's Territorial battalions. His cap and lapel badges are clearly the RWF's flaming grenade. Infantry officers often had to ride so it would not have been unusual for them to wear riding breeches and boots. As for his cap, officers in Territorial battalions often retained 'soft' caps, and one can see that his cap is slightly crumpled. In place of a swagger stick, he has a hunting crop–quite unlike the short whip issued to cavalry officers. This is probably an affectation on the part of this officer, who —one assumes—had probably hunted a great deal before the war.

practised trench-to-trench attacks, throwing German hand grenades and Lewis gun firing.

Cyril had a period of home leave during this break from the front line. The *Denbighshire Free Press* reported, under its regular 'Home on leave' column, that he had been home on 14 days leave —but had returned to France by the time the report was published.[15] His leave dates were probably 23 September to 6 October as this would explain why the War Office later credited him with a ration entitlement for these days —presumably, he was not entitled to a separate ration allowance when with his battalion. During this leave, he 'delighted his fellow-school friends by playing football for them in one of their matches.'[16]

Whilst 2RWF was out of the line, a British offensive further north around Cambrai resulted in the strong German defensive Hindenburg Line being stormed and the Germans retreated eastwards pursued by the British first towards the Beaurevoir-Masnières Line, which was the Germans' last formal position in the area, and then towards the scratch defences of the Hermann Line and the river Selle.

Bulgaria dropped out of the war on 30 September. On 4 October, after Ludendorff had had a nervous collapse and had insisted that the German armies could fight no more and that Germany must seek an armistice, Germany approached President Wilson of the USA to seek an armistice and declared that it was prepared to give up all occupied territory. Hindenburg, Chief of the German General Staff, considered that it was vital for Germany to hold the Hermann Line so as to improve its negotiating position in discussions surrounding the requested armistice.

Notwithstanding the on-going discussions concerning an armistice, the Allies continued their forward pressure on the German positions. The period 17–25 October saw the crossing of the river Selle and the end to fighting in Picardy. On 26 October, when Ludendorff

15. 12 October 1918, FP.
16. 16 November 1918, FP.

resigned as Quarter-Master General of the German army, the British were already pushing through the Hermann Line. Elsewhere, the British had liberated Lille and, on 18 October, the Belgians recovered Ostend and Zeebrugge. Once through the Beaurevoir-Masnières and Hermann Lines, the British could debouche into open countryside and the war became, once again, one of movement and fluidity.

After its rest period, 2RWF moved in quick succession from 3 October to trenches outside Lempire (some 12 miles south of Cambrai), through trenches east of Bony to lines three miles further east on the western outskirts of Le Catelet. Having moved pretty much in a due easterly direction since August to Le Catelet, the Battalion now swung almost due north for a couple of miles to lines due west of Pienne before swinging eastwards again on 8 October when the Battalion co-operated in an attack on the village of Villers-Outréaux. From Depree, it would appear that D Company played little or no part in the capture of this village.[17] After the village's capture, the Battalion spent the night in billets there. This was the first time that the troops 'had seen or entered a habitable house' since the advance had started back in August.[18]

Sometime between 6 and 9 October, Cyril re-joined the Battalion from his Home leave and, on 9 October, replacement officers arrived and the Battalion spent the day re-organising and resting.

The Battalion's next moves until November were in a north-easterly direction by route march through billets in Bertry and Troisville until, on 13 October, it took up a front line position on the river Selle just north of Le Cateau–Cambrésis where, between 14 and 22 October, preparations were made to bridge, and cross, the river. The Battalion had occasional days out of the front line to rest and bathe. On one occasion, D Company was loaned to 17RWF on the Brigade's left.

Cyril must have been interested to know that 6 Cavalry Brigade,

17. Depree, pages 349–53.
18. ibid, page 359.

his former cavalry brigade, was part of the forces being pushed forward as part of the Third Army with the aim of operating against the German flank and rear positions and cutting German communications.[19]

Come 23 October, the Battalion was again advancing. First to Richemont and Croix-Caluyau before, on 25 October, the Division completed the capture of Englefontaine, a village midway along the western edge of the Forêt de Mormal, where a concentration of German forces put up a 'stubborn resistance.'[20] As the British troops advanced, they were greeted by such of the local population as were still there and had defied German orders to evacuate and retire along with the retreating German forces.[21]

On reaching Englefontaine, the Third Army paused while its rear communications were made more secure. Meanwhile, troops were rested —but remained available to move forward again at short notice. The Battalion took over the front running through the village's eastern outskirts where it had the twofold task of consolidating a defensive line and acting as the advance guard. As advance guard, it was to maintain contact with the German forces if they retreated again. Additionally, it was ordered, if possible, to push posts out past the German rearguard. 2RWF spent two days on 27 and 28 October trying to effect this infiltration policy but was checked by heavy defensive machine-gun fire.[22] In several places, the opposing forces were so close that British and German troops occupied adjacent houses while the local inhabitants sheltered below in cellars.[23]

By now, the Central Powers were in a state of collapse. The Ottoman Empire signed an armistice on 30 October, followed by Austria-Hungary on 3 November. In Flanders, between 31 October

19. ibid, page 454.
20. ibid, page 68.
21. ibid, page 478.
22. ibid, pages 169–170.
23. Munby, page 78.

and 4 November, the Allies launched a series of attacks on the German lines from the north, south, and centre; in Belgium, they reached the Scheldt while, on 2 November, Valenciennes, a railway junction and the last major French town in enemy hands, fell to Canadian forces. The final element was the Battle of the Sambre when, on 4 November, British forces attacked across the Condé-Mons canal and through the Forêt de Mormal.

In preparation for this last advance, 2RWF was relieved from its front line position at Englefontaine during the evening of 29 October and returned to billets in Croix-Caluyau area where it spent the next four days resting and cleaning up before training in close country fighting and attacking —particularly through local woods and orchards— and marching on compass bearings.[24]

It was during this spell out of the line that Cyril wrote the last letter that we have.[25] Cyril's principal purpose in the letter was to thank his father for having obtained an engagement ring for Cyril's fiancée. He went on to suggest that the price of the ring that his father had obtained 'was a little high' before saying that 'a few weeks of [his] extra pay will knock that off.'

News of his engagement was a surprise to his family for they knew nothing of his fiancée, Norah. Cyril explained that she was the orphan sister of a fellow officer trainee at Romford through whom he had met her. It would appear that they had become engaged during his most recent furlough and he said that he would not have got engaged to her so quickly had he not been coming back out to France.

Cyril then covered more domestic matters by consoling his father over his aunt Josephine's recent death and hoping that his mother's health improved so that 'before very long she will be more like her old self again.' This would seem to confirm that her stroke had been a relatively recent one. He then tackled the subject of his younger brother's education and raised the possibility of John's

---

24. Depree, pages 171–2.
25. Letter from Cyril to his father, 1 November 1918; see Appendix II.

being sent away to school. He suggests that John was missing 'the influence of Mam that we had.' This does rather hint that his mother was a somewhat forceful character (or a 'tiger mother' in modern terminology) who pushed her children.[26] That he made this suggestion may indicate that Cyril had observed the effect of a public school education on many of his fellow officers and thought that young John might benefit.

Finally, Cyril sent home with the letter a parcel of underclothing for which he no longer had a need and asked that his sister Phyllis arrange for it to be washed and kept for him.

During this break, Cyril's path crossed with that of a school friend from his Love Lane School and County School days for Thomas Davies later wrote[27] to Cyril's father that they had had a lengthy conversation two days before Cyril's death. Davies was a corporal in the Divisional train so, presumably, had been in the process of delivering supplies to 2RWF.

24. *Cyril's 38 (Welsh) Divisional shoulder patch, a Red Dragon on a black background (the red has now faded to a deep golden colour).*

26. This certainly conforms to the aura of an imposing and forceful woman that other family members have reported, second or third hand.
27. Letter from Thomas E. Davies to Cyril's father, 22 November 1918; see Appendix II. Thomas Davies appears, with the number 3 pinned to his chest, in the photograph (N[o.] 5) of the Love Lane School boys who passed the 1907 scholarship examinations to Denbigh County School.

12. THE FINAL BATTLE

After this break, 115 Brigade took over a three-battalion front in trenches at Englefontaine during the night of 2/3 November with 2RWF on the right. The Battalion spent 3 November quietly preparing for the next day's advance through the orchards to the village's east and north-east.

The war was clearly coming to an end as the Division's staff noted that instructions had been received that no further applications were to be accepted for commissions (except for the Special Brigade and the Tank Corps). Nonetheless, on 4 November, the Battalion was engaged in some of the heaviest fighting in which it was involved in the period Cyril was with the Battalion and the Battalion's war diary entry for that day is the second longest entry during that period. It was the last big push by 38 (Welsh) Division and 2RWF.

The Division was to attack on the south-eastern outskirts of Englefontaine and into the Forêt de Mormal with its final objectives being the bridle-paths in the forest running north-east and south-east from Les Grandes Patures, a hamlet in the middle of the forest. This particular assault must have been redolent with thoughts of the BEF's initial foray to France as Maubeuge, the BEF's initial concentration point in 1914, was at the forest's north-eastern end and the forest had played its part in the Retreat from Mons.

The attack was to be on a one brigade frontage with each brigade having an objective to capture and hold until the brigade in the rear leap-frogged through: 115 Brigade was to capture the first objective, 113 Brigade the second and 114 Brigade the third and final objective.

The offensive was timed to begin at 0530 with 17 Division, on 38 (Welsh) Division's left, opening the attack. 38 (Welsh) Division then joined the battle 45 minutes later when 115 Brigade launched its attack. 2RWF formed the Brigade's right wing, 17RWF its left wing and 10SWB were in the centre. A tank had been allotted to each battalion but the tank allotted to 2RWF had failed to appear. So, the Battalion intercepted, and appropriated, a tank that had been allotted to another division but which had lost its way.

2RWF's final objective was a bridle-path running roughly north and south 500 yards east of the western edge of the Forêt de Mormal (described as the Blue Line —because drawn in blue crayon on the planning map). This was not an easy objective (indeed, Munby described it as 'especially difficult'[1]) as two changes of directions needed to be carried out over a front which would vary from 300 yards to 800 yards owing to the Battalion's right resting on a stream (the ruisseau des Eclusettes) which twists a great deal in its course at this point. This meant that, at one turning point, A Company was required to leap-frog through D Company and join C and B Companies in the front while D Company remained on the leap-frog line in reserve. The Battalion's headquarters company was to be responsible for the final mopping-up of the houses.

At 0500 on 4 November, 2RWF formed up to advance in the following order:

- right front company—C;
- left front company—D (with Cyril in command);
- right support company—B;
- left support company—A.

2RWF moved to attack at 0615 behind what the war diaries describe as a very heavy and accurate 'creeping' barrage put up by 38 (Welsh) Divisional Artillery. This 'ingenious and skilful' barrage was planned to be placed 300 yards ahead of the advancing troops and to move forward at the rate of 100 yards every six minutes. In

---

1. Munby, page 79.

addition, the Corps' heavy artillery was also engaged and balloon spotters sent up to report on it.²

To maintain the momentum of the advance as the Division attacked through the forest, the creeping barrage was planned to continue throughout the whole advance. This necessitated half of the Division's field artillery ceasing fire at one point while they moved forward to resume their part in the barrage once the remaining field artillery had reached its maximum range. This tactic avoided the need for any pause in the barrage or the advance —which would otherwise occur if, as had happened with the advances on 8 and 23 October, the whole of the field artillery battery was obliged to cease firing and move to new, forward, positions.³

The Division's tactical instructions to unit commanders emphasised the importance of ensuring that the proper direction of advance was maintained through the orchards and the woods. This required that the various units be kept well concentrated under their platoon commanders and every officer needed to make full use of his compass to keep direction.⁴

That morning's heavy mist made keeping the correct direction even more difficult—but it also hampered the enemy's movements and helped the Battalion to overcome opposition that was particularly heavy in machine gun and trench mortar fire —especially on the Battalion's right. Here, a gap of about 400 yards opened up at one point between it and the division on its right which enabled the Germans to enfilade the Battalion but the appropriated tank rendered considerable assistance in suppressing this enfilading fire.

The Battalion achieved all its objectives that day and, by 1600, had returned to the billets it had vacated in the morning. In all, it had captured 1 field gun, 6 trench mortars and 28 machine guns (light and heavy). It recorded enemy casualties as: killed —about

2. Depree, pages 174–6.
3. ibid, pages 326–7.
4. ibid, pages 78–9.

40; and prisoners— 4 officers and approximately 120 other ranks.

Among its own casualties were Cyril who was killed and 2nd Lts. G. P. Jones MM, C. H. Aslam, R. E. Griffiths and Ll. W. Llewelyn who were wounded. Ten other ranks were killed and 65 were reported wounded or missing. Another of that day's casualties was Wilfred Owen, the war poet, who was killed crossing the Sambre-Oise canal to the south of the Forêt de Mormal.

At a divisional level, the Division had achieved its final objective before 1700 and pushed so far forward as to reach beyond the line of the next day's first objective and place itself 5,000 yards[5] ahead of troops on either flank. In all, the Division captured about 500 prisoners and 23 guns for casualties of about 600.

Clayton shows how 38 (Welsh) Division advanced rapidly and with confidence to reach —and go beyond— its objective for that day with limited casulaties whereas 17 Division to its left was handled far less surely and suffered many casualties. This difference highlighted the depth of 38 (Welsh) Division's training and its experience. It was one of only five out of 13 divisions to reach its objective that day.[6]

The attack at Englefontaine was 2RWF's last engagement of the Great War and the Battalion was in billets at Aulnoye on 9 November as the Kaiser abdicated and crossed by train into exile in neutral Holland before the Armistice came into effect at 1100 on 11 November 1918.[7]

Dunn[8] provides additional detail on Cyril's death over and above the war diaries. On 3 November, Cyril and Captains Howells Evans, commanding C Company, and Butler had been out reconnoitring when Cyril mentioned that he did not like the look of a farm on his right and asked Evans to help from the flank. The next day, after C Company had completed its mopping up, Evans

---

5. The Division's Field Ambulance war diary suggests just 4,000 yards.
6. Clayton, pages 233, 344 and 347.
7. It remained at Aulnoye until 28 December 1918.
8. Dunn, page 565.

went over to the farmhouse that Cyril had identified. Its only occupant was all that remained of Cyril. D Company had had a clean run through its objectives but, in the fog, had run into the Division's barrage and had taken casualties. Cyril was the only one killed —when a piece of shell that had burst behind him penetrated his heart. His batman, Edwards —another Denbigh man, later wrote to Cyril's father about how they had gone 'over the Top' together and had been talking to each other just a few minutes before he saw Cyril fall.[9] These two accounts would suggest that someone had moved Cyril's body from where he fell to rest inside the farmhouse.

Cyril could have run into friendly fire for a number of reasons. We must remember that he and D Company were advancing under a creeping barrage. They would have been expected to 'lean into' the barrage and follow as closely behind it as possible —a point emphasised in the Division's tactical instructions in advance of the attack.[10] The misty morning could well have caused them to lose their way and so get ahead of the barrage. Equally, if the Germans retreated more quickly, D Company may have advanced ahead of the barrage.

If it were not a case of his having got ahead of the barrage, the most probable explanation would have been a shell hitting a branch, exploding and fragmenting. The barrage consisted of the divisional artillery's firing high explosive shells with percussion fuses, as opposed to shrapnel with time fuses. Firing in support in a wooded area always carried the risk that, given the rather flat trajectories of the contemporary field guns, a shell would strike a branch rather than explode on the ground further on. This risk was known —and explained why soldiers disliked being in wooded areas under a barrage. The whole area around Englefontaine was planted with many fruit orchards so, even without the forest itself, trees abounded.

9. Letter (undated) from Tom Edwards to Cyril's father; see Appendix II.
10. Depree, page 178.

After the reconnaissance on 3 November, Cyril had, according to Dunn, expressed a feeling that the chances of living to a ripe old age were distinctly rosy for those who came through the 4 November attack as it looked as though a German collapse was very near and this must be the Germans' last despairing stand. Had Cyril had a sense of foreboding? Family lore[11] certainly suggests yes: he had told his batman that he was leery of the attack, but had no choice but to lead D Company as so many other officers were unavailable. To be leery is understandable but to say that he had no choice is a strange comment, for it was his job to lead his men that day —and he gave no evidence of feeling fey or anxious in the 1 November letter to his father. Of course, the tale may have become garbled in the telling; or, there may have been a degree of sugar-coating for his grieving parents' benefit. Nonetheless, it does suggest that Cyril had a prior sense of foreboding about that day.

Richards also describes the attack at Englefontaine[12] and how the company that advanced from the orchard suffered heavy casualties. He then recounts how a German doctor captured by the Battalion in that morning's fighting explained that if the British had not attacked, all arrangements had been made for the German troops to withdraw from the village that evening through the Forêt de Mormal to prepared positions the other side of the river Sambre.

Cyril had the somewhat unenviable distinction of being one of the last of 2RWF to be killed during the Great War. In this, he was all the more unfortunate as he appears to have come through the war uninjured to this point. The only relevant entry on his 'Casualty Form – Active Service' is a reference to an attack of scabies during the period 29 March to 3 April 1916 when he would appear to have been hospitalised before being discharged back to 3DG by the RAMC.

Given that armistice negotiations were well under way by the

---

11. Recounted in the late 1960s to the author's mother by Cyril's younger brother, John.
12. Richards, pages 309–11.

time that the British decided upon their attack along the Sambre, Cyril's family must surely have wondered whether the whole battle had been necessary and had Cyril died needlessly. Clayton suggests that, without the British having forced the issue and joined the battle, the German Army would not have withdrawn from its defensive positions around the Forêt de Mormal and the Sambre–Oise Canal, and in doing so effectively applied greater pressure on Germany to agree an armistice.[13]

25. Cyril's grave at Englefontaine.

---

13. Clayton, page 350.

13. NEWS OF CYRIL'S DEATH REACHES HOME

It was not until 13 November that his commanding officer made a Field Service Report of Death to the War Office which received the report on 15 November. An interesting aside here is that this is the only occasion in his records where the Regiment's name is spelt 'Welch.'

The standard War Office administrative machinery then ground into action and his parents were telegraphed[1] on 15 November:[2]

> To: Keepfer, Derwenfa, Denbigh. Deeply Regret 2nd Lieutenant WRC Keepfer Welsh Fusiliers killed in action November fourth Army Council express sympathy.

His death was the second loss his father had suffered within a month for, in October, Cyril's aunt, his father's sister, Sister Mary Josephine, a nun at St. Clare's convent in Pantasaph, had died — just days after Cyril had returned to France from leave.[3]

As a child, I was told that the telegram arrived at Derwenfa on 11 November while the town's church bells were being rung to celebrate the Armistice and that the news effectively killed his mother who was ill in bed at the time. A dramatic tale; but one that

---

1. Officers' next of kin were given the news by telegram; other ranks' next of kin were informed in writing on a pre-printed form (Army Form B1014-82).
2. It is just possible, judging from the list of dates at the beginning of Cyril's War Office file, that the telegram was sent on 18 November. However, 15 November seems far more likely because both the *Denbighshire Free Press* and *Baner ac Amserau Cymru* carried a report of his death in their 16 November editions.
3. 12 October 1918, *FP*.

is not literally true even if the broad outline may have had some basis. The telegram was not sent until 15 November and his mother did not die until 1925 —although, following a stroke, she was confined to bed for several years before her death. Even here, Cyril's final letter suggests that his mother had already suffered a stroke before his final visit home —so it could not have been a case of the news of his death having caused her stroke.

Unquestionably, news of Cyril's death must have been a shock to his family. By 14 October, with the news that Germany had sought an armistice, the London newspaper boys had been crying out 'The War Over ! The War Over!' and, by early November, the newspapers were clear that the war was all but over and happy faces were seen on the London streets.[4] It would, therefore, hardly have been surprising if the family had not been swept up in this optimistic mood and been looking forward to Cyril's return from the field of battle only to be shattered by the news of his death.

One must also doubt whether, in fact, this telegram was the first intimation to reach Denbigh of Cyril's death. Certainly, the news was quickly bruited around Denbigh and the *Denbighshire Free Press*, in its 16 November edition, had an article about Cyril, describing his upbringing and schooling in Denbigh and a summary of his military career. The article contained information that could only have come from the family and it quoted verbatim the text of the letter that his parents had received from the major then in acting command of the Battalion. The most likely explanation is that it was this letter that brought the news to Denbigh ahead of the War Office's telegram —quite possibly, even before 11 November, as, in those days, the postal service was very efficient and prompt.

Certainly, the news was back in England before the Field Service Report of his death was sent by his commanding officer to the War Office. We know this because the first item on the agenda for the Law Fire Insurance Society Limited's board meeting on 12 November

---

4. *Zeppelin Nights*, page 266.

was to note formally the news of Cyril's death.⁵ Then, on 22 November, the company's Secretary wrote to his father requesting details of Cyril's war service as part of the Secretary's exercise in recording details of all the company's staff's war service.⁶

A fellow subaltern, Charles Larson, in 2RWF's D Company also wrote⁷ to Cyril's parents on 12 November about his death and assumed that his parents had already been informed by the Battalion of Cyril's death. He said that Cyril held a high reputation in the Battalion for his 'good work and leadership.' He informed them that Cyril had been buried at Englefontaine and that the burial party consisted of 2RWF's commanding officer, and the officers and men of D Company. The burial would have been conducted by one of the Division's burial parties.

The *Denbighshire Free Press* described Cyril as 'a nice, bright loveable Denbigh boy, very much esteemed by young and old and a great favourite with his former young school fellows.'⁸ It explained that, during 1916, he was in the Somme, five times mounted and five times on foot. It said he was one of six men chosen by 3DG to take up a commission in the infantry and he succeeded well at Romford and was at the top of the weekly examinations and passed out second in the whole draft at the final examinations. He 'earned distinction as one of the steadiest officers' in 2RWF and had experienced three winter campaigns and four birthdays in France.

At the time of his death, the newspaper said that Cyril had been commanding 'D' Company for the last three months and was the third longest serving officer with the Battalion.⁹ The Battalion's acting commander wrote:

---

5. CLC/B/192/MS/15010/041 (LMA), Board Minutes, 1917–1920, vol P, page 277.
6. Letter made available to the author.
7. Letter C. Larson to Cyril's parents, 12 November 1918, see Appendix II.
8. 16 November 1918, *FP*.
9. The newspaper says 'regiment' but it must mean battalion as the RWF comprised many battalions.

Dear Mr Keepfer, —I regret very much to have to tell you that your son was killed in action on November 4th, 1918. We are all terribly sorry about it, as he was one of the best officers in the regiment, and we miss him badly as a friend and a good soldier.

I am personally very grieved as he was a great friend of mine.

You have at least the great consolation of knowing that he died as a soldier should, leading his men in action against the enemy.

Please accept my deepest sympathy in your bereavement, and the sympathy of the Regiment. —Yours sincerely,

E. R. de Mercinout,[10] Major, 2 R.W.F.

A former army officer has suggested that this letter goes beyond the usual formalities of such letters. Thus, one may take it that Cyril was, genuinely, regarded as a good officer and, despite the difference in their substantive ranks, a good friend of the letter-writer.

The *Baner ac Amserau Cymru's* report was much briefer and simply reported that Cyril and another Denbigh boy, Sgt. Tom Davies, had died:[11]

Dinbych
Daeth y newydd i'r dref yn ystod y dyddiau diweddaf fod y Sergt. Tom Albert Davies[12] *... wedi ei ladd ar faes y rhyfel; hefyd, yr Is-gadben Cyril Keepfer, mab cyntaf Mr a Mrs W. Keepfer. Yr oedd y naill a'r*

---

10. Sic. This may well be a mis-spelling for G. E. R. [Guy Egon Réné] de Miremont— an officer who had a somewhat mixed reputation within the Battalion: see Dunn pages xliii-xliv and Duty Done, pages 75–6.
11. 16 November 1918, *Y Faner*: Denbigh. The news came to the town in recent days that Sgt Tom Albert Davies had been killed on the field of battle; also Lieutenant Cyril Keepfer, the first son of Mr and Mrs Keepfer. Both were well known boys in the town and well-liked by all who knew them. It is sad to lose the boys when peace is imminent. The first named of the two was married. We sympathise deeply with their families in their loss.
12. Sgt. Davies had two brothers and one sister in Denbigh. Both brothers subsequently acted as municipal trumpeters on occasions in Denbigh. His sister named her son

llall yn fechgyn adnabyddus i'r dref, ac yn hoffus gan eu holl gydnabod. Trist yw colli'r bechgyn pan ar fin heddwch. Yr oedd y blaenaf o'r ddau yn briod. Cydymdeimlir yn ddwfn a'u teuluoedd yn eu colled.

The Times of 19 November included Cyril's name in its daily Roll of Honour of officers who had fallen.

Put in context, by 1918, some 250 officers had passed through 2RWF; 68 of whom died[13] —Dunn says 39.[14] The difference may be explained by Dunn looking at deaths in the Battalion and Langley looking at deaths at any time of officers who had served in the Battalion. Whichever, a greater number of officers associated with the Battalion were killed during the Great War than the Battalion had had on its strength at the outbreak of the war. Similarly, Dunn suggests 1,106 other ranks were killed —again, higher than the Battalion's establishment level in 1914. Cyril was one of 31,000 Welshmen who sacrificed their lives during the war out of the 272,000 who enlisted in the Army. While Cyril served with 2RWF, the Battalion achieved battle honours in 14 battles, of which three are borne on the Battalion's Sovereign's Colour[15] (out of 28 and five respectively earned throughout the whole war).

Appendix I provides a breakdown of Cyril's service during the war. He served from 7 September 1914 to 4 November 1918, a total of 1,525 days or just short of four years and two months. Of this period, 398 days were spent immediately after enlisting in training for the cavalry before reaching 3DG in France. In 1917, he spent a further 225 days at home on a mixture of leave, officer training and attachment to 3RWF before, again, going to France, this time with 2RWF. In all, a total of some 623 days were spent at Home —plus two further short furloughs in 1918.

Thus, he spent 902 days on active military service in France; 504

after him. This nephew died serving in the RAF in the Second World War. Information provided to the author by R. M. Owen.
13. *Duty Done*, page 250
14. Dunn, page xlii.
15. Ypres 1917, Somme 1918 and Hindenburg Line.

days with 3DG and 398 days with 2RWF. As to his time with 3DG, it is not possible to square the statement in the *Denbighshire Free Press* notice of his death of his having been in action five times mounted and five times dismounted with the relevant war diaries for 3DG. Of course, it may be a question of definition, both as to what constitutes 'being in action' and how the occasions are counted. Servicemen usually interpret 'being in action' broadly so as to equate to being in harm's way. There were only two recorded occasions during the Somme battles of 1916 when 3DG was at readiness for action: at the opening of the Somme offensive on 1 July and, again, in connection with the Battle of Flers in September 1916 —but there was no gap on either occasion for the cavalry to exploit and 3DG were quickly moved back behind the rear areas.

As for being at the Front dismounted, there are two possibilities. Either this is a reference to his having served in 6 Dismounted Cavalry Battalion —of which there is no specific confirmation— or it is a reference to his being in a working party at the Front. Certainly, the Dismounted Cavalry's war diaries record three occasions when 6 Dismounted Cavalry Battalion served in front line trenches. Further, there are numerous references —in the war diaries of both 3DG and the Dismounted Cavalry Division— to working parties being detached at, or near, the Front and Cyril may well have been a member of one or more of such working parties.

Even the reference to 'in the Somme' is unclear. Is it intended as a narrow reference to the series of battles which, together, usually fall within the term 'the Battle of the Somme'? Or, is it, in journalese, a more generic reference to fighting in the general area of the Somme —or, even, to the battlefields of France in general?

Today, we are accustomed to think in terms of the Great War as being a life in the trenches. Certainly, apart from three months at the beginning and again at the end of the war, trench warfare dominated the Western Front; but, this did not mean that soldiers spent all their time in the trenches. Without detracting from the horror that trench warfare often entailed, it is important to realise that, in fact, quite a small proportion of a soldier's time was actually spent in the trenches. By the time Cyril went to France with the infantry, the staff had developed sophisticated rotation schedules to equalise time spent at the front between the different units; billets had been established so that the men could sleep under cover when not at the front; baths and laundries had been established[16] and, as we have seen, there was even a programme of entertainments.

In terms of battlefield action, Cyril's time with 2RWF —at 116 days in front line trenches and some twelve days in action or advancing on the battlefield— somewhat exceeded the average that has been estimated for a typical unit at just five to ten days a year in intensive action and 60 to 100 days in front-line trench activities without action[17] with the remainder spent at rest or in reserve — with the inevitable fatigue duties and training exercises. In Cyril's case, this would have been due to the general advance during the last three months of the war: a period unlike any other for the British in the war as it was one of constant advances.

---

16. Rawson, page 22.
17. See discussion in *The Long, Long Trail* on battle reality.

14. BACK AT HOME

On 15 November, the Registry at the War Office calculated the amounts due to Cyril's estate[1] in respect of his service as follows:

		£. s. d.
Gratuity under Articles 496 and 497	97.13.00	
Less: Overpaid 13.13.00		
I.T. (1.00.00)		
Net Gratuity:		85.00.00
Ranker's Grant		16.10.00
Allowances:		
Lodging, Fuel and Light		
7 October–4 November	8.02.01	
Rations		
23 September–6 October	1.09.02	
Other Credits		9.11.03
Total		111.01.03 (£111.06)

On 29 November, his father, who was listed as his next of kin, signed an undertaking in favour of the War Office for Cyril's personal effects against undertaking to pay all his debts and, on 12 December 1918, the War Office credited the above monies to Cyril's account at Messrs Cox & Co —the Army's traditional bankers who

---

1. The file note mistakenly refers to 'WRC Keepfer of the South Wales Borderers.' This is, presumably, simply a clerical error as the 10th Battalion South Wales Borderers were another of the battalions in 115 Brigade.

also acted as the Battalion's agents and administered its officers' accounts.

On 27 January 1919, the War Office wrote to the National Provincial and Union Bank of England Ltd (NP Bank) branch in Denbigh (until its recent closure, the Royal Bank of Scotland plc branch in Vale Street) giving more detail as to the above calculation. As a 2nd lieutenant, his pay had been 10/6 (52.5p) per day.[2] As he had been killed in action, he was entitled to a gratuity of 186 days pay from which was deducted £13/13/00 (£13.65) in respect of the period 5–30 November for which he had already been paid (less Income Tax (or Income Duty) of £1 thereon), leaving a credit due to Cyril's estate of £85 which the War Office's accounts department then noted as having been credited to Cyril's effects on 20 February 1919. It was noted also that the Grant of £16/10/- (£16.50) for service in the ranks was also to be credited to his effects.

On 4 February, the War Office wrote again to the NP Bank asking if it was now able to forward the Letters of Administration for the estate to the War Office which would register and return them and issue the amount due. The District Probate Registry at St Asaph only issued Letters of Administration to his father on 22 September 1919. The Letters of Administration record Cyril as having died intestate on Active Military Service with a gross estate valued at £162/16/3 (£162.81).

For his war service, Cyril was entitled to, and received, three standard medals: the 1914–15 Star for service with the British Expeditionary Force as from 5 October 1915, the British War Medal 1914–1918 and the Allied Victory Medal.[3] In the 1920s, his family would also have received a Memorial Plaque, which was given to the next of kin of all Empire service personnel who were killed in the war. It was cast of bronze and was five inches in diameter. Similar in style to (although considerably larger than) the pre-

---

2. It is unclear whether or not this sum included the extra pay and allowances to which he was entitled as acting company commander.
3. Somewhat irreverently known as Pip, Squeak and Wilfred respectively.

decimal coinage penny, it was commonly referred to as the Dead Man's Penny, or *Y Geiniog Fawr*.

From one-sided correspondence,[4] we can tell that, in February 1919, Cyril's father wrote to the parish priest at Englefontaine to seek further information about Cyril's grave, and to enquire whether or not the letters R.I.P. (*requiescat in pace*) had been placed over it and was it cared for? The priest, curé Flament, responded immediately that there were a great many soldiers' graves dispersed throughout the orchards around Englefontaine so, at Mass, he had asked his parishioners to search their properties to look for Cyril's grave. He soon had the required information and went immediately to inspect the grave and was able to report that it was with about 30 other graves in an orchard adjoining the house of a local widow whose husband had been killed in the defence of Maubeuge. A small fence surrounded the graves and would protect them from accident.[5] He confirmed that, although the cross above Cyril's grave was very strong and —unlike some others— the inscription very clear, it was not superscribed with the letters R.I.P. He went on to assure Cyril's father that the grave would be well tended by the widow.

Curé Flament proceeded to offer his thanks to Cyril's father for the gift of his son in the defence and recapture of their poor little village. He also suggested that, should Cyril's father wish it, he would approach the British and French authorities so as to have Cyril's body exhumed and prepared for transportation back home; and, pending such transportation, offered to have it kept in his own family's vault. Even had Cyril's parents wished it, this would not have been possible. In the First World War, the British government decided that, unlike in earlier wars, no remains would be returned home for burial but all the Fallen should be buried where they fell.

---

4. Letters curé Flament to Cyril's father, 2 and 30 March 1919; see Appendix II.
5. Although the priest describes the site as in the village of Englefontaine on the road to Hecq, other (British) sources refer to the grave as being in the 'Hecq cemetery.'

This was because, in earlier wars, it had been only the wealthier families who could afford for the remains to be returned home for interment. This decision led to the establishment of the Imperial War Graves Commission[6] which has subsequently cared for the graves of the British war dead. In contrast, the French authorities were compelled, by public opinion after the war, to allow French families to exhume the remains of their lost ones and have them reburied closer to their families.

Cyril's father quickly responded and asked curé Flament to have the letters R.I.P. engraved on the cross above the grave and to thank the widow for her care of the grave. He also asked curé Flament to say Masses for Cyril and sent him £1 for this purpose. It is likely that he also sought further information about the village and the area where Cyril had been killed for curé Flament gave a brief description of Englefontaine as a place of orchards—mainly apple trees—on the edge of the forest with a small manufacturing industry in relation to clay tiles and drain pipes.

The priest concluded by describing how both Englefontaine and the other villages bordering the forest were devastated and how the local population were living amidst ruins. He sent a sketch map of the village detailing where Cyril's grave was to be found but apologised for not being able to send a photograph as there were no British troops then stationed in the village. Such troops would have had photographic apparatus whereas the villagers' cameras had all been seized by the Germans. Although he had secreted two cameras beneath the floorboards, these had been destroyed when a shell (British) had exploded near their hiding place and then the rain had ruined the rest of the apparatus, which he only discovered on his return to the village in December 1918. He, nevertheless, undertook to have the grave photographed at a later date. He must have done so for there is a photograph of this grave amongst family papers but there is no accompanying letter.

---

6. Renamed as the Commonwealth War Graves Commission in 1960.

The other graves in the small cemetery where Cyril was buried were those of British soldiers who fell in battle during October and November 1918. After the Armistice, the smaller cemeteries in the area were consolidated and Cyril's remains were transferred from that cemetery (which was closed) to Plot II.D.24 in the British War Cemetery at Montay-Neuvilly Road, Montay (just outside Le Cateau-Cambrésis) which had been created by the 23 Brigade, Royal Garrison Artillery on 26 and 27 October —mainly for men from his own, 38 (Welsh), Division, the 33 Division and the 6 Dorsets.

This cemetery was designed by Charles Holden. Cyril's grave is on the far left just before the middle ranks of the cemetery as you enter from the gate off the Montay-Neuvilly road. After the war, the Imperial War Graves Commission erected its by now famous headstones and, where the family so wished, included a brief phrase chosen by the fallen soldier's relatives. The relatives could choose this inscription but they were required to pay for it —at a rate of about 3½d (1.5p) per letter. Where a headstone bears no such inscription, it is a case of either the Imperial War Graves Commission's being unable to trace the soldier's relatives or the family's being unable to pay for an inscription.

Cyril's simple headstone, which bears a Latin cross,[7] is headed by the badge of the RWF and his identity. The family's chosen inscription consisted of 37 characters and cost his father 10/9 (54p). The instruction form issued by the Imperial War Graves Commission for the engraving of that cemetery's headstones includes a specific note to the engraver as regards the circumflex —the family were not charged extra for this.[8] The inscription, at the base of the headstone, reads:

---

7. See Marshall, "'Big Cross', 'Little Cross' Why?" published in *Stand To*, issue N°· 108 (published by The Western Front Association) for a discussion of the use of Broad crosses and Latin crosses on servicemen's headstones.

8. Imperial War Graves Commission Report of Inscriptions for the Montay-Neuvilly Road Cemetery, Schedule B, page 21.

*Ei enw'n perarogli sydd a'i hûn
mor dawel yw*[9]
R. I. P.

In the years to follow, various commemorative services were held and memorials set up to record the Fallen from Denbigh. In March 1919, a meeting of the Committee of the Denbigh Free Reading and Recreation Rooms, of which Cyril's father was a member, expressed their deep sympathy and condolence to him on Cyril's death in action 'and the fact of it occurring within a couple of days of the Armistice being signed making the same the more painful.'[10] In early August 1919, an open air United Service at the Town Cross to commemorate all the Denbigh Fallen was organised by the Discharged and Demobilised Sailors and Soldiers Foundation.[11]

26. *Cyril's grave at the Montay-Neuvilly War Cemetery.*

Memorials which list Cyril among the Fallen include a memorial shrine, the Denbigh War Memorial and the County School's Roll of Honour.[12]

9. 'His name smells most sweetly for his sleep is most peaceful.'
10. 22 March 1919, *FP*.
11. 9 August 1919, *FP*.
12. The Roll of Honour hung originally just inside the main entrance to the old Denbigh County School in Middle Lane. It is now in the new Denbigh High School building on Ruthin Road. The Roll of Honour was erected by subscribers. No member of the Keepfer family subscribed to the erection of this memorial; information provided to the author by R. M. Owen who has a copy of the list of subscribers.
13. 16 November 1919, *FP*.

27. Memorial Shrine to the Denbigh War Dead. Cyril's name is at the top of the column on the centre right hand side. The shrine was presented to the town by Mrs Burton of Gwaenynog in 1917 and hung originally inside the entrance to the Town Hall. As it had been presented to the town during the war, additional names were inscribed as time passed. After the Denbigh War Memorial was erected in 1922, this shrine was moved to the Territorial Army's Drill Hall in Lenton Pool until that closed when it was removed to Council storage. Rediscovered in 2016, it was placed in the Denbigh Museum as part of its exhibition on Denbigh and the Great War.

Cyril is one of 49 Denbigh men listed on the town's war memorial as having given his life in the war. He was one of only two Denbigh boys killed during November 1918 —although a number died subsequent to the Armistice from wounds or accidents. The *Denbighshire Free Press* commented that 'for a school of its size' the names recorded on the County School's Roll of Honour were 'very numerous' in that 32 old boys had fallen out of the 180 or so who had joined up. It noted that 'the latest two heroes were Lieut. (sic) Cyril Keepfer, son of Mr and Mrs W. Keepfer, Denbigh and Pte. Glynne Edwards, son of Mrs Edwards, The Shop,

28. Denbigh War Memorial. This was erected on Crown Square in 1922. Its exact position on the square has changed several times over the years.

Llanelidan.'[13] Cyril's name is also included on the Capel Mawr memorial to those of its congregation who had fallen in the war.

A stone cross outside the parish church of St Marcella's (Llanfarchell, Whitchurch or Eglwyswen) in Denbigh commemorates, very simply, 'the Officers and Men' from the parish who fell in the war. At Bangor, Cyril's name is also to be found on the North Wales Heroes' Memorial which commemorates all those who fell from the area of North Wales that equates to the old principalities of Gwynedd and Powys.

His parents remembered him in November 1919 and placed an In Memoriam notice in the *Denbighshire Free Press* on 8 November:

> KEEPFER —In proud and loving memory of 'Cyril', the eldest beloved son of W. L. and E. Keepfer, Derwenfa, Denbigh, Sec-Lieut. 2nd R.W.F., killed in action in France November the 4th, 1918, buried at Englefontaine, Nord (over 4 years service) 'R. I. P.'

---

1. Their sleep is most peaceful.

15. EPILOGUE

Cyril's sister, Josephine, followed him to London during the war to work in a bank. Here, she met Grier Lloyd, one of the American soldiers who came through London in 1917 and 1918. Shortly after the war's end, she became one of the first 'GI brides' and moved back with Grier to live in Chattanooga, Tennessee.

Cyril's mother passed away on 28 January 1925 and was buried in the cemetery at St Marcella's. The inscription on her gravestone also commemorates Cyril:

> In
> Loving Memory of
> ELIZABETH
> beloved wife of
> W. L. KEEPFER
> Derwenfa, Denbigh
> Died 28 Jan. 1925, aged 56
> Also their son
> Lieut. W. R. Cyril Keepfer
> killed in action
> Englefontaine, France
> 4th Nov. 1914, aged 24
> *'Eu hûn mor dawel yw'*[1]

In the 1920s, Cyril's father, sister Phyllis and younger brother John, along with Phyllis's husband, Sydney Watkins, went over to France to pay their respects at Cyril's graveside. Cyril's name was remembered by his young brother, John, who named his second son after him.

When, just over 20 years after Cyril had been killed, Britain was again at war with Germany, conscription was imposed from the very start of the conflict. Cyril's younger brother, John, was called up to serve as a signalman on the corvette HMS *Clarkia* before becoming a petty officer and a signals instructor at the Royal Navy's shore based training establishment, HMS *Arthur*. Unlike Cyril, he declined to apply for a commission. Cyril's nephew, Ivor Watkins —the son of his sister Phyllis— served throughout the war in the 1st Battalion of the Hertfordshire Regiment where he became the senior major. After the war, he returned to Denbigh where, like his father and great-grandfather before him, he served on the Town Council. In 1949, he joined the 4th Battalion, RWF (Territorial Army) as a major and had charge of the Drill Hall in Denbigh before becoming a colonel in the Territorial Army in 1966, responsible for North Wales.

29. Cyril's mother's grave, St Marcella's, Denbigh

The Second World War had an even greater impact on the civilian population back home and Cyril's father, who had played no part in the First World War, served in the local Air Raid Protection service in Denbigh even though, by then, he was in his 70s. He had remarried in 1927. He died in 1945, leaving a widow, Clarice, and two young daughters, Pauline and Yvonne.

Cyril's sister, Phyllis, subsequently became Governor and

Chairman of the Board of Governors of Denbigh Grammar School —the successor to the County School which Cyril, his brother and younger sisters had attended. This was ironic as Phyllis was the only one of the siblings not to attend a County School —having been educated at Howell's School.

As to the units with which Cyril had served, 3DG merged, in 1922, with 6 Dragoon Guards into a single regiment known as 3rd/6th Dragoon Guards while both regiments were stationed in India. In 1928, the new regiment's name changed to 3rd Carabiniers (Prince of Wales's Dragoon Guards). It merged again, in 1971, with the Royal Scots Greys (2nd Dragoons) to form the Royal Scots Dragoon Guards (Carabiniers and Greys) with its base in Edinburgh Castle.

Meanwhile, the spelling of 'Welch' was restored to the RWF by Army Order N[o.] 56 of 1920. 2RWF was disbanded in 1948 when the Regiment again became a single battalion regiment before merging, on St David's Day in 2006, with the Royal Regiment of Wales to become 1st Battalion, The Royal Welsh (Royal Welch Fusiliers).

In 2014, L'Anneau de la Mémoire (or the Ring of Remembrance) was opened at France's largest military cemetery at Ablain-Saint-Nazaire, just north of Arras to commemorate the nearly 600,000 soldiers of all nationalities who fell in the Nord and Pas-de-Calais departments during the war. It consists of 500 upright metal panels in an ellipse pattern on which are inscribed, in alphabetical order, the names of all those soldiers who fell there —including Cyril.

APPENDIX I
Breakdown of Cyril's wartime service

Unit	Period	Billets	Trenches		Bivouac	Camp/ Hutments	Battlefield or advancing	Unclear/ marching	Leave	Total days
			Front	Reserve or Support						
						Days				
3 Cav Res	07.09.14 to 09.10.15	Training at the Depot in Canterbury and then awaiting posting to France							A	398
3DG	10.10.15 to 01.01.16	84								84
DCD	02.01.16 to 11.02.16	27	12	2						41
3DG	12.02.16 to 25.02.17	320			47	11		1		379
	19.02.17 to 01.10.17	Home leave (duration unclear), officer training in Romford (approximately 140 days) and posting to 3RWF in Litherland (approximately 60 days)								225
2RWF (with 33 Div)	02.10.17 to 05.02.18 (trench warfare in the Ypres, Messines, Paschendaele area))	43	16	13	2	51		1	B	126
2RWF (with 38 Welsh Div)	06.02.18 to 01.04.18 (trench warfare in the Wez Macquart area)	29	20			6				55
2RWF (with 38 Welsh Div)	02.04.18 to 07.08.18 (trench warfare in the river Ancre area)	22	34	5	30	30		7		128
2RWF (with 38 Welsh Div)	08.08.18 to 04.11.18 the "hundred days" advance	16	34		7	6	12		14 (while Cyril on leave, 2RWF in huts/camp for 11 days and trenches for 3 days)	89
TOTAL		541	116	20	86	104	12	9		1,525

Notes:

A — There are no records of Cyril's having any leave during his period of training or after he had completed his training. However, various photographs of him and his family in Denbigh suggest that he must have had at least one period of leave during this time—presumably between completing his training and being posted to France.

B — He was reported as having had some leave during January 1918, but the period is unclear.

APPENDIX II
Transcripts of various letters referred to in the text

Item	Date	Page
1. Cyril to his brother, John Lloyd, on his birthday	20 April 1915	166
2. Cyril to his parents	End May/early June 1915	167
3. Cyril to his parents	4 October 1915	169
4. The 'Boll postcard'	10 August 1918	172
5. Cyril to his father	1 November 1918	173
6. 2nd Lt. C. Larson to Cyril's parents	12 November 1918	175
7. T. E. Davies to Cyril's father	22 November 1918	176
8. Tom Edwards to Cyril's father	undated, 1918	177
9. Curé Flament to Cyril's father, plus translations	2 and 30 March 1919	178

Written on embossed 3rd Dragoon Guards notepaper

20 April 1915

> 4th Troop
> C Squadron
> 3rd Dragoon Guards
> Canterbury

My dear John Lloyd,

I am writing you a short note John to wish you very many happy returns of your birthday and trust you will have very many more.

I hope you are quite well and enjoying yourself as you ought to.

I expect you have found a good many nests. I have found one or two with "cuwion"[1] in them when we have been leading our horses through a wood. Yesterday they told me to look after a nice chestnut horse that has come all the way from the Argentine. Do you know where that is John? Well ! you look at a map of the world and find South America and near the top of South America I think you will find a big stretch of country called the Argentine. It is noted for its Horses and Sheep and Cattle. But this is not a geography lesson is it?

How are you getting on in school now? Are you going to learn the Piano John. If I was you I would and learn to play well. I know it would be very hard to practice when you want to go out to play —but it would be worth it.

Well! John I must go to bed now & so good night.

Wishing you again a very happy birthday —with custards for tea— & many many more.

With best love from
Your loving brother
Cyril

---

1. Sic. Spelling should be *cywion*, meaning chicks.

APPENDIX II: TRANSCRIPTS OF LETTERS

Written on pre-printed forms provided by Y.M.C.A. With H.M. Forces on Active Service (For God and For King and For Country).

Dated Tuesday but otherwise no indication of date. However, the reference to the riots at Rhyl means that the letter must have been written after 21 and 22 May 1915, when they occurred. The reference to warmer weather also suggests that this letter was probably written at the end of May/early June 1915. It was written while Cyril was still at the Canterbury barracks.

Tuesday

4th Troop C Squadron
3rd Dragoon Guards
Canterbury

My dear Mam & Dad,
Thank you all very much for letters cakes & money &c all of which I have received safely.

    I did not get Dad's Sunday letter until this afternoon. I am sorry I have not written before this. I meant to write yesterday but we were out from 2. o'c until 6 at night and I was too tired to go out. We rode to Whitstable—had some competitions there & cooked our grub on the beach. It was a lovely day.

    I will do my utmost to get leave this next weekend —if I am not successful I shall try the following weekend— glad Mam will stay for 2 weeks or so and do hope the change will do her a great deal of good. I read about the riot at Rhyl in one of the Sunday papers. It must have been serious. Glad to know all are well at Litherland. Am writing WE[2] a long letter tonight —I cannot say if he is still at 81 or in his new house— but he is sure to get the present as they will forward to him. Thank you immensely for your trouble Dad.

---

2. It is unclear to whom the initials WE might refer. It may be to his father's sister, Winifred Eva (also known as Aunty Winnie) —in which case the subsequent references to a male must be a non-sequitur response to a question raised in the letter that Cyril was answering. If, however, the initials are linked to the following phrases, it is unclear to whom Cyril is referring.

Fancy Norman Green in France. I had a long letter from Bishop on Thursday and he said he was going to write you. I don't think he will go out for some time.

The promotion in all these new Regiments is so quick because they have not got the old Non Coms in them. Ours are nearly all old soldiers and Non Coms who have served in the Regmt. before.

Will write to Tom Gee. Glad J Ll is alright does well to be 4th on the ladder. Yes ! thank you I enjoyed the cakes.

There is an interesting thing happening here. On Saturday they asked for volunteers to go to the Infantry. They want 400 in all—100 per Squadron —but did not get many volunteers in "C" Sqdn. This afternoon we were paraded but nothing further was done except take a few names. I think that they have the choice of Regmt —and if they want me to go I shall try and transfer to L'dn Welsh. But I don't think somehow they will want me to go. They seem to have realised that they won't want so many cavalry. I don't think they can make you transfer. Those who do go will only be attached to the Infantry Regmt. & should cavalry be wanted they will have to get together again I think. I am interestedly awaiting events.

Well! have no more news.

Conclude with my best love to you all

Your loving son

Cyril

Appendix II: Transcripts of Letters

Written on embossed 3rd Dragoon Guards notepaper.

The envelope in which it was sent is embossed with the 3DG crest on the back. The postage was 1d (½ p) and the letter was franked at 10 pm at Canterbury on 4 October 1915 and franked again at Denbigh at 5.00pm the next day.

Cavalry Barracks
Canterbury

Monday morning

Oct. 4th 1915

My dearest Mam and Dad,

I trust you have received my last night's letter and I know you have received my wire. I received your wire today wiring me another £1 for which I thank you immensely —and also for your message.

My regimental no. & name is now '7255 Pte. W. R. C. Keepfer 3rd Reserve Cavalry Regiment.' I hope the letter & parcel will come in time.

Well! I believe we go at 4 o'c tomorrow morning & shall, I expect, be at Southampton until nighttime and will try & drop you a line from there. If you do not hear from me for a week or more don't worry & get over-anxious as you will understand I may not always have opportunities for writing.

Have got everything and don't want anything now —but should I want something over there I'll let you know. The weather here is beautifully fine & means to give us a good send off I think. We are doing nothing but sleep & writing letters today. I am sending a word to the Office now.

I am going as I told you with a very decent lot of chaps & hope to meet Jack Gill also. So please Mam & Dad don't worry overmuch —I know you will be a little troubled— but let us all trust & pray & all will be well. I am going quite gladly —alive to all the dangers & risks— but perfectly trained. So God bless and keep you all. That will be my prayer & I know you will say a few for me.

Tell all at Denbigh —I mean all that matter. Thank Phyllis immensely for her letter & say that we are postponing my birthday festivities & presents until my Continental Tour is over. But thank you all immensely. We'll talk of this later. Have got rid of all my things here—taking only necessaries. Everything else is in the care of Mrs. Simpson at Calabria Rd. I have had a Princess Mary's Gift Box[3] —that is also in safe keeping. I have given Dad as my next of kin so he'll know if I get a little damaged in some mix up. But I would ask you this favour that supposing Dad should hear of something like this —one of you will wire to that effect to Miss B. M. Hayes— 3 Liberia Rd., Highbury, London N —a friend of mine who probably you will not have heard about.

I suppose this will be my last letter from Canterbury. Will give you my new address as soon as possible.

So JLl has been eating too many apples has he! Naughty boy!

Tell him Cyril will try to bring him a helmet or something.

Again please let me impress that no news is good news Mam. Don't be sad —will you try & be a little proud instead— as proud as I am of you dearest Mam.

But there I must not become downhearted. It is my first touch of that. Mark you I go with a good heart —a clear conscience & a complete faith in the Cause for which I am now making this effort.

Well! I hope things will continue to prosper in Denbigh & that you will all enjoy the very best of health & a full measure of God's blessing.

I suppose we shall be at the Base for some little time until the Regiment comes down again.

Give my very best love & wishes to all at Haulfryn —Park Cottage— 45 & Schwarzwald. I'm wondering if I shall be seasick or not!!

Will write as often as possible & don't forget all of you to be at the

---

3. A brass gift box (officers received a silver box) provided by a Fund whose patroness was Princess Mary, daughter of George V and later the Princess Royal. Originally intended as a Christmas Gift for all those serving overseas or afloat at Christmas 1914, eligibility was gradually extended to all who were serving in the forces in 1914, and the next of kin of 1914 casualties. The contents were, generally, an ounce of pipe tobacco, 20 cigarettes, a pipe, a lighter, a Christmas card and a photograph of the princess. Given the increased numbers and the practicalities surrounding distribution, many of these boxes were still being distributed well after Christmas 1914.

Station to meet me when 'the boys come home!'

I trust the sudden news did not shock you too much. I was only warned of it at midday on Saturday & have been busy doing things & getting equipped —have told you on previous occasions that the call would be a sudden one haven't I ?

Well! let us all face it cheerfully & bravely you & I. It had to come & to face the sad inevitable bravely is one of the greatest deeds.

I must draw to a close now. Nos dawch i gyd.

With my fondest love to you both —Jo Phyllis & John & all the family.

Be brave & God bless you all for always.

Ever your loving son

Cyril
xxxx

Postcard dated 10.8.18 from Boll addressed to "Herrn Küpfer." The front of the postcard has a picture of the village of Boll bei Bonndorf in the Black Forest area of Germany (Schwarzwald) and a cross marking a window in a farmhouse — but no explanation as to what the cross represents. The suggestion is that the recipient should have known what it was meant to represent (or the sender, at least, wishes to sow this impression).

Herrn
Küpfer Uhrmacher
Denbigh
England

Boll 10.8.18

Mit Ihrem Sohne sind wir recht gemütlich beisammen.
Freut mich, dass noch etwas deutsches Blut in Walles [sic] herrscht.
Ihr Sohn fühlt sich bei uns jedenfalls gut aufgehoben.
Recht viele Grüsse aus dem Schwarzwald.
Rŭd. Hŭgel[4]

TRANSLATION

Mr Küpfer Watchmaker
Denbigh
England

Boll 10.8.18

We are comfortably together with your son.
Happy that there is still some German blood in Wales. Your son at any rate feels well looked after.
Warm greetings from the Black Forest.

Rud. Hugel.

4. Rud is a diminutive and is probably short for Rudolf or Rudiger. The stroke across the u is distinct from an umlaut and is a function of the script (or Schrift) in which the card was written.

Cyril to his father dated 1 November 1918

BEF
1st Nov. 1918

My dear Dad,

Now this is a letter all for yourself. Just let me tell you, I am quite fit & well & still in charge of the Company —for which work I get extra pay & allowances. The rank may come along later & I should have had it long ago but for that old Army bugbear of 'seniority' —but I'm not too badly off & have a good reputation (tho' I say it!) which is something.

My real reason for writing is to tell you a little about Norah —you took my word for everything on my last leave & I don't think I told you very much in the hurry of the moment. She is an orphan & lives with her elder sister who has 'mothered' the family. She has two brothers —one married & in the Excise in Dublin & the other (whom I knew at Romford) is now out here with the {M}. G.C. She is a secretary now to one of the 'heads' at the Head Offices of the Fordson Tractor people & has rather a good job. I met her thro' her brother whilst at Romford. She is a Wesleyan by religion. I don't think I can tell you any more Dad —next time I come over I will bring her to Denbigh to see you all & then you can criticise my taste!!

How is John getting on—do you think it would be a good idea to send him to some good school —something like you yourself had Dad— he has not got to the same extent the influence of dear Mam that we had. Of course Dad there are the pecuniary considerations — but he would like it I think & it would mould him into shape. This is only my point of view & I don't wish to interfere Dad. You can see best.

I would thank you again for the trouble you took over getting the ring —it was a little high— but a few weeks of this extra pay will knock that off —& its once in a lifetime. As I told you —had I not being coming back here I would have waited —but there were sentimental reasons (which you will understand) why I wished it then.

Also I pray God Dad that he will give you —in particular— & all of us —strength in the loss of poor Auntie Josephine. I can at times feel her watching when I've been in some nasty places —& it is most comforting. God keep her. I trust that dear Mam improves & hope that before very long she will be more like her old self again.

I quoted your message to Norah & she was contented & replied that; 'time would certainly show she would be what you wished!'

I have heard from Jo & am writing her tonight. Tomorrow I am sending home a parcel of underclothing which I cannot use now. Will you please ask Phyl to have washed the dirty stuff & keep the whole lot for me. I don't want anything back now.

We are resting at present altho' there's plenty to do —all the little details & refitting to be attended to. But I have some worthy helpers so its all O.K.

I still have Edwards & he is quite well. My best love to Mam Phyl John & Babies & to you dear dad my love & thanks for all.

Nos dawch & God bless you

Your loving son

Cyril

APPENDIX II: TRANSCRIPTS OF LETTERS

From 2Lt C Larson. Although dated 12th October 1918; this must be an error and the date should be November.

B.E.F. France,
12th October [sic] 1918

Dear Mr & Mrs Keepfer,

You have probably had intimation from the 2nd Bn. RWF of the death of your Son in action, but being a brother officer of the same Company as your Son since October 1917, I wish to extend to you my deepest sympathy in your sad bereavement.

Your Son was dearly loved by all the officers of the Battalion and especially those of the same Company some of them at the present time are in England wounded and knew him for a considerable time. He was a splendid Soldier and one who held a high reputation in the battalion for his good work and leadership, and at the time of attack was in charge of the men of his Company.

He was buried in 'ENGLEFONTAINE,' west of a large forest called 'FORET DE MORMAL' and his burial was attended by the Commanding officer, Company officers, and men.

I wish to again extend to you all my deepest sympathy and hope that God will give you all strength and Grace to bear your great loss.

Yours sincerely

C Larson 2 Lt. 2 RWF[5]

---

5. Listed as Charles Frederick Larson, MC in *Duty Done*, page 125. He is also mentioned in Dunn pages 526, 527 and 532 in connection with the attack on Sailly-Saillisel. He was commissioned as a Temporary 2nd Lt. R.W.F. on 1 August 1917 and was awarded the Military Cross (*London Gazette* 2 December 1918 — 'For conspicuous gallantry in action. When his company came under point blank machine gun fire from a ridge, he went forward and captured the entire post. Throughout operations he showed great initiative and courage). He relinquished his commission as a lieutenant in 1920.

Cyril Keepfer, 1894–1918

From Corporal Thomas E. Davies, dated 22 November 1918

Corpl T. E. Davies, 069907
4 Coy., 38th Div Train
B.E.F.
22/11/18

My Dear Mr Keepfer,

I sincerely regret that the occasion has ever arrived for me to write you these few lines. I beg to offer you my true & heartfelt sympathies in your recent bereavement. Sickness has prevented me from writing you sooner. The news of poor Cyril's death came as a terrible blow to me, as an old school pal, and to everyone else who ever came in contact with him, for a finer example of manhood never left the old country. It will be some consolation for you to know that as an Officer and a man he was idolised by his regiment and he was classed as one of the best Officers ever posted to the Battalion. The news came after a great rush by our brigade. Two days previous I had a lengthy conversation with him. As you are well aware, of late years our friendship had been partially severed owing to our business circumstances, but the years of our schooldays together I shall never forget, and will always be dear to me.

No doubt you have had all the particulars available from his brother officers. I very much regret that owing to the great rush by our brigade at that particular time, I was unable to obtain any reliable information, our work of delivering supplies to his regiment being terribly difficult owing to tremendous opposition by enemy artillery.

I again beg to offer you all my deepest sympathy, and can only say that to me his death has been a personal loss which can never be replaced.

Please offer my kindest regards to Mrs Keepfer & John Lloyd, and also please accept same yourself.

Believe me to be
Yours very Sincerely
Thos. E. Davies

Appendix II: Transcripts of Letters

From Tom Edwards: undated but probably November 1918

> High Field In Hospital

Dear Mr. Keepfer

I am writing in answer to your letter which I received this morning to Sympathies with you in the sad news of your young Son's death.

I am very sorry for you but I hope you will all have strength to bare it. I was with him when he got killed. We were attacking in Mormal Forest & I was going over the Top by his side & was talking with him a few minutes before his death. He had just left me & had gone about five yards when he fell I ran over to him & I found that he was dead and a few minutes later I was wounded. I have been thinking a lot about him after as we were great Friends. I am very sorry I cant give you any more information about him as I was unlucky to be wounded but the best thing I could advise you to go would be to write to our Quarter Master of the Company as they were big Friends. His name is CQMS. Jones, D Company
Perhaps he can give you more information.

I am very glad to inform you that I am getting on allright although my arm is rather painful but I hope to be home soon & I we shall meet so in Concluding I again send you

My Deepest Sympathy to you & the Family in your loss

I remain
Your Friend Tom Edwards.

From Curé Emile Flament to Cyril's father in March 1919 with contemporaneous translations prepared by Curé Flament's sister, Sister Mary Joseph of the La Sagesse sisters (Daughters of Wisdom).

Sister Mary Joseph's translations are somewhat freehand, and not literal, translations. They provide a good sense of her brother's letter, but she omits some of the detail and adds other items or changes phrases—presumably because she knows the locality and is well aware of what her brother is writing.

I have had a more literal translation prepared for each letter.

1. Updated translation of Curé Flament's letters of 2 and 30 March 1919.
2. Curé Flament's original letters of 2 and 30 March 1919.
3. Sister Mary Joseph's translations of her brother's letters.

Updated translations of Cure Flament's letters of 2 and 30 March 1919

Englefontaine, 2 March 1919

Dear Sir,

Your letter reached me yesterday evening and I am happy enough to be able to reply this very day.

I read English easily, but I fear that in replying in your language I would express myself badly. So I apologise for doing so in French. My sister who is a nun with the Convent de la Sagesse at 221 Golders Green Road, London N.W.4, provides a translation on the opposite page and will send it on to you.

There are a great many graves —English or German— in all the orchards. In order to answer your question, I asked my congregation at Mass this morning to look for your son's name on the graves in their own properties. A short time later I had the required information and was able to go to your son's grave.

That grave, along with 30 others —many of which sadly no longer have names— is in an orchard near the home of Mme. Vve. Trannoy-Gorisse whose husband was mobilised and killed at the assault on Maubeuge and whose brother is a priest. The grave is near the road from Englefontaine to Hecq, near a chapel at a place called Le Terneau. The home forms a corner of the above road and Green Lane. Moreover, if you like, I could send you a sketch of the position which you can locate on a map. The cross shading the grave bears the words: In the Memory of (name and rank). There is no R.I.P. The letters and writing are, and will remain, very clear. Anyway we know now the exact spot and you need not worry about finding it. The graves are surrounded by a small fence protecting the area and Mme. Trannoy's home from accidents. If you wish, I will ask the English and the French authorities to exhume the body of your dear son and place it in a coffin which may be transported to England, if that is your intention and in the meantime I will have it placed in my family tomb, as I come from Englefontaine. In which case, kindly give me the requirements under English law on the matter.

Allow me, Dear Sir, in ending this letter, to express my religious and respectful condolences and to thank you for the gift of your son in the defence and recapture of our poor village. We live in the midst of ruins, and go in mourning, weep for many dead, not only for our own but also for the brave young men who gave their lives for France and for mankind and whose remains have not yet been honoured as they deserve.

Yours sincerely, with my warmest regards in the Name of Our Saviour.

Em. Flament
Curé d'Englefontaine (Nord)

Englefontaine, 30 March 1919

Dear Sir,
I received your kind letter a few days ago. Thank you for the details you give me to understand your fine and excellent son and your good sister, the nun, and whose mortuary keepsake I shall carefully preserve.

Mme. Trannoy-Gorisse thanks you too for the sentiments you asked me to pass on to her. The grave of your son will be well preserved. Alas, we have a great number of graves of English and German soldiers scattered everywhere over the grounds of the Parish, many with the epitaph: 'unknown British soldier.' The grave of your dear son, however, has a strong cross and the knowledge we have of its exact location allows us to point it out to you whatever happens.

If it is possible I will have a photograph taken of the spot and send it to you, but at the moment we no longer have any English troops here and our cameras have been seized by the Germans. I had two that have been hidden under a floor for 4 years. Unfortunately, a [British] shell shattered the floor near the cameras and everything was demolished; rain completely damaged them —for all purposes they are worthless, because I only found them when I returned at the end of December.

I send, while waiting on a photograph of the grave, the broad plan of the village.

Englefontaine is located in the Nord Department in the district of Avesnes, canton east of Quesnoy. It is a large village of 16 to 1800 souls, an area of 450 hectares, 2/3 of which are pastures, almost entirely planted in fruit trees, mainly apples. There were a lot of manufactures there —pantiles, tiles, drains in fired clay. Hence the name Tuileries that you have seen from British Headquarters despatches about 24 October. The area borders in the south-west the Forest of Mormal which is very large (about 10,000 hectares) and one of the most beautiful in France. It is today completely devastated, along with many towns that border it to the South.

As you requested, I shall have R.I.P. put on the grave Cross of your dear son and celebrate the Masses you asked for as soon as possible. Thank You for the £1.

Yours sincerely, Dear Sir, with my religious condolences and deep respect.

Em. Flament

Curé Flament's original letters of 2 and 30 March 1919

Englefontaine (Nord) le 2 mars 1919

Cher Monsieur,
Votre lettre m'est arrivée hier soir et je suis assez heureux de pouvoir vous répondre aujourd'hui même. Je lis facilement l'anglais, mais je craises, en vous répondant dans votre langue, de m'emprise mal. Aussi je vous priè de m'excuser de la faire en français. Ma souer religieuse au Convent de la Sagesse 221 Golder's Green Road, London N.W.4 fera la traduction sur la page ci contre et vous l'enverra.

Il y a un très grand nombre de tombes disperser dans tous les vergers, tombes anglaises ou allemandes. Afin de pouvoir respondre plus rapidement à votre question j'ai demandé ce matin à la Messe, à mes paroissiens de chercher le nom de votre fils sur les tombes qui se trouvent dans leurs propriétés respectives et peu de temps après, j'avais le renseignement demandé et je pouvais me rendre sur la tombe de votre cher fils.

Cette tombe se trouve avec 30 autres, dans dont plusiers malheureusement ne portent plus de noms, dans le verger et auprès de la maison de Mme. Vve.

Trannoy-Gorisse dont le mari mobilisé et été tué au siège de Maubeuge et dont le frère est prêtre.

C'est vous dire, cher Monsieur, que le tombe de votre fils est bien gardée —Elle se trouve auprès de la route allant d'Englefontaine à Hecq, près d'une chapelle à l'endroit nommé le Terneau—la maison forme l'angle du chemin que je viens d'indiquer et du chemin vert. D'ailleurs si vous le désirez je pourrai vous envoyer la cruquis de la position que vous poussez repérer sur une carte—La Croix qui ombrage la tombe porte les mots : In Memory of — (le nom et le titre)—Il n'y a pas de R.I.P. Les caractères de l'écriture restent et resteront très visibles—D'ailleurs nous connaissons maintenant exactement la place et vous pouvez être sans inquiétude sur le possibilité de le retrouver —Les tombes sont entourés d'une petite clôture qui les protége et le voisinage de la maison de Mme. Trannoy empêchera tout accident.

Si vous le désirez, je demanderai aux autorités anglaises et françaises, d'exhumer le corps de votre cher fils et de le mettre dans un cerceuil qui puisse être transportér en Angleterre, si vous en avez l'intention, et en attendant, je le ferai deposer dans mon caveau de famille, car je suis originaire d'Englefontaine. Dans ce cas veuillez me donner les indications sur les exigences de la loi anglaise à ce sujet.

Permettez moi, cher Monsieur, en terminant cette letter de vous presenter mes sentiments & religieuse et respecteuse condoléances et à vous remercier d'avoir donné votre fils pour défendre et reconquerér notre pauvre village — Nous vivons au milieu des ruines, nous avons bien des deuils à porter, bien des morts à pleurer, deuils et morts qui sont notres mais nous pleurons aussi ces valeureux jeunes gens qui ont donné leur vie pour la France et l'humanité et dont la sépultures n'est pas encore l'honneur qui leur est dû.

Agréez, cher Monsieur, l'expressions de mes sentiments d' affecteux respects en N. S.

Em. Flament,
curé d'Englefontaine (Nord)

Englefontaine (Nord), le 30 mars 1919.

Cher Monsieur

J'ai bien reçu il y a quelques jours votre bonne lettre. Je vous remercie des détails que vous me donnez pour me faire connaître votre bon et excellent fils et votre bonne souer religieuse dont je conserverai avec soin le souvenir mortuaire.

Madame Trannoy-Gorisse vous remercie aussi des sentiments que vous m'avez demandé de lui expresser. La tombe du M. votre fils sera bien gardée —Hélàs, nous avons en très grand nombres des tombes de soldats anglais et aussi soldats allemands dispersée un peu partout sur la territoire de la paroisse —et pour beaucoup c'est toujours les mots 'soldat anglais inconnu'— Quant à la tombe du votre cher fils la Croix très solide et la connaissance que nous avons de la position très exact, nous permetter de vous le désigner dans façon certain quoi qu'il arrive.

S'il est possible je ferai prendre la photographie de l'endroit et je vous l'enverrai, mais en ce moment nous n'avons plus ici de troupe anglaise et nos appareils de photographie ont été pris par les allemands —J'en avais deux qui sous resté caché 4 ans dans un plancher. Malheureusement un obus anglais a cassé le plancher près de appareils, et la tout était démoli, la place a complètement détériore les appareils qui sont pour l'instant hors d'usage, car je ne les ai retrouvés qu' à mon retour fin de Décembre.

Je vous envoie, attendant une photographie de la tombre, le plan développé du village.

Englefontaine est situé dans le Department du Nord, arrondisement d'Avesnes, canton est le Quesnoy. C'etait une bourgade de 16 à 1800 âmes – . Superficie de 450 hectares de territoire, dont le 2/3 sont en paturages presque entièrement plantés d'arbres fruitiers, principalement pommiers —on y fabriquant beaucoup de pannes ou à carreaux du drains en terre plain cuite —De là le nom de Tuileries que vous avez vu dans les communiqués du quartier général anglais vers le 24 Octobre— la territoire bord au sud oeust la Forêt de Mormal qui est très grande (environs 10,000 hectares) et qui était l'une des plus belles de France. Elle est aujourd'hui complètement dévastée —aussi que beaucoup de communes qui la bordait au Sud.

Comme vous me le demandéz je ferai mettre R. I. P. sur la Croix de la tombe du votre cher fils et célèbrerai les Messes qua vous me demandez aussitôt que possible. Bien reçu la Livre—Merci.

Veuillez agréer, cher Monsieur, avec mes religieuses condoléances l'expression de mon profond respect.

Em. Flament

Sister Mary Joseph's translations of her brother's letters

Englefontaine
2 March / 19

Dear Sir;
Your letter reached me yesterday & I am happily able to reply at once. —I can read English but do not know it well enough to write. My sister —a nun— at La Sagesse Convent Golders' Green Rd. London— will translate my reply.

There are a great many graves dispersed through all the orchards of Englefontaine —they are either English or German.— In order to be able to answer you quickly I gave out the name yesterday at Mass. I desired my parishioners to examine the graves they have —many alas are nameless— Very shortly after, I obtained the required information & was able to visit your dear son's grave.

It is with a group of 30 others, several without names, in an orchard near the home of Mme. Vve. Trannoy-Gouise whose husband was killed at Maubeuge & whose brother is a priest. —That is sufficient, my dear Sir, to assure you that your son's tomb will be well tended.

It is placed near the road from Englefontaine to Hecq, close to a little shrine at a spot known as Le Terneau. Mme. Trannoy's home forms a corner between the High road & Green Lane. If you like I could send you sketch which would enable you to find the exact spot on an ordnance map. The cross at the head bears the words In memory of 2nd Lieut. W. R. C. Keepfer 2nd Batt. Royal Welsh Fusiliers —there is no R. I. P. The writing is very clear & will remain so for a long time.—

Now we know the exact spot you would have no difficulty in finding it. The graves have a little fence round them & they are protected by Mme. Trannoy's house.—

If you wish it, I can ask the English & French authorities to exhume your son's body, & place it in a coffin suitable for removal to England if such is your intention; —the coffin could be put pending its return in my own family vault.

If you wish the body exhumed please let me know very exactly the English law in such a case.

Allow me, my dear Sir, to end my letter by offering you my respectful & religious condolences & my sincere thanks for having given your son to defend & recapture our little village.

We live in the midst of ruins, & very numerous are our losses & the dead we mourn; but, as well as our own dead, we mourn the valiant young men who gave their lives for France & for humanity & whose burial places are not yet honoured as they should be.

Yours with affectionate respect in J. C. {Jesus Christ}

Emile Flament
Curé d'Englefontaine

Dear Sir,
May I add my sympathy to that of my Brother.
        Sr. My. {Mary} Joseph

Golders Green

March 8

Englefontaine
March 30/19

Dear Sir,
Your kind letter reached me a few days ago. Many thanks for the details you give me of your dear & excellent son; & of your good sister the nun, whose souvenir I will keep carefully.

Mme. Trannoy-Gorisse thanks you for the sentiments you asked me to express to her on your behalf.

Your son's tomb will be well looked after. —Alas, we have a large number of graves of English soldiers (& also Germans,) dispersed all over the parish —many bearing the epitaph 'Unknown British soldier.'— As to your son's tomb the good strong cross & the exact knowledge of its position would always make us to point it out.

If possible I will have it photographed later; & will send you the picture; but, for the moment, we have no more English Troops & all our photographic apparatus was taken by the Germans. I had 2 cameras hidden under a floor —Unfortunately a shell (British) crashed through the floor just there & all was smashed— all other apparatus has been ruined by the rain —I only found them on my return at the end of December.

In default of a photo, I enclose a plan of the village & have marked the tomb.

Englefontaine is in the Department known as le Nord in the district of Avesnes —& canton of Le Quesnoy.— It is a large village of 1600-1800 inhabitants. It is almost entirely made up of meadows planted with fruit trees, chiefly apples. Large quantities of tiles, drain-pipes etc. were made here —hence the name Tuileries often given in British despatches last October.— On the south west Englefontaine borders on the Forest of Mormal which is very large; & was one of the most beautiful in all France. —Today it is utterly devasted with many villages on its southern edge.

I will have the letters R. I. P. put over your son's grave & will say the Masses asked for, as soon as I can —many thanks for £1— duly received.

Please accept, with my religious condolences, the assurances of my deep respect.

Em. Flament

Golders Green April 5/19

I add my best thanks for letter & memorial card to those of my brother. Very sincerely yours in JC.

S. Marie Joseph

APPENDIX III

Composite extracts from war diaries relating to 3rd Dragoon Guards and 2nd Battalion, Royal Welsh Fusiliers for the time which Cyril Keepfer served with them

Notes on the war diaries and the extracts

General Comments on the war diaries:
Inevitably, regimental war diaries concentrate solely on the regiment concerned and do not place them —or the action in which they were involved— in a wider context. Here, the brigade and divisional war diaries are (slightly) more helpful.

The war diaries are all hand-written (or —particularly later in the war— typed up) on pre-printed forms. There is, thus, a degree of standardisation about them. However, much does depend upon the writer. The 2RWF war diary is often very well, and literately, written up.

The war diaries all engage in heavy use of capitalised terms and I have reflected such usage in this summary —but not in the main body of this book.

Amalgamation:
The following are not always strictly verbatim transcripts from the relevant war diaries. I have amalgamated the battalion, regiment, brigade and divisional war diaries, as the case may be, so as to produce an amalgam of a summary and verbatim accounts from them.

There are occasional divergences between the various units' war diaries as to the exact date on which a certain event occurred. This is usually no more than a day's difference and reflects, probably, an error on the part of a compiler or a difference in the dates on which the war diaries were completed. Where they do arise, the differences have no material bearing on the overview of events.

With the 2RWF, I have concentrated on D Company and, largely, ignored entries relating to its other companies.

Location:

The regimental war diaries state the unit's location on the night in question.

For 3DG, location is the place where 3DG's regimental headquarters passed the night. The 3DG war diary does not start giving locations (even though the printed form includes space for the location) until 5 January 1916. Where possible, the locations have been deduced from 6 Cavalry Brigade's war diary.

For 2RWF, the location is given as its location at the start of the day —which is, usually, the same as where the Battalion passed the night; although, where it was involved in a relief in the trenches, the reliefs took place overnight so the location is where 2RWF was at the start of the day before any relief.

Timings:

I have used a 24-hour clock throughout —although, more often than not, the war diaries do not.

Sources:

The relevant war diaries are all in the National Archives at Kew.

WO 95/1153: War diary of 3DG covering the period 10 October 1915 – 28 February 1917. It must be said that this war diary is not completed quite as fully as several others. This may reflect the fact that little of impact occurred in relation to the Regiment during the period covered. The war diary gives no indication of the Squadron to which Cyril was attached or who was in which working/digging party or which Squadron was detached in January and February 1916 to form part of 3DG Squadron of 6 Dismounted Cavalry Battalion. *Note:* a facsimile copy of this war diary has been published by The Naval & Military Press Limited.

WO 95/1152: War diary of the Brigade Headquarters of 6 Cavalry Brigade, October 1915–February 1917. I have extracted items of relevance to 3DG.

The Brigade's war diaries state the Brigade's location as the location of the Brigade's headquarters on the night in question. This location is not included in the Summary save where it is of particular relevance to 3DG.

WO 95/1141: War diary of the General Staff of 3 Cavalry Division, October 1915–February 1917. Again, I have concentrated only upon items of relevance to 3DG. As before, the locations in the war diary are given as for the Division's headquarters' staff. It is noticeable that its war diary for October 1914 to September 1915 is voluminous —in significant contrast to that for the period October 1915–February 1917.

WO 95/1143: War diary of Adjutant and Quartermaster's Branch of 3 Cavalry Division, October 1915–February 1917. The Adjutant and Quartermaster General's branch dealt with routine administration.

WO 95/1189: War diaries January–February 1916 of:
   6 Dismounted Cavalry Battalion;
   3 Dismounted Cavalry Brigade;
   Dismounted Cavalry Division;
   Headquarters General Staff, Dismounted Cavalry Division; and
   Adjutant and Quartermaster of the Dismounted Cavalry Division.

WO 95/2423: War diary of 2RWF, October 1917–November 1918. *Note:* a facsimile copy of this war diary has been published by The Naval & Military Press Limited.

WO 95/2421: War diary of 19 Infantry Brigade Headquarters, October 1917–February 1918.

WO 95/2406: War diary of 33 Division's General Staff, October 1917–February 1918.

WO 95/2409: War diary of 33 Division's Adjutant and Quartermaster's Branch, October 1917–February 1918.

WO 95/2410: War diaries of 33 Division's Assistant Director of Medical Service; Commanding Royal Artillery, October 1917–February 1918.

WO 95/2411: War diary of 33 Division's Divisional Engineers, October 1917–February 1918.

WO 95/2560: War diary of 115 Infantry Brigade, February–November 1918. I have extracted items of relevance to 2RWF from 12 February 1918, when 2RWF joined the Brigade, until 11 November 1918. The Brigade's war diaries state the Brigade's location as the location of the Brigade's headquarters but, except where relevant, this location is not included in the following Summary.

WO 95/2540: War diary of 38 (Welsh) Division General Staff, February–November 1918. I have extracted items of relevance to 2RWF (and, occasionally, 115 Brigade) from 12 February 1918, when 2RWF and 115 Brigade joined the Division, until 4 November 1918. The Division's war diary provides a more detailed overview account of the 4 November advance than the Brigade's war diary.

WO 95/2541: War diary of Adjutant and Quartermaster's Branch of 38 (Welsh) Division, February–November 1918.

WO 95/2500: War diaries of 38 (Welsh) Division's Field Ambulance Section; Sanitary Section and the Divisional Train, February–November 1918.

WO 95/2542: War diary of 38 (Welsh) Division's CRA (Commanding Royal Artillery), February–November 1918.

WO 95/2544: War diary of 38 (Welsh) Division's CRE (Commanding Royal Engineer), February–November 1918.

WO 95/2549: War diary of 129 Field Ambulance Section, February–November 1918.

Cyril Keepfer enlisted on 7 September 1914 and joined 3 Cavalry Reserve Regiment training depot at Canterbury, Kent on 9 September 1914. He left Canterbury on 5 October 1915 and reached his first regiment, 3rd Dragoon Guards, in France on 10 October 1915.

3rd Dragoon Guards, 6th Cavalry Brigade, 3rd Cavalry Division

Date	Location	Accommodation	Principal activity
1915			
Oct			
10	Raimbert	Billets	Draft of 4 NCOs, 41 men (including Cyril) and 34 riding horses joined the Regiment from Rouen. 3 Cavalry Division was under the orders of the First Army until 3 October 1915 when it moved back behind the line, Lillers – Burbure – Cauchy-à-la-Tour. On that date, 6 Cavalry Brigade marched into billets.
11 to 13	Raimbert	Billets	
14	Raimbert	Billets	Regiment training at counter-attack.
15	Raimbert	Billets	Squadron arrangements.
16	Raimbert	Billets	Squadron arrangements. The Divisional Sanitary Section conducted a sanitary inspection of the regiment. From time to time, this Section conducted routine inspections and disinfection of the billeting huts.
17	Raimbert	Billets	Squadron arrangements. On 17 October, 3 Cavalry Division came under the orders of the Cavalry Corps (I).
18	Raimbert	Billets	Squadron arrangements. The Divisional Sanitary Section conducted a sanitary inspection of the regiment.
19	Beaumetz-les-Aires		Regiment marched from Raimbert to Beaumetz-les-Aires.
20	Beaumetz-les-Aires	Billets	
21	Westrehem, Nedonchelle, Fontaines-les-Hermans	Billets	Regiment paraded at 1015 and then marched to permanent Winter billets. It arrived in the billeting area at 1215. A Squadron billeted at Westrehem. B Squadron " Fontaines-les-Hermans. C Squadron " Nedonchelle. Further reinforcements arrived for the Regiment in the form

			of 2 Officers and 100 Other Ranks. Its establishment was now 26 Officers and 651 Other Ranks.
22	"	Billets	Cleaning up billets and stables.
23	"	Billets	Squadron arrangements.
24	"	Billets	
25	"	Billets	Began building horse shelters.
26 to 31	"	Billets	
Nov			
1 and 2	Billets at Sercus for the digging parties. Otherwise, as above.	Billets	2 Officers and 32 (the Brigade's War Diary states 40) men sent to Sercus for digging.
3	"	Billets	Another 76 men sent to Sercus for digging.
4	"	Billets	Assistant Divisional Vetinerary Officer inspected the Regiment's horses.
5	"	Billets	The two digging parties at Secus re-joined the Regiment.
6	"	Billets	A further 167 men sent to Sercus for digging.
7 and 8	"	Billets	
9 and 10	Billets at Ouderdom for the digging party. Otherwise, as above.	Billets	150 men to Ouderdom for digging communications trenches.
11	"	Billets	The Divisional Sanitary Section supervised the Regiment bathing and disinfected their clothes whilst they were bathing by use of disinfecting powder in the seams of trousers. Petrol cans were also delivered to the Regiment for use as latrine pails.
12 to 16	"	Billets	
17	Offin/ Loison and digging party at Ouderdom	Billets	On 16/17 November, 3 Cavalry Division moved to billets west of Fruges. 3DG paraded at 0900 at Fontaine-les-Hermans and marched to Offin arriving at 1730 where it went into fresh billets: A and C Squadrons at Loison; and B Squadron at Offin.
18 to 20	"	Billets	Improving new billets.

21	"	Billets	Improving new billets plus medical inspection.
22	Offin/ Loison	Billets	The digging party returned by bus from Ouderdom arriving back at 2130.
23	Offin/ Loison and digging party at Ouderdom	Billets	A new party of 5 officers and 183 men went to Ouderdom under the Regiment's Commanding Officer as a digging party under V Corps. They travelled by rail from Maresquel to Poperinghe. *Digging parties were not immune from casualties. Two men from 3DG were wounded during November.*
24 to 29	"	Billets	
30	Offin/ Loison	Billets	Digging party returned from Ouderdom. All the Regiment's blankets were disinfected. The Divisional Sanitary Section supervised the construction of an incinerator and the digging of latrine and general sanitary conveniences.
Dec			
1	Offin/ Loison	Billets	Mens' clothing dis-infected.
2	Offin/ Loison	Billets	
3	Offin/ Loison	Billets	Mens' clothing dis-infected.
4 to 7	Offin/ Loison	Billets	
8	Offin/ Loison	Billets	Medical inspection of working parties detailed to proceed to La Belle Hotesse for digging purposes.
9	Offin/ Loison	Billets	
10	Offin/ Loison and Lynde	Billets	3 Officers and 86 (the Brigade's War Diary states 107) other ranks sent as digging party. They were bussed to Lynde in order to continue work on the La Belle Hotesse Line.
11 and 12	Offin/ Loison and Lynde	Billets	
13	Offin/ Loison and Lynde	Billets	A second digging party of 1 officer and 92 other ranks was sent to La Belle Hotesse to join the digging party.
14 to 21	Offin/ Loison and Lynde	Billets	
22	Offin/ Loison and Lynde	Billets	The Divisional Sanitary Section inspected a farm where men from 3DG were billeted and where there were suspected cases of Foot & Mouth disease; removing the troops from that farm.

23	Offin/ Loison and Lynde	Billets	
24	Offin/ Loison	Billets	The two digging parties returned to billets.
25	Offin/ Loison	Billets	Christmas Day.
26	Offin/ Loison	Billets	
27	Offin/ Loison	Billets	3 Cavalry Division received orders regarding the immediate formation of a Dismounted Division of the Cavalry Corps. As from midday on 29, it was to be ready to move to billets at 3½ hours' notice. The Brigade received orders to create 6 Dismounted Battalion forthwith and to remain in billets awaiting orders to move.
28 and 29	Offin/ Loison	Billets	
30	Offin/ Loison	Billets	A suspected case of typhoid in 3DG was considered by the Division's Sanitary Section.
31	Offin/ Loison	Billets	

6th Dismounted Cavalry Battalion, 3rd Dismounted Cavalry Brigade, Dismounted Cavalry Division, First Army

1916			
Jan			
1	Offin/ Loison Mares-quel	Billets	From 1 January – 11 February, 3DG remained at Offin/Loison with a standard War Diary entry of: General daily routine in billets and training. *For this period, the summary extracts and summaries below are taken from the fragmentary comments of 3DG's War Diaries (which include a few scattered references to 6 Dismounted Battalion) and relevant extracts from the War Diaries of 6 Dismounted Cavalry Battalion, 3 Dismounted Cavalry Brigade and the Dismounted Cavalry Division. The concentration is upon 6 Dismounted Cavalry Battalion.* *Interestingly, the writer of the 6 Dismounted Cavalry Battalion's War Diary starts off the War Diary with some of the most detailed accounts of minutiae in any of the War Diaries examined. Quite uniquely, he also starts by identifying other ranks by individual name. Both such detail and such identification drop off as time passes.* The Division's HQ was at Chateau des Pres and the Reserve Brigade's HQ was at Sailly-la-Bourse (sometimes referred to simply as La Bourse), with one battalion stationed at Sailly-la-Bourse, another at La Bourse and the third at Verquin.

			The Division's Left Brigade would be stationed so that one battalion would be in the Front Lines, a second in the Support sector and the third in Reserve at Sailly-la-Bourse. The Division came under the command of I Corps. The Division was ordered to take over the line from Devon Lane to Mud Trench (east of Bethune) as from 1400 on 4 January 1916. To the Division's south was IV Corps.
			The Dismounted Cavalry Machine Gun Section went by train to Fouquereuil to form part of the 3 Dismounted Cavalry Brigade.
2	Offin/ Loison	Billets	6 Dismounted Cavalry Battalion marched to Maresquel and billeted there for the night. The remainder of the Regiment stayed at Offin/Loison in permanent billets.
	Maresquel		At 1430, 6 Dismounted Cavalry Brigade's Transport was brigaded at Offin and proceeded by rail to Maresquel where it was billeted for the night.
3	Maresquel	Billets	At 0530, the Transport commenced to entrain at Maresquel to join 3 Dismounted Brigade at Fouquereuil.
			3DG and 3DG's commanding officer, Lt. Col. A Burt, were joined at Maresquel by the other companies that were to form 6 Dismounted Battalion. At 0830, they began to entrain. The train left at 0915 and arrived at Fouquereuil station (two miles west of Bethune) at 1215. There, the Battalion disentrained and marched to billets in *L'Orphanage*, Bethune, arriving at about 1330.
			The remainder of the day was spent in cleaning up the orphanage and getting settled into the billets.
			The Division's Adjutant arranged that 10% of the Division's smoke blankets should be sent up to the trenches daily. Washing of clothes was arranged at Lumbres.
	.		A cinema theatre, a coffee bar and a theatre were arranged at Sailly-la-Bourse to be carried on for the benefit of the Reserve Brigade.
4	Bethune	Billets	Initially, 3 Dismounted Cavalry Brigade formed the Division's Reserve and it moved up to the Sailly-la-Bourse – Verquigneul area in support, arriving by 1300.
			The Battalion marched from Bethune at 1030 and took over billets at Sailly-la-Bourse at about 1200 in relief of 141 Brigade.
5	Sailly-la-Bourse	Billets	In Reserve. Work done—fatigues, carrying stores to the trenches, etc.
			The Division noted that a great deal of work was required to be done on the defences of the portion of the line occupied and the time and energy of the troops was fully taken up in making the necessary improvements. Enemy snipers were

			active and, at that time, enjoyed a superiority.
6	Sailly-la-Bourse	Billets	The Battalion marched from Sailly at 1000 arriving at Bethune at about 1130 where it went into billets in L'Orphanage. Work done—fatigues, carrying stores, digging, etc. Meanwhile, the Division noted that a great improvement had been made to the trenches and they were now practically dry. The weather was fine with a mild south-westerly wind.
7 and 8	Bethune	Billets	Work done—fatigues, carrying stores, digging, etc. Weather remained fine and mild.
9	Bethune	Billets	The Brigade relieved 1 Dismounted Brigade. Guides met the head of the columns at Vermelles at 0830. The Battalion was to be in Brigade Reserve and left Bethune at 0830 for the Brigade's Reserve Trenches. It arrived about 1200 when 3DG took position at Vermelles (the other companies were at Lancashire Trench and Sailly-la-Bourse). The Brigade noted that, although 1 Dismounted Cavalry Brigade had improved the trenches, there was still a lot of attention needed and working parties started work at once. From 1600, 3DG detached men for work: ■ 50 men to Clarks Keep; and ■ one NCO and three men to Battalion HQ for guard duty 1600 – 0700. At 1700, a further 40 men were sent to Clarks Keep. The Division noted that operations were practically confined to artillery exchanges and that enemy snipers were less active. The whole front line had been strengthened and many fire loopholes had been made. Weather was fine but colder.
10	Vermelles	Trenches (reserve)	*6 Dismounted Battalion's headquarters were at Lancashire Trench. However, where different, I have included, under Location, the location of 3DG Squadron.* During the day, 3DG Squadron was involved in the following work: -- From 0930, one officer and 40 men worked as carriers for the Tunnelling Company at Clarks Keep; -- From 1200, one officer and 50 men were at Clarks Keep under the Royal Engineers carrying sand bags, boards and wood; -- At 1330, one NCO and 12 men were ordered to report to 3 Dismounted Cavalry Brigade's bomb stores to carry bombs to 8 Dismounted Cavalry Battalion; -- At 1530, one officer and 50 men went to Vermelles cross-roads to work under the Royal Engineers;

			-- At 1600, an NCO and three men went to Battalion HQ for guard duty 1600 – 0700; and -- At 1700 an officer and 30 men were at the Quarries on fatigues for the Royal Engineers. The weather remained 'wonderfully fine.'
11	Vermelles	Trenches (reserve)	At 0730, the Battalion began to relieve 8 Dismounted Cavalry Battalion in the front line trenches. The relief was complete by 1115. 3DG was holding the line on the Right. During the day, a German Biplane flew over the line in a westerly direction but returned on being fired on. The afternoon passed quietly, although a few rifle grenades were fired by 3DG. The night, which was cold but moonlit, passed without incident, a little machine gun fire and a little sniping by the Enemy occurred.
12	Front Sector D1 (near Vermelles, Bethune)	Trenches (front line)	The day opened with fine weather. At 0730, the Enemy fired three mortar shells into Crown Trench blowing in about three yards (but causing no casualties), which were immediately repaired. At 0845, the Enemy sent over a few whizz-bangs.[1] At 0930 a shrapnel shell burst over 3DG in the trench and wounded a private. At about 1230, a detachment of 3DG was taken from the front line trench to allow a bombardment by howitzers and Royal Horse Artillery to commence at 1300. Hostile aircraft also active during the day. The Adjutant reported a shortage of coke at the front (evidently used more in the rear trenches than in the front) and of Vigilant periscopes.
13	Front Sector D1	Trenches (Front)	Weather fine with a north-westerly wind. Nothing of interest occurs. Light shelling, machine guns, etc.
14	Front Sector D1	Trenches (Front)	Morning was fine but dull. 1130, Enemy fired some class of aerial torpedo which caused a great deal of damage to Kaiserin Trench. 3DG suffered casualties [Cyril was not among those casualties listed]. Brigade described all this as the enemy being 'unusually active.' At 1445 a British aeroplane flew very low over the German lines and although heavily shelled continued its

---

1. The term generally used for High Explosive shells, particularly small German ones.

Appendix III: War Diaries (Extracts)

			reconnaissance.
			Some grenades fired at a German working party.
15	Front Sector D1	Trenches (Front)	The Battalion was relieved at 1000 (complete by 1115) by 2 Dismounted Battalion and marched to billets in Bethune. A very fine day but the wind was still cold. A lot of salvage work was undertaken—especially by the Battalion.
16 and 17	Bethune	Billets	*No Battalion entries.*
18	Bethune	Billets	The Headquarters of The Royal Dragoons proceeded to Bethune by rail to relieve 3DG who had until that time provided the Battalion's headquarters. The Battalion was billeted in *L'Orphanage* and the Battalion's HQ was established close to the *Eglise du Perroy*.
19	Bethune	Billets	The Battalion found working parties daily whilst in Reserve in Bethune, the chief being a party of 200 men who were employed in carrying stores from Vermelles.
20	Bethune	Billets	No Battalion entry but the Division noted a bombardment of Alexander and Crown trenches at 1100.
21	Bethune	Billets	At 0700, the Battalion moved from Bethune by road. Companies were distributed in the local Brigade Reserve with 3DG to Sailly-la-Bourse. The weather was fine. From 1700, 3DG found 75 men to work under 180 Tunnelling Company.
22	Sailly-la-Bourse	Billets	At 0800, the same working party. At 1700, 10 men were found for machine gun emplacement work. Weather fair. During the morning, the Enemy shelled Vermelles and also Noyelles and Sailly with small 'crumps' but without much damage. Orders were received that the Battalion was not to relieve 7 Dismounted Cavalry Battalion in the trenches until the afternoon of 23.
23	Sailly-la-Bourse	Billets	At 0730, all men's feet were rubbed with anti-frostbite grease. Weather fine and clear. The Battalion relieved 7 Dismounted Cavalry Battalion in D1 Sector in the afternoon. 3DG relieved the Leicestershire Yeomanry company. Four platoons were in the front line in Alexander Trench and two platoons were in the support line in Crown Trench.

			During the night, parapets and fire trenches were repaired and improved. Wire was put up.
			The enemy was active with trench mortars and rifle grenades.
24	Front Sector D1	Trenches (front line)	Weather fine, rather dull.
			At 1200, the Enemy shelled Crown Trench. British guns replied with effect and silenced the enemy.
			At 1700, the Enemy exploded a mine close under their own parapet (so as to create a crater which they could develop as an outpost) and occupied the crater in the dark. Also opened heavy fire by trench mortars for five minutes on our support trenches.
			At 2045, British trench mortars opened on the new crater with good effect—five dead Germans were later found there by a British patrol.
25	Front Sector D1	Trenches (front line)	At 0830, an exchange of trench mortars. Then, at 0900, the Enemy shelled Alexander and Crown Trenches which were damaged a good deal. (The Division's account states that the shelling was between 1030 – 1230.) At 1000, British Heavies opened but the enemy continued to shell Crown Trench with HE and 5.9". (The horse batteries could not open fire on account of hostile aeroplanes.) The hostile shelling ceased at 1130.
			During the night, 3DG filled in Farmer's Hole with wire and loose earth. 3DG suffered three Other Ranks killed and three wounded.
26	Front Sector D1	Trenches (front line)	Weather fine.
			At 1600 there was a heavy bombardment of the British front line being chiefly directed on Crown and Alexander Trenches. British artillery replied effectively. There was lots of damage so, during the night, working parties had to clear up and repair the damage. More wiring put down in front of Alexander Trench.
			3DG suffered four Other Ranks killed and 12 wounded.
			Division noted that it was at 1215 that 3 Dismounted Cavalry Brigade reported that the Sector was being very heavily bombarded; British howitzers were ordered to retaliate and the enemy shelling ceased.
			A further very heavy hostile bombardment commenced at 1630.
			At 1730, the Kink (held by the Brigade) was attacked and the X Hussars company was ordered up from the Reserve. At 1750, the Battalion's commanding officer reported that the bombardment was particularly heavy and the front and

Appendix III: War Diaries (Extracts)

			support trenches had suffered considerably. At 1800, the Brigade's commanding officer reported that the Battalion's lines were still holding and the bombardment was gradually ceasing. During the day, the Division recorded several intercepts of German telephone conversations.
27	Front Sector D1	Trenches (front line)	Weather fine. At 1030, the Battalion was relieved by 1 Dismounted Cavalry Battalion and marched back to its old billets in Bethune. The Division noted that, at 0500, the Brigade reported that the situation was much quieter in the Left sector and, at 0630, the Brigade's relief by 1 Dismounted Cavalry Brigade began.
28 and 29	Bethune	Billets	The Battalion remained in Bethune and fatigue parties were found as before.
30 and 31	Bethune	Billets	In Reserve billets. Work involved fatigues in carrying stores to the trenches, digging etc. A very misty day and the Division noted less enemy activity than usual.
Feb			
1	Bethune	Billets	(As on 30 and 31 January).
2	Bethune	Billets	The Brigade relieved 1 Dismounted Cavalry Brigade in the Left Sector. At 0500, the Battalion marched out from Bethune and took over support trenches and billets from 2 Dismounted Battalion at 0915. 3DG was allotted Sailly. From 1230 – 2330, about 500 men in all were required for carrying stores and ammunition etc. to the front lines.
3	Sailly-la-Bourse	Billets	At 0430, two platoons from 3DG moved from Sailly to Vermelles. For the remainder of the morning, the rest of the Battalion rested. From 1500, work on fatigues. A quiet night.
4	Sailly-la-Bourse	Billets	At 0500, the Battalion commenced moving up to the front lines and relieved 7 Dismounted Cavalry Battalion by 0915. 3DG had four platoons in Alexander Trench (front line trench) and two platoons in Crown Trench (support trench). It was quiet until 1200. Occasional enemy trench mortars on the right side but no damage done.
5	Front Sector D1 (near	Trenches (Front)	Quiet, weather fine. Satisfactory work carried out on wire in front of Alexander Trench.

	Vermelles and Bethune)		
6	Front Sector D1	Trenches (Front)	Front line distribution as on 4 February.
7	Front Sector D1	Trenches (Front)	The whole Division (including the Battalion) had a practice gas attack at 0700. Situation quiet except for the usual rifle grenades—mostly in Kaiserin Trench.
8	Front Sector D1	Trenches (Front)	At 0700, relief by 2 Dismounted Cavalry Battalion started and complete by 0920. The Battalion reached Bethune at 1200 from the trenches and was billeted in Reserve Billets in *L'Orphanage* (replacing 1 Dismounted Cavalry Battalion). Rested during the afternoon and night. Meanwhile, the Division was notified that it would be relieved by 12 Division.
9 and 10	Bethune	Billets	In Reserve billets. Baths. A digging party of 400 men.
11	Bethune	Billets	The Brigade, which was in Reserve, was relieved by 36 Infantry Brigade. The Battalion entrained at 1025 at Bethune for, and arrived at, Maresquel at 1736 and each company then re-joined its original regiment in permanent billets west of Fruges.

3rd Dragoon Guards, 6th Cavalry Brigade, 3rd Cavalry Division

12 to 14	Offin	Billets	General daily routine in billets and training.
15	Offin	Billets	General daily routine in billets and training. *12 Division relieved the Dismounted Cavalry Division—which was then disbanded.*
16 to 29	Offin	Billets	General daily routine in billets and training.
Mar			
1 to 7	Offin	Billets	General daily routine in billets and training.
8	Offin	Billets	Regiment inspected in marching order by the Commanding Officer of 6 Cavalry Brigade.
9	Offin	Billets	General daily routine in billets and training.
10	Offin	Billets	Tactical exercise at Boris Jean.
11	Offin	Billets	General daily routine in billets and training.

APPENDIX III: WAR DIARIES (EXTRACTS)

to 22			
23	Offin	Billets	Tactical exercise at Sempy.
24 and 25	Offin	Billets	General daily routine in billets and training.
26	Offin	Billets	Divine Service at Loison at 1000.
27 to 31	Offin	Billets	General daily routine in billets and training.
April			
1 to 30	Offin	Billets	General daily routine in billets and training. On 6 April, the Cavalry Corps was abolished as a Corps and 3 Cavalry Division formed a reserve under the command of the GOC Reserve Corps (i.e. GHQ).
May			
1 to 14	Offin	Billets	General daily routine in billets and training.
15	St. Riquier / Oneux	Billets	6 Cavalry Brigade marched to St. Riquier area where it went into billets in order to take part in five days of Divisional training. This was part of a move by 3 Cavalry Division for a week's Divisional training. 3DG was billeted in Oneux.
16 to 20	St. Riquier / Oneux	Billets	Divisional Training.
21	St. Riquier / Oneux	Billets	After the week's training, the Division retraced its march route back to its billets.
22 to 24	Offin	Billets	General daily routine in billets and training.
25	Paris-Plage, L'Etaples	Camp	3DG proceeded to Le Touquet camp. (Permission had been obtained by 6 Cavalry Brigade to establish this Brigade camp so that the Brigade's regiments could use the sands at Paris-Plage for drill, there being no suitable ground in the permanent billeting area.)
26 to 31	Paris-Plage	Camp	Training
June			
1 to 4	Paris-Plage	Camp	Training
5	Offin	Billets	General daily routine in billets and training. 6 Cavalry Brigade's War Diary states that 3DG returned to permanent billets on 5 June whereas 3DG's War Diary suggests that they only returned to permanent billets on 7 June—and 3

			Cavalry Division's War Diary suggests 10 June.
6 to 23	Offin	Billets	General daily routine in billets and training.
13			*3 Cavalry Division came under the First Army for administrative purposes but was to remain under the orders of the GHQ Reserve.*
18			*Brigade received orders to ensure that it was concentrated in billets by 22 June.*
24	Dom-vaast		Regiment complete with transport proceeded to Brigade Rendezvous at T roads 220 yards south of P in Point St. Vaast. Noted that 3DG's strength was: 		Officers	Other Ranks	Horses	Wagons
---	---	---	---	---
Fighting Troops	23	380	433	
A Echelon	2	71	109	10
B Echelon	2	25	24	5
Total	**27**	**476**	**566**	**15**	 Brigade marched to Domvaast via Hesdin – Regnaville – La Broye.
25	Marcheville	Billets	Brigade assembled at cross roads 700 yards north of Yvrencheux and marched to St. Leger-les-Domarts via Yvrencheux – Domquer – cross roads at La Chaussee – Runehaut – Domart-en-Ponthieu. This was all part of 3 Cavalry Division's move by march to the Bonnay and La Neuville areas. Dismounted men were moved by rail. 3 Cavalry Division was under the orders of the Reserve Army.
26	St. Leger-les-Dormarts	Billets	3DG arrived here at 0200 and went to billets At 2130 the Brigade re-assembled at the north-west entrance to Vignacourt and marched to Corbie East area.
27	Bonnay	Bivouac	After a very fast march the Brigade bivouacked just east of Bonnay just south of east on D'Ancre at 0430. The Brigade was being held in readiness to exploit any opportunities that opened up during the forthcoming Somme offensive.
28	Bonnay	Bivouac	The Brigade remained in Bonnay on what was described as a very wet day. At 1000, Brigade Headquarters received orders to be ready to move at 0730 on 29 June; but, at 1730, the readiness order was postponed by 48 hours.
29	Bonnay	Bivouac	Brigade in readiness.
30	Bonnay	Bivouac	Brigade in readiness. The Divisional Quarter-master General (**QMG**) issued 1,500 steel helmets to 6 Cavalry Brigade.
July			

APPENDIX III: WAR DIARIES (EXTRACTS)

1	Bonnay	Bivouac	1 July was Z Day for commencement of the Fourth Army's attack in the neighbourhood of Albert. 3 Cavalry Division was ordered to be ready to go into action in the case of an advance. Brigade formed up at 0730 awaiting orders to move. At 0745, the whole Brigade off-saddled and stood ready to move at half-an-hour's notice. But, at 1730, a message was received altering the readiness level to two hours and, at 1900, a message was received that the Brigade would not be advancing from the area of concentration the next day.
2	Bonnay	Bivouac	At 2040, the Brigade was ordered to be ready to move at four hours' notice.
3	Bonnay	Bivouac	The Brigade remained at Bonnay in bivouac. 3 Cavalry Division was ordered to move west of Amiens on 4 and to come under the orders of the Fourth Army for tactical and administrative purposes.
4	Meerlesart	Billets	At 0100, the Brigade received orders to march at 0515 to the Hallencourt area. It set off then and marched via the Neuville – Amiens – Ailly-sur-Somme – Soues – Airaines route to Allery. *En route*, the Brigade halted and off-saddled and fed at Dreuil-les-Amiens. The long march was much interfered with due to movements by other troops. It arrived in the Hallencourt area at 1600 when the regiments all went to billets, with 3DG allocated Meerlesaart.
5	Meerlesart	Billets	At 0530, the Brigade was ordered to provide an officer and 58 men to form a dismounted squadron (as part of a 500 men contribution by 3 Cavalry Division) to proceed by rail from Longpre to Mericourt for clearing the battlefield duties under the orders of the Fourth Army. *During July, the Divisional QMG considered the question of dropping one of the three days' rations carried by each trooper if they were to carry extra bombs with them when they were going into the Trenches.*
6	Meerlesart	Billets	The Brigade was ordered to 1½ hour's readiness but this order was cancelled the next day.
7	Meerlesart	Billets	Church of England service was held in camp
8	Meerlesart	Billets	At noon, 6 Cavalry Brigade (and the remainder of 3 Cavalry Division) was ordered to march at once to the Corbie area.
9	Vaux-sur-Somme	Bivouac	The Brigade reached Corbie at 0200 and bivouacked west of the town. At 1630, it moved on to bivouac at Vaux-sur-Somme. *3DG's War Diary simply has the regiment at Meerlesart. The diary has no further information so it is not possible to reconcile the War Diaries of 3DG and those of the Brigade.*
10	Vaux-sur-	Bivouac	

11	Vaux-sur-Somme	Bivouac	An officer and 70 men were detached from the Brigade to Mericourt for salvage duties under XV Corps.
12 to 18	Vaux-sur-Somme	Bivouac	
19	La Neuville	Bivouac	*(3DG's War Diary suggests that the regiment moved here only on 20 June.)* Dismounted parties employed on burying duties on the battlefield were relieved by new parties. The reliefs were carried out by bus.
20 to 24	La Neuville	Bivouac	On 22 July, the Divisional QMG received a further supply of steel helmets and issued another 435 to each brigade (presumably, meeting each brigade's need).
25 and 26	La Neuville	Bivouac	A party of 3 Officers and 93 men from 3DG were detached to Becourt to work under III Corps digging and improving trenches in the neighbourhood of Contalmaison. This detachment was part of a group of 500 men supplied by 3 Cavalry Division. The Divisional QMG noted that Divisional working parties had been detailed on 24 as follows: a. 117 Burial, salvage work and clearing the battlefields around Mametz and Fricourt—under XV Corps; b. 110, " c. 142 " under III Corps; d. 71 at Mericourt working under the Royal Engineers; e. 234 at Contay loading ammunition; f. 271 at Menencourt under the Royal Engineers; g. 516 at Contalmaison working on Trench Lines.
27	La Neuville	Bivouac	A similar sized party (as part of another 700 men from 3 Cavalry Division) was sent to join the first party for work on the line between Hametz and Contalmaison.
28 and 29	La Neuville	Bivouac	
30	La Neuville	Bivouac	An officer and 45 men from 3DG went to Becourt to relieve the two working parties.
31	La Neuville	Bivouac	The working parties returned to their regiments.
Aug			
1	La Mesge	Billets and Bivouac	6 Cavalry Brigade marched from La Neuville to La Mesge where it was billeted and bivouacked. The route was by the Daours – Vequement road just south of Amiens Citadelle to La Chausee thence via Pequigny-Soues to Soues and La Mesge.
2	Caours	Bivouac	The Brigade marched via Airaines – Sorel – Liercourt – Pontremy – Buigny L'Abbe – Vauchelles to Neuf Moulins where it went to bivouac, with 3DG bivouacking at Caours. *This was part of a 3 Cavalry Division move to the St. Riquier area. The weather was reported as being very hot.*

Appendix III: War Diaries (Extracts)

3	Caours	Bivouac	Note that 3DG's War Diary suggests that the march to Offin occurred over 5 and 6 July. The Brigade's War Diary has nothing of relevance for 3 July. It may be that the march took place over a couple of days.
4	Roussent	Bivouac	The Brigade continued its march and 3DG bivouacked overnight at Roussent.
5	Offin	Billets	The Brigade assembled just north of Maintenay and marched via Buire-le-Sec to the Beurainville area where it went into permanent billets in the Fruges area. 3DG was listed as being billeted at Offin, Loison and Pt. Beaurain whereas 3DG's War Diary simply states Offin. It may be that the regimental headquarters was at Offin and some Squadrons were billeted at Loison and Pt. Beaurain.
6 to 12	Offin	Billets	General daily routine in billets and training.
13	Offin	Billets	General daily routine in billets and training. 2 officers and 59 men (as part of 500 men supplied by 3 Cavalry Division) were detached as a working party to the II Corps area for laying cables.
14 to 23	Offin	Billets	General daily routine in billets and training.
24	Offin	Billets	General daily routine in billets and training. 3 Cavalry Division supplied a working party of 147 men to the Bouzincourt area to work under II Corps.
25 to 30	Offin	Billets	General daily routine in billets and training.
31	Offin	Billets	General daily routine in billets and training. The working party was relieved by a similar sized party.
Sept			
1 to 9	Offin	Billets	General daily routine in billets and training.
10	Argoules	Billets	The Brigade marched in two columns to the valley of the River Authie. The march went via Gouystandre – Saul Choy – Manbus – St. Josse – Douriez. 3DG were billeted at Argoules.
11	Le Plessiel	Billets and Bivouac	The Brigade continued its march in two columns to Le Plessiel. One column marched via Vironcheaux – Crecy – Forêt L'Abbaye while the other marched via Ligescourt and Crecy-Clanchy. 3DG was billeted and bivouacked at le Plessiel.
12	La Chaussee	Bivouac	The Brigade marched via Vauchelles – Epagne – Pontremy – L'Etoile – Flixecourt to La Chaussee West. 3DG bivouacked here.

13	La Chaussee	Bivouac	
14	North of Bussy	Bivouac	At 0800, the Brigade set off on march to the Bussy area via St. Sauveur – Amiens northern outskirts – Rivery – Camon and Lamotte (where it watered at 1100) arriving at Bussy at 1400.
15	West of Bonnay	Bivouac	At 0800, the Brigade marched to a point just south-west of Bonnay where it off-saddled and fed. At 1000, the Brigade was ordered to 30 minutes readiness but at 1845 it was ordered to bivouac for the night and to be ready to move at 30 minutes' notice on 16.
16	West of Bonnay	Bivouac	At 2340, orders were received to move at 0700 on 17 September.
17	Pont Noyelles	Bivouac	At 0700, the Brigade moved as ordered through a very thick fog until 0900 when it reached Pont Noyelles where it bivouacked.
18	Pont Noyelles	Bivouac	The weather was not pleasant for troops in bivouacs as it was a very wet day.
19	Pont Noyelles	Bivouac	A wet night.
20	Pont Noyelles	Bivouac	A wet morning.
21	Pont Noyelles	Bivouac	
22	La Mesge	Bivouac	The Brigade marched by Vequemont – Lamotte – Amiens station – Picquigny to bivouacs at Soues-le-Mesge.
23	Wavans	Bivouac and Billets	The Brigade marched to Flixecourt – the north bank of the Somme – Domart-en-Ponthieu to the Bealcourt/ Beauvoir/ Wavans area and on to billets and bivouacs.
24	Maintenay	Billets	The Brigade marched by Auxi-le-Chateau – Le Ponchel – Labroye to billets on the north bank of the River L'Authie between Raye-sur-Authie and Roussent. 3DG were billeted at Maintenay.
25	Maintenay	Billets	
26	Maintenay	Billets	An officer and 21 men from 3DG replaced another officer and 44 men on attachment to the Fourth Army.
27 to 30	Maintenay	Billets	General daily routine in billets and training.
Oct			
1	Maintenay	Billets	General daily routine in billets and training.
2	Maintenay	Billets	General daily routine in billets and training. 2 officers and 46 men from 3DG dismounted and entrained at Hesdin for attachment to the Reserve Army as a working

Appendix III: War Diaries (Extracts)

			party. This was part of a 579 man working party supplied by 3 Cavalry Division.
3 to 19	Maintenay	Billets	General daily routine in billets and training.
20	Maintenay	Billets	General daily routine in billets and training. Another officer and 65 men from 3DG went to Bouzincourt to relieve the earlier working party working under the Reserve Army.
21	Maintenay	Billets	General daily routine in billets and training. The earlier working party re-joined the regiment.
22	Campigneilles les Grandes	Billets	There was a change in the billeting areas with 3DG being distributed between Campigneilles-les-Grands, Airon Notre Dame, Airon St. Vaast and Rang du Fliers.
23 to 31	Campigneilles les Grandes	Billets	General daily routine in billets and training.
Nov			
1	Campigneilles les Grandes	Billets	General daily routine in billets and training. 3 Cavalry Division's War Diary records that the various working parties were relieved. 600 Mackintosh capes were issued to each Brigade within 3 Cavalry Division.
2 to 5	Campigneilles les Grandes	Billets	General daily routine in billets and training.
6	Berck Sands	Billets	General daily routine in billets and training. 6 Cavalry Brigade's War Dairy makes no mention of the changed venue of the billets. In fact it states that there was no change throughout November from the billets arranged on 21 October.
7 to 27	Berck Sands	Billets	General daily routine in billets and training. On 11 November, the working party from 20 October now re-joined the regiment. On 14 November, the Division's War Diary noted that Ordinary leave was permitted and that 13 vacancies per day had been allotted to the Division. On 20 November, one Company from 3DG was transferred to

			Maresquel.
28 and 29	Bois de Vertun	Billets	General daily routine in billets and training. *28 and 29 November were reported as being at Bois de Vertun but no explanation for the move is given*
30	Berck Sands	Billets	General daily routine in billets and training. *Again, no explanation is given for the changed location.*
Dec			
1 to 19	Campigneilles les Grandes	Billets	General daily routine in billets and training. *A scheduled inspection of 3DG on 12 December by the Commanding Officer of 6 Cavalry Brigade on the sands at Merlimont Plage was cancelled owing to the weather.*
20	Airon-St. Vaast	Billets	General daily routine in billets and training. *6 Cavalry Brigade's War Diary records this as being part of a wholesale change of billeting areas with 8 Cavalry Brigade. 6 Cavalry Brigade's War Diary states that 3DG were now billeted at Aix-en-Issart – Marant Marenna – Marles-sur-Canche.*
21 to 31	Airon-St. Vaast	Billets	
1917			
Jan			
1 to 31	Airon-St. Vaast	Billets	General daily routine in billets and training. *A cinematograph entertainment is recorded as having taken place in the evening of 3 January.* *On 17 January, the Brigade's Commanding Officer inspected 3DG'shorses.*
Feb			
1 to 28	Airon-St. Vaast	Billets	General daily routine in billets and training. *Cyril's War Office personnel file suggests that he was transferred to England "as Candidate for temporary commission in Infantry" on 18 February or, possibly, 22 February.* *There is also a statement that he was posted to 6 Cavalry Reserve Regiment of Dragoons on 26 February.*

Background to Cyril's rejoining the Front

Sept			
20			*The Second and Fifth Armies attacked. 33 Division was in reserve to X Corps which attacked with 23, 39 and 41 Divisions. 23 and 39 Divisions took all their objectives but 41 Division failed to take its final objective until it made a second attack in the evening.*
25			*There was a strongly organised German counter-attack all along the Divisional front. 33 Division received the first news of this attack by a pigeon message at 0715 from 1 Queens. At 1220, 19 Brigade was ordered to despatch 19 Scots Rifles to support 98 Brigade.*

26			33 Division attacking forward but being strongly counter-attacked. At 0805, 2RWF was placed at the disposal of 98 Brigade to ensure that any gaps were filled at all costs. Only one battalion was left in the Division's Reserve. At 1440, 2RWF opened its attack.
27			At 1300 the situation was not absolutely clear and 2RWF was preparing to attack. At 1430, the Blue Line was captured.
28			33 Division relieved by 23 Division. 19 Brigade moved to the Racquinghen – Blaringhem area. The buses and trains were late and the battalions did not arrive in most areas until the morning of 29. Congratulatory telegrams were received from Gen. Plumber and Sir Douglas Haig.
29 and 30			Divisional brigades resting.

2nd Battalion of the Royal Welsh Fusiliers, 19 Brigade, 33 Division, X Corps (2 October – 5 October 1917); VIII Corps 5 October 1917 - 6 February 1918

Oct			
1			
2	Blaringhem	Billets	The components of 33 Division trained near their billets. 2RWF had a practice parade for inspection by Field Marshall Sir Douglas Haig (Commander-in-Chief of British Armies in France). 33 Division Royal Engineers obtained flagpoles for the inspection parade from St. Omer and, afterwards, returned them to the *mairie* at Blaringhem. Lt. W. R. Smith, 2nd Lieut. W. R. C. Keepfer and 2nd Lieut. D. A. Jones joined from base.
3	Blaringhem	Billets	Brigade was inspected by Haig who expressed entire satisfaction with appearance and turnout of the Battalion. Capt. Redford lectured all officers on the recent operations.
4	Blaringhem	Billets	Parades under company arrangements.
5	Acquin		Brigade (and the remainder of 33 Division) moved by road to Acquin and the Tilque Training Area—a 16 mile march. Only two men fell out from the Battalion. On the march, orders received transferring the Division from X Corps to VIII Corps.
6	Acquin	Camp	Moved by road to Wizernes, entrained and went to Bailleul, detrained and marched to Kortepyp Camp (between Bailleul and Neuve Eglise). Very cold night.
7	Kortepyp Camp	Camp	All watches put back one hour for Winter Time—rained all day.
8	Messines	Trench (Support)	19 Brigade relieved 42 Brigade in Messines Sector. The Battalion relieved 5 South Wales Borderers (**SWB**) in Support Line, Messines Left Sub-Sector. Very bad night for relief, dark

			and wet.
9	Messines	Trench (Support)	Enemy shelled a little in early morning.
			Shortly after the relief, a small party of the enemy succeeded in raiding the Right Battalion in an exposed and isolated position and capturing two men and wounding a third.
10	Messines	Trench (Support)	All Companies employed in carrying from the Belle Farm Dump to Swaynes Farm Dump and from there after dark to the Front Line.
			Generally quiet in Brigade sector apart from some shelling on tracks and communication trenches after dark.
11	Messines	Trench (Support)	Carrying as yesterday.
			Again, a very quiet day but, at night, intermittent artillery fire on the communications trenches and machine gun fire on tracks near the front line.
12	Messines	Trench (Support)	An uneventful day.
			2RWF relieved 5 SWB in the front line. During the relief, from 1930 – 2115, the enemy shelled the front line all along the sector and the communications trenches causing some casualties in the Left Sub-sector. D Company got caught in the barrage on Fanny.
			Winter clothing issued to all men.
13	Messines	Trench (Front)	Battalion HQ shelled with 5.9 howitzers from 0900 until dark, several direct hits. New HQ in the Support Company's HQ.
14	Messines	Trench (Front)	19 Brigade relieved by 100 Brigade. 2RWF was relieved by 16 Kings Royal Rifles. A very quick relief. D Company had three Other Ranks wounded coming out. Marched back to billets in Neuve Eglise.
15	Neuve Eglise	Billets	Resting and clearing up.
16	Neuve Eglise	Billets	Company training; baths in the afternoon; sent three working parties (total 100 men) for work up the Line under the Royal Engineers.
17	Neuve Eglise	Billets	Company training; same working parties.
18	Neuve Eglise	Billets	Moved by bus to Menin Gate, Ypres and took over camp from 4 King's Liverpool Regiment. Attached to I ANZAC Corps for work on roads and railways.
19 to 22	Ypres	Camp	2RWF found 400 men for road making and timber carrying in the forward areas.
23 and 24	Ypres	Camp	Same working parties (less 50 men).
25	Ypres	Camp	Same working parties (less 50 men).
			2RWF relieved by 2 Worcestershire Regiment at 1500 and embussed at 1600 back to Neuve Eglise and occupied Bulford Camp.

APPENDIX III: WAR DIARIES (EXTRACTS)

26	Bulford Camp (Neuve Eglise)	Camp	Clearing up and resting. Palmer Baths at the disposal of the Battalion. *Second and Fifth Armies attacked and improved their lines north-east of Ypres in pouring rain.*
27	Bulford Camp	Camp	Parades under Company arrangement and training.
28	Bulford Camp	Camp	Church Parade in YMCA tent.
29	Bulford Camp	Camp	Parades under Company arrangement and training.
30	Bulford Camp	Camp	19 Brigade relieved 98 Brigade in the Messines Sector and 2RWF relieved 1 Argyle & Sutherland Highlanders in Messines Left Sub-Sector Support Line. Night very cold and wet.
31	Messines	Trenches (Support)	Enemy artillery displayed considerable activity in the Left Battalion (i.e. 2RWF) area—especially after dark when some damage was done to trenches and a battalion working party was considerably interfered with.
Nov			
1	Messines	Trenches (Support)	On carrying duties day and night.
2	Messines	Trenches (Support)	Quiet and uneventful.
3	Messines	Trenches (Front)	2RWF relieved 5 Scots Rifles in the front line. A, B and C Companies in the front; D Company in support.
4	Messines	Trenches (Front)	Left of Battalion's trenches very wet, otherwise in very fair condition.
5	Messines	Trenches (Front)	Quiet day.
6	Messines	Trenches (Front)	
7	Messines	Trenches (Front)	19 Brigade relieved by 100 Brigade and the Battalion, after being relieved by 9 Highland Light Infantry, marched to billets in Bulford Camp.
8	Bulford Camp (Neuve Eglise)	Camp	Clearing up and checking deficiencies. The Brigade became VIII Corps Reserve Brigade. The Brigade's War Diary noted that there were practically no facilities for training in the area so the time from 8 – 13 November was spent in cleaning up and close order training around the camps.
9	Bulford Camp	Camp	Baths allotted to Battalion 0800 – 1200. Small working parties.
10	Bulford Camp	Camp	Small working parties.
11	Bulford Camp	Camp	Small working parties; Church Parade.
12 and 13	Bulford Camp	Camp	Training in Camp area.
14	Line of		19 Brigade marched by route march to Strazeele via Bailleul.

		march		
15 and 16	Straz-eele (Rouge Croix)	Billets	There were no facilities for training so time was spent in close order drill.
17	White Chateau Ypres	Bivouacs	Moved by bus to White Chateau area of Ypres. The Brigade debussed at Ypres Asylum and marched into bivouacs around White Chateau. Owing to hostile bombing, all tents had to be struck at 0700 daily.
18	White Chateau Ypres	Bivouacs	Encampment shelled by German long-range gun.
19	Potijze	Camp	19 Brigade moved by bus to camp in Potijze Support area.
20	Potijze	Camp	In Support. Reconnoitred the Paschendaele Sector. Large working parties were found from 2RWF for work on roads and trenches in the forward areas.
21 to 23	Potijze	Camp	Working parties.
24	Pasch-endaele	Trenches (Support)	19 Brigade relieved 98 Brigade in the front line. 2RWF relieved the Cameronians and 5 Scots Rifles in Support Left Sub-Sector. B and D Companies at Hamburg.
25	Pasch-endaele	Trenches (Support)	Still in Support. Shelling intermittent. Morning quiet but, in the afternoon, the enemy shelled Paschendaele and Crest Farm heavily. Shelling increased and, at 1900, the SOS call went up on the * Division front. Our barrage came down promptly and no infantry action followed.
26	Pasch-endaele	Trenches (Support)	Hostile artillery active during the day—especially on Crest Farm—where a company from 2RWF relieved a company of Cameronians.
27	Pasch-endaele	Trenches (Front)	2 RWF relieved Cameronians in Front trenches, Paschendaele Left Sub-Sector. D Company Right front company. Hostile artillery through the night resulted in an SOS call from the Right Division front but no infantry action developed.
28	Pasch-endaele	Trenches (Front)	Generally a quieter day. 2RWF was still in the Front Line where shelling continued in bursts but Paschendaele and the back areas suffered heavy fire.
29	Pasch-endaele	Trenches (Front)	Front Line. One company was relieved during the day at Crest farm. Hostile artillery against Paschendaele and our guns around Abraham Heights.
30	Paschen daele	Trenches (Front)	100 Brigade relieved 19 Brigade, including 2RWF. A good relief and quiet journey back to Potijze where 2RWF spent the night and on the next day took train from St. Jean for the Brandhoek No. 2 Area.
Dec			

1	Brand-hoek (Erie Camp)	Camp	19 Division was the Divisional Reserve. Each battalion carried out training in the vicinity of its respective camp.
2 to 6	Brand-hoek	Camp	Training.
7	Menin Gate	Camp	Moved to the Support Area Potijze near Menin Gate, Ypres by road.
8 to 10	Menin Gate	Camp	In camp. Working parties. On 10 November, 33 Division became the Corps Reserve.
11	Watou area		Brigade proceeded by train to the Watou.
12	Watou area	Billets	Clearing up. Billets very scattered but good.
13	Watou area	Billets	Clearing up area, etc.
14 to 19	Watou area	Billets	Training
20	Watou area	Billets	Training GOC 33 Division lectured 19 Brigade on 'Lessons to be drawn from the recent Cambrai fighting.'
21	Poper-inghe	Billets	Left Watou by road for Poperinghe where 19 Brigade relieved 100 Brigade working on VIII Corps roads and railways. Transport and classes under instruction left in Watou area.
22 to 24	Poper-inghe	Billets	Working parties.
25	Poper-inghe	Billets	Christmas Day. Whole day observed as a holiday. GOC 33 Division visited 2RWF to convey his good wishes.
26 to 28	Poper-inghe	Billets	Working parties.
29	Poper-inghe	Billets	Route march to Watou. Occupied billets vacated on 21.
30	Watou	Billets	Church Parade at HQ.
31	Watou	Billets	Baths allotted to Battalion at Watou. From 1000 – 1600, all Officers attended a lecture by the Corps' Commanding Officer on training, etc. in the cinema hall at Steenvoorde. Another officer then lectured on platoon work.
1918			
Jan			
1	Watou	Billets	Holiday.
2	Watou	Billets	All men passed through the Gas Hut at Steenvorde.
3	Brand-hoek		Moved by rail to Toronto Camp. Brigade took over as the Divisional Reserve.
4	Brand-		Moved by bus to Ypres thence by route march to Alnwick

	hoek		Camp where 2RWF spent a few hours in the Support Brigade Area. Moved to Hamburg Trench in the evening and relieved 7 Durham Light Infantry as Left Support.
5	Paschendaele	Trenches (Front)	19 Brigade relieved 151 Brigade in the front line. 2RWF relieved 5 Border Regiment in Left Sub-Sector Paschendaele. D Company in reserve at Haalen Support.
6	Paschendaele	Trenches (Front)	Evening quiet. Snowed all day. During the day, the Enemy shelled in the vicinity of the Left Support Battalion lightly with 4.2" artillery.
7	Paschendaele	Trenches (Front)	Evening quiet. Snow and frost. D Company relieved C Company in Right Front.
8	Paschendaele	Trenches (Front)	Enemy quiet. Snowed all day.
9	Paschendaele	Trenches (Front)	Enemy heavily shelled Battalion HQ and working parties in the rear from 1000 – 1300. 100 Brigade took over from 19 Brigade in the line. 2RWF relieved by 9 Highland Light Infantry (relief complete at 0130) and moved to billets in Ypres.
10	Ypres	Billets	Moved by light railway to Brandhoek (St. Lawrence Camp). Remainder of the day spent clearing up.
11	Brandhoek	Camp	Whole Battalion bathed. And cleaned equipment etc.
12	Brandhoek	Camp	Clearing up and booking deficiencies.
13	Whitby Camp	Camp	Moved by light railway to Whitby Camp in the Support Brigade Area.
14	Whitby Camp	Camp	From 0530 – 1130, 2RWF was detached as a Working Battalion at Manners Junction and making light railways between Hamburg and Abraham Heights.
15	Whitby Camp	Camp	The same. Very wet.
16	Whitby Camp	Camp	Working parties cancelled due to floods.
17	Whitby Camp	Camp	Working parties as on 14. Snow and rain.
18 to 25	Whitby Camp	Camp	Working parties as on 14. On 20 January, Sunday church services. Many Church of England services were scheduled; Roman Catholic Masses were half the number of Anglican services; while just two Wesleyan Services were scheduled: for 1000 at the Dressing Station in Vlamertinghe, and at 1100 in the Divisional Rest Station in Brandhoek. On 22 January, baths at Ypres. On 25 January, baths at Ypres for D Company.
26	Whitby Camp	Camp	2RWF moved to Longuenesse (St. Omer) by train from St. Jean station at 1620 arriving at St. Omer at 2020.

27	Longue-nesse	Billets	Billets very good and clean.
28 and 29	Longue-nesse	Billets	Companies cleaned up.
30	Longue-nesse	Billets	Battalion training near billets. Command of the Paschendaele Sector passed to 50 Division.
31	Longue-nesse	Billets	Specialist classes and training near billets.
Feb			
1	Longue-nesse	Billets	Specialist classes and training near billets.
2	Longue-nesse	Billets	Training.
3	Longue-nesse	Billets	Church Parade.
4	Longue-nesse	Billets	At 1315, 2RWF commenced a three day march to join 38 (Welsh) Division, First Army in Merville Area. First, it marched to Renescure where it was addressed by Maj. Gen. R. J. Pinney and Brig. Gen. C. R. G. Moyne. *This move was part of a wholesale re-organisation of Divisions on a '9 battalion' system.* Orders required each company to march 100 yards apart and there to be 500 yards between the Battalion and its transport, with a 25-yard gap between each group of six vehicles. 33 Division was responsible for sending rations for the Battalion's consumption on 6 February at Thiennes. Four lorries filled with blankets were to accompany the Battalion until it arrived at its final destination.
5	Renescure	Billets	Battalion moved to Thiennes. Billets good.

2nd Battalion Royal Welsh Fusiliers; 115 Infantry Brigade; 38 (Welsh) Division; First Army

6	Thiennes	Billets	2RWF moved to Robermetz. Massed bands and drums of 115 Brigade played the Battalion into billets and through Merville where the Battalion was met by the Acting Assistant Adjutant of 38 Division. 2RWF now became part of 115 Brigade and 38 (Welsh) Division and under the orders of the First Army. *(Notwithstanding the 2RWF War Diary and 38 Division's General Staff's entries for 6 February, it is not until 12 February that 115 Brigade's War Diary records 2RWF's joining the Brigade (and 16 Welch Regiment and 11 SWB leaving the Brigade).)*
7	Robermetz	Billets	Billets very good. Whole Battalion bathed.

8	Robermetz	Billets	Working parties. Construction of new Corps line—100 diggers.
9	Robermetz	Billets	Inspection of Battalion in drill order by XV Corps commanding officer.
10 to 12	Robermetz	Billets	Continued working parties. On 10 February, Church Parade at Concert Hall in Merville.
13	Hollebecque Camp	Camp	38 Division moved into the Line to relieve 57 Division with 115 Brigade relieving 170 Brigade in the Wez Macquart Section. The disposition was one battalion from Chards Fme to Rue du Bois with two companies in the Front, Support and second Support Lines and two companies in the Subsidiary Line; one battalion from Rue du Bois to Burat Fme with one company in the front system of trenches and one in the subsidiary system of trenches and two companies in the Fleurie Surtal (rue Allee to Lavesace) and one battalion in Reserve at Hollebecque Camp. 2RWF (now Reserve Battalion) proceeded by route march to Hollebecque Camp in the Steenwerck area where the Battalion relieved North Lancashire Regiment at night. Very wet.
14	Hollebecque Camp	Camp	Battalion cleaned up and booked deficiencies. Enemy artillery and machine guns were active.
15	Hollebecque Camp	Camp	Enemy artillery and machine guns were active. 2RWF trained at Camp and fired on the range. Officers reconnoitred L'Armee and Fleurie Switches in the rear of Wez Macquart Sector of the Line.
16	Hollebecque Camp	Camp	Training. Meanwhile, in the forward trenches, Enemy aircraft, machine guns and trench mortars were active.
17	Hollebecque Camp	Camp	Church parade.
18	Hollebecque Camp	Camp	2RWF to Rolanderie area where they took over hutments at Rolanderie Farm. Men crowded but comfortable.
19	Rolanderie	Billets	The company commanding officers reconnoitred the front line while the companies trained near the billets.
20	Rolanderie	Billets	Full day's work.
21	Rolanderie	Billets	2RWF relieved the 17RWF in the Centre-Left of the Wez Macquart sector. C and D Companies were in the line: C Company of the right. *Therefore, D Company must have been on the Left.*
22	Wez Macquart	Trenches (Front)	Hostile artillery was very active. In addition, machine guns and trench mortars were active. Enemy shelled the Left Company *(i.e. D Company)*.
23	Wez	Trenches	Front Line. Quiet.

Appendix III: War Diaries (Extracts)

	Macquart	(Front)	
24	Wez Macquart	Trenches (Front)	Fine and mild. Continuous heavy shelling of the Wez Macquart Sector by enemy artillery and trench mortars. The shelling almost amounted to a box barrage of the Left battalion sector—but no action followed.
25	Wez Macquart	Trenches (Front)	A Company relieved D Company in Left sub-sector. Only a little activity on the part of enemy artillery, machine guns and trench mortars was reported.
26	Wez Macquart	Trenches (Front)	Trenches. Enemy aircraft, artillery, machine guns and trench mortars all engaged. (The Brigade's War Diary recorded that the enemy aircraft had not been very enterprising and tended only to cross the British lines at a very high altitude.)
27 and 28	Wez Macquart	Trenches (Front)	Enemy aircraft, artillery, machine guns and trench mortars all engaged.
Mar			
1	Wez Macquart	Trenches (Front)	St. David's Day. The Division held a St. David's Day concert in the YMCA Hut at Steenwerck. 2RWF relieved by 17RWF and marched to Rolanderie Farm. Sir Douglas Haig visited 38 Division's HQ.
2	Rolanderie	Billets	Rest and clearing up.
3 to 8	Rolanderie	Billets	3 companies went as working parties to the L'Armee Switch.
9	Rolanderie	Billets	Continued working parties. 2RWF relieved 17RWF in Centre Left of Wez Macquart Sector. Before the relief, the Battalion HQ at Artillery Farm had been shelled, which delayed the relief.
10	Wez Macquart	Trenches (Front)	Front Line. The Battalion reported scattered shelling whereas the Brigade recorded that enemy artillery, aircraft, machine guns and trench mortars were very active. At 0400, the enemy placed a heavy barrage on the Brigade's lines but no action materialised.
11	Wez Macquart	Trenches (Front)	Back areas, very heavily shelled. Great difficulty in delivering rations to the troops.
12	Wez Macquart	Trenches (Front)	Quiet—although the Brigade reported enemy artillery, machine guns and trench mortars as well as aircraft activity.
13	Wez Macquart	Trenches (Front)	Early morning (0515), under cover of a heavy barrage, a large enemy Raiding Party of about 300 attempted to raid the extreme Left part of the Battalion's position and about 20

			succeeded in getting through the artillery barrage and attacked Evelyn Post held by D Company who repulsed them, inflicting losses and capturing one prisoner.
14 and 15	Wez Macquart	Trenches (Front)	Enemy artillery active.
16	Wez Macquart	Trenches (Front)	Enemy shelled subsidiary line—principally C Company—with gas.
17	Wez Macquart	Trenches (Front)	2RWF relieved in the Front Line by 17RWF. Battalion HQ at La Rolanderie Farm. Slight shelling of the back areas.
18	Rolanderie	Billets	
19	Rolanderie	Billets	Battalion working parties on the L'Armee Switch.
20	Rolanderie	Billets	Battalion working parties on the L'Armee Switch. Enemy artillery continued. Killed two Other Ranks and wounded three.
21	Rolanderie	Billets	In the early morning, the whole area was gas shelled. The working parties on the L'Armee Switch worked for three hours in respirators: two were killed and one wounded. After some time, the work was postponed and did not resume until 1800 and, again, the men were obliged to stop work because of shelling. Some men (including one platoon from D Company) were kept off the working parties in order to practice for a raid.
22	Rolanderie	Billets	Working parties and Raid practice.
23	Rolanderie	Billets	
24	Rolanderie	Billets	Company commanders reconnoitred Wez Macquart. Divine Service—Church of England at 0930; Non-Conformists at 1100—in the Signallers' Billets at La Rolanderie.
25	Rolanderie	Billets	2RWF relieved 17RWF in Centre and Left Sectors of Wez Macquart. D Company on the Right. Very quiet.
26	Wez Macquart	Trenches (Front)	Altered the dispositions in the Line.
27 and 28	Wez Macquart	Trenches (Front)	Quiet day. Shelling at night. The Divisional front line was now held by two brigades with the third brigade in the Corps Reserve. 115 Brigade held the Wez Macquart Sector (Bailleuil – Lille railway to the road Divisional boundary). The sector was divided into three: --10SWB on the Right --2RWF in the Centre --17RWF on the Left. Each battalion was organised in depth back to the Fleurie Switch.

Appendix III: War Diaries (Extracts)

Date	Location		Notes
29	Wez Macquart	Trenches (Front)	2RWF relieved by 1/5 The Loyal North Lancashire Regiment. Marched to Sailly; last arriving at 0530.
			The Brigade recorded that 2RWF had carried out a raid on a German trench but had found it to be unoccupied. *(There is no mention of this raid in the Battalion's War Diary.)*
30	La Sart	Billets	38 Division relieved from the line on night 29/30. 115 Brigade relieved by 170 Brigade and moved by road to the Nouveau Monde – Sailly area.
			2RWF marched to La Sart. Comfortable billets although rather scattered.
31	La Sart	Billets	Battalion at rest in La Sart. Engaged in clearing up.
			Easter Sunday voluntary Church of England and Non-Conformist Services.
April			
1	La Sart	Billets	Moved by rail. Entraining at Calonne to Doullens. Marched Doullens to Villers-Bocage 97 miles north of Amiens).
2	Villers-Bocage (Amiens)		Moved to Hedauville.
3	Hedauville	Billets	38 (Welsh) Division, which was today transferred to V Corps, was in V Corps Reserve with 115 Brigade under the command of 2 Division in the case of an emergency.
			2RWF's billets—fair. Working party of 175 men on trenches North of Englebelmer. Very wet.
4	Hedauville	Billets	Range allotted to Companies. Rain. Working party of 350 men at Englebelmer.
5 and 6	Hedauville	Billets	38 (Welsh) Division in Army Reserve and 115 Brigade not to be involved in fighting except under the orders of 38 (Welsh) Division.
			Range allotted to Companies.
7	Hedauville	Billets	Moved by route march by road to Hérissart.
8	Herissart	Billets	Billets in Hérissart. Rain.
			38 (Welsh) Division to be Right Supporting Division and 115 Brigade to be prepared to assemble at Henencourt and Senlis with a view to occupying the Millencourt – Engelbelmer Line.
9 and 10	Herissart	Billets	
11	Herissart	Billets	38 (Welsh) Division took over the Right Divisional Sector with 115 Brigade relieving 114 Brigade in reserve.
			2RWF relieved 13 Welch Regiment as Right Battalion of the Brigade in reserve near Milencourt.
			Battle surplus (about 15 officers and 144 men) to Contay.

12 and 13	Milencourt	Bivouac	Battalion in bivouac near Milencourt.
14	Milencourt	Bivouac	2RWF detailed for work on Corps line from 1900 to 0100. Very dark night.
15	Milencourt	Bivouac	All Battle Surplus bathed at Contay. 2RWF in bivouacs near Milencourt. Working on Corps line near Senlis 2200 – 0200.
16	Milencourt	Bivouac	Bivouacs near Milencourt. No working parties.
17	Milencourt	Bivouac	Bivouacs near Milencourt. Working parties cancelled.
18	Milencourt	Bivouac	Lewis gun class fired on the range. 115 Brigade relieved 113 Brigade in the line. 2RWF relieved 13RWF in the Brigade's Right Sector near Bouzincourt. D Company on the Right. Quiet night. HQ very uncomfortable. Men in disconnected trenches.
19	Bouzincourt	Trenches (Front)	Lewis gun on long range in the morning; at 30 yards in the afternoon. Battalion in trenches. Quiet and put up a little light shelling and machine gun (MG) fire. Very cold; sharp frost.
20	Bouzincourt	Trenches (Front)	Lewis gun. Battalion in trenches. Very cold. Slight shelling throughout the night.
21	Bouzincourt	Trenches (Front)	115 Brigade less 2RWF relieved by 113 Brigade and back in reserve. 2RWF under command of 113 Brigade and in trenches. Usual MG and artillery fire. Bright moonlit night. Fine day. Church Parade: Church of England at 0945 and Non-Conformists at 1030.
22	Bouzincourt	Trenches (Front)	Battalion in trenches. Minor operations carried out by 113 Brigade.
23	Bouzincourt	Trenches (Front)	At about 1400, 2RWF ordered to reinforce 13RWF with 3 more platoons. Enemy Lively.
24	Bouzincourt	Trenches (Front)	Battalion expected to be relieved but relief cancelled.
25	Bouzincourt	Trenches (Front)	2RWF relieved by 10SWB and moved to sunken road near Bouzincourt in Support and the Brigade's Reserve.
26	Bouzincourt	In support	2RWF relieved by 10SWB and moved to sunken road near Henencourt Wood.
27	Henen-	Bivouac	In evening, 2RWF moved to sunken road south of Senlis.

Appendix III: War Diaries (Extracts)

	court		
28	Senlis	Bivouac	Battalion near Senlis; supplied working party of three companies for work on Corps line and old French line South of Senlis Mill. Enemy active.
29	Senlis	Bivouac	Battalion still near Senlis. Three companies as working parties.
30	Senlis	Bivouac	Battalion still near Senlis. Three companies as working parties. Battle Surplus to Domquer le Plouy.
May			
1	Senlis	Bivouac	Battalion in sunken road near Senlis. Working party of three companies on Corps line south of Senlis.
2	Senlis	Trenches (Front)	2RWF in sunken road near Senlis. Relieved 17RWF in Right Sector of Brigade. D Company in Reserve
3	Senlis	Trenches (Front)	Battalion in trenches. Quiet—although the Brigade War Diary notes some enemy artillery and patrols.
4 and 5	Senlis	Trenches (Front)	Battalion in trenches.
6	Senlis	Trenches (Front)	B company attempted a raid on enemy trenches. Failed because of weather conditions and alertness of enemy. About 2250, Lt. J. T. S. Evans and one Other Rank captured.
7	Senlis	Trenches (Front)	Battalion in trenches. Very quiet night.
8	Senlis	Trenches (Front)	2RWF relieved by 17RWF. Relief seen and heavily shelled. No casualties. To sunken road South of Senlis to take over 17RWF's position.
9	Senlis	? Bivouac	Battalion in sunken road South of Senlis. Enemy attacked the battalion on the Right of the 17 RWF and occupied the front line.
10	Senlis	Bivouac	Battalion in sunken road South of Senlis. Supplied working parties on old French and Corps lines: one company wiring and three companies digging. Enemy driven out of front line by 23 London Regiment.
11 to 13	Senlis	Bivouac	Supplied four companies for work as on 10 May.
14	Senlis	Bivouac	2RWF relieved 10 South Wales Borderers in Left Sector of Brigade East of Bouzincourt. Quiet relief. D Company Left Front.
15	Bouzincourt	Trenches (Front)	HQ shelled.
16	Bouzincourt	Trenches (Front)	Quiet day. HQ moved to sunken road South of Bouzincourt.
17	Bouzincourt	Trenches (Front)	Quiet day.
18	Bouzincourt	Trenches (Front)	Enemy lightly shelled the area near the Battalion. At 1100, enemy heavily shelled the Left Company and support in retaliation for raid carried out by Left Battalion (14RWF).

			Very hot weather.
19	Bouzin-court	Trenches (Front)	At 0300, enemy heavily shelled whole Battalion area. A heavy barrage was laid down on the Brigade's lines at 0400 - 0430.
			Very hot weather.
20	Bouzin-court	Trenches (Front)	2RWF relieved by the North Staffordshires. Relief shelled and heavily gassed. Relief complete at 0220.
21	Harpon-ville	On march	115 Brigade relieved by 105 Brigade. 2RWF marched to a position near Harponville for breakfast. Marched to reserve camps south-east of Hérissart.
			Very hot.
22	Héris-sart	Camp	Battalion in Camp near Hérissart. Battalion cleared up.
			Many cases of gas poisoning.
23	Héris-sart	Camp	Whole Battalion bathed and clothes put through disinfector.
24	Héris-sart	Camp	Commenced training and rifle competitions.
25	Héris-sart	Camp	Continued training.
26	Héris-sart	Camp	Church Parade.
27	Héris-sart	Camp	Battalion and transport inspected by the Corps Commander. Both were congratulated on their clear turn-out.
28	Héris-sart	Camp	Tactical scheme in co-operation with tanks. 2RWF and 17RWF carried out a practice attack on trenches in co-operation with six Whippet tanks.
29	Héris-sart	Camp	Continued training. Rifle and sports competitions.
30	Héris-sart	Camp	Half the Battalion bathed. Continued training.
31	Héris-sart	Camp	The remainder bathed. Brigade tactical schemes for Officers, runners and signallers.
June			
1	Héris-sart	Camp	Battalion in camp. Voluntary Church Services.
			Brigade competitions all day.
2	Hérissart	Camp	Battalion in camp.
			In the afternoon, an Officers' jumping competition was held.
			The Divisional GOC held an At Home.
3	Hérissart	Bivouac	Battalion marched to Acheux Wood where tents were pitched. Battle Surplus to Hiermont.
4	Acheux Wood	Bivouac	2RWF relieved Hawke Battalion No. 63 Naval Division on Centre Mesnil Sector. D Company Left Support. Quiet Relief.
5	Mesnil Sector	Trenches (Front)	Beautiful weather. Quiet day.
6	Mesnil	Trenches	Change in dispositions. Left ½ Battalion relieved by 14RWF.

	Sector	(Front)	Very late relief—completed at 0520.
			New dispositions with the Battalion taking up positions in depth. D Company No. 3 Defences Locality.
7	Mesnil Sector	Trenches (Front)	Quiet day. Heavy bombardment on our Left in evening.
8	Mesnil Sector	Trenches (Front)	14 Division raided with two battalions on our Left. 2RWF co-operated by discharging rockets etc. and drawing artillery fire.
9	Mesnil Sector	Trenches (Front)	Quiet. Slight rain.
10	Mesnil Sector	Trenches (Front)	Fine day with slight rain.
11	Forceville	Trenches (Front)	During the night of 10/11, a change in dispositions. D Company No. 3 defended locality.
12	Forceville	Trenches (Front)	During the night of 11/12, D Company was relieved in the Front Line by another company. 2RWF then moved to Purple System (as Reserve Battalion).
13	Forceville	Bivouac	During the night of 12/13, 2RWF moved to be Divisional Reserve near Forceville.
			A, B and D Companies had Baths.
			Battalion to practice for contemplated raid. Training area West Lealvillers.
14 to 19	Forceville	Bivouac	Battalion continued to practice for contemplated raid. Training area West Lealvillers near Kiwi Wood.
20	Forceville	Bivouac	Battalion rested and was addressed by the Brigadier ahead of the raid.
21	Forceville	Bivouac	At 0250, 2RWF carried out a raid on enemy lines North of Aveluy Wood.
			It was a very wet night.
			A good protective barrage was laid down on the forward slopes of Thièpval Ridge. Trench mortars co-operated and the Division's machine gun companies fired very effective machine gun barrages.
			Zero was 0200. The forming up took place without incident or opposition and, at zero hour, the troops advanced. On the left, the objective was reached, but the enemy trenches were found deserted and none of the enemy was found. No prisoners or material captured. On the right, the troops were unable to reach the objective owing to heavy trench mortar fire.
			The Battalion suffered some 22 killed and wounded.
			On 2RWF's left, 14RWF also raided at the same time with their objectives being contiguous with those of 2RWF. 14RWF

			also found its objectives to be unoccupied; but found and captured a machine gun.
22	Englebelmer		Battalion clearing up. On the night 22/23, 115 Brigade relieved 113 Brigade in Mesnil Left Sector. 2RWF moved to a position East of Englebelmer in Support and relieved 13RWF.
23	Englebelmer		Working party—290men—under the Royal Engineers on rear defences.
24	Englebelmer		Working party as on 23 June. Each night (24 - 27 June), B and C Companies tried to raid and capture prisoners but the enemy trenches were, again, found to be unoccupied.
25	Englebelmer		Working party as on 23 June. Tonight, the raiding party was just two platoons in strength.
26	Englebelmer		Working party as on 23 June. Tonight's raiding party was at company strength—but, again, found the enemy trenches unoccupied.
27	Englebelmer		Working party as on 23 June. The raiding party was held up by bombs and heavy machine gun fire.
28	Mesnil	Trenches (Front)	2RWF relieved 13 Welch Regiment in Mesnil Right Sector: D Company Right Front.
29	Mesnil	Trenches (Front)	Quiet day. Patrols continued to be active—but without meeting the enemy.
30	Mesnil	Trenches (Front)	Quiet day.
July			
1	Mesnil	Trenches (Front)	2RWF relieved during night of 1/2 by 13 RWF. Enemy raided Post in Aveluy Wood at 2200—repulsed by D Company. Casualties: six. Relief held up on account of raid; completed at 0415. Battalion to bivouacs at Forceville
2	Forceville	Camp	Clearing up.
3	Forceville	Camp	Baths at Forceville.
4	Forceville	Camp	Working party—cable burying.
5	Forceville	Camp	Company training and range practice. The Battalion constructed a new range south of Forceville.
6	Forceville	Camp	Company training and preliminary training for a Raid.
7	Forceville	Camp	Company and Battalion training; preliminary training for a Raid on special training ground.
8 and	Forceville	Camp	Company training and preliminary training for a Raid.

Appendix III: War Diaries (Extracts)

9			
10	Force-ville	Camp	Final practice. Lecture on Artillery Barrage. Shelled on way back to Camp; two men of D company wounded. 2RWF moved into Intermediary System part of Englebelmer and occupied Quacker Alley and front line Intermediary System.
11	Force-ville	Camp	Companies moved up to assembly trenches at 2100 and were in position by 2200. Tapes laid out and all Raiding Companies assembled outside our wire and in front of the Hamel outposts by 2245. Zero was 2300 when four Companies, under an accurate artillery and machine gun barrage, raided the village of Hamel (where they were scheduled to remain for one hour). The objectives were reached at all points. 19 prisoners and one machine gun and a few rifles were taken; 50 enemy killed and 20 enemy dug-outs blown up. The Raiding Parties were out one hour and withdrew in good order. Very successful Raid. One officer and two men killed; 44 men wounded; and three men missing. (The Division's Adjutant suggests that four officers were wounded and a further five men were missing.) Battalion returned to camp at Forceville.
12	Force-ville	Camp	Resting. Battalion addressed by Divisional GOC and complimented on their splendid work.
13	Force-ville	Camp	Baths at Forceville. Battalion marched up to support occupying Intermediate System and relieved 13 RWF. Good relief.
14	Force-ville	Trenches (Supp-ort)	Quiet day. All Companies on working parties at night.
15	Force-ville	Trenches (Support)	Quiet day. Working parties. Establishing Reserve in trenches.
16 and 17	Force-ville	Trenches (Support)	Quiet.
18	Force-ville	Trenches (Support)	Battalion relieved. Quiet relief.
19	Hérissart	Billets	Marched to billets in Hérissart during the morning and rested for the remainder of the day.
20	Hérissart	Billets	Training. Congratulatory letter from Gen. Byng, Third Army commander, on success of the Raid.
21 to 25	Hérissart	Billets	Training. In addition, baths on 23 July.
26	Hérissart	Billets	Battalion inoculated. Very wet.
27	Hérissart	Billets	Training half the day. Wet.
28	Héris-	Billets	Church Parade.

	sart		The Brigade received a warning order that it would be moving back to the Front Line.
29	Hérissart	Billets	Holiday all day. Brigade Sports meeting.
30	Hérissart	Billets	2RWF moved forward to area near Forceville and Acheux. Camp. Very hot march. Regimental goat died of heat stroke.
31	Forceville	Camp	Training.
Aug			
1 and 2	Forceville	Camp	Whole Battalion digging Brown Line near Beaussart.
3	Forceville	Camp	Whole Battalion digging Brown Line near Beaussart. 38 Divisional Sports. News arrived in the afternoon that the Enemy had withdrawn from the Western bank of the River Ancre at 1400 near Aveluy.
4	Forceville	Camp	Training and Baths in morning. Divisional Horse Show in afternoon.
5	Forceville	Camp	Dull morning. The Brigade and Battalion worked and trained during the morning. At night, the Brigade relieved 50 Brigade in the Front Line (former German trenches) with forward patrols holding the railway line. 2RWF relieved 6 Dorsets in Bouzincourt Sector. D Company Right Support. Good relief.
6	Bouzincourt	Trenches (Front)	Fine day. Night patrols by B and C Companies. The Enemy shelled Aveluy and its former trenches.
7	Bouzincourt	Trenches (Front)	Quiet day. Night patrol to examine the River Ancre and crossing.
8	Bouzincourt	Trenches (Front)	Beautiful weather. No enemy activity apart from slight shelling. Inter-Company relief. D Company relieved C Company. Patrols as usual. 38 Division's Commander of Royal Engineers (**CRE**) reconnoitred the River Ancre and possible crossings with a view to the Enemy's retiring.
9	Bouzincourt	Trenches (Front)	Quiet day on our front. Army on our right attacked. *Interestingly, while the Battalion reports little enemy action,*

Appendix III: War Diaries (Extracts)

			the Brigade War diary talks of heavy Enemy bombardments during these three days, 7 – 9 August.
10	Bouzin-court	Trenches (Front)	Bouzincourt heavily shelled during afternoon—otherwise no activity on our front. Army on the Right continued its attack.
11	Bouzin-court	Trenches (Front)	2RWF relieved by 17 RWF and went into Reserve behind Senlis. Poor relief. New camp very comfortable.
12	Senlis	Camp	Baths for ½ Battalion.
13	Senlis	Camp	Baths for the remainder. Company training in areas around the camp.
14	Senlis	Camp	Company training: close and open order. During the day, news was received of an Enemy withdrawal near Serre and Puisieux and even indications that it might withdraw from opposite the Brigade's front.
15	Senlis	Camp	Company training in the morning. 2RWF relieved 13 and 15 Welsh Centre Divisional Sector at Martinsart and Aveluy Wood.
16	Martin-sart.	Trenches (Front)	Quiet day. Two patrols at night to the river bank. Despite the earlier reports, there were no signs of an impending German withdrawal.
17	Martin-sart.	Trenches (Front)	Working party under the Royal Engineers—60 men from A and D Companies.
18	Martin-sart.	Trenches (Front)	Working parties of 75 men from each of A and D Companies. One patrol to the river.
19	Martin-sart.	Trenches (Front)	Working parties. Inter-Company relief. A and D Companies relieved C and B Companies respectively. A patrol under 2 Lt. Morris crossed the River Ancre and reconnoitred a track. Working parties from A and D Companies and night parties from B and C Companies.
20	Martin-sart.	Trenches (Front)	Working parties recalled on account of expected move across the River Ancre. A patrol by 2 Lt. J. O. Smith and A Company successfully reconnoitred a crossing of the Ancre.
21	Martin-sart.	Trenches (Front)	The remainder of the Third Army attacked at dawn on a seven-mile front from Beaucourt north of the River Ancre and penetrated to a depth of three miles, but there was no move forward by 115 Brigade.

			During the morning, a thick mist prevailed and, under cover of the mist, the Battalion pushed out patrols across the River Ancre to ascertain whether the Enemy had withdrawn and to establish crossings at Aveluy. One patrol was held up by rifle fire and further patrols were cancelled as the Enemy were evidently holding their line. 2 Lt. Diggle of D Company killed by a shell on the railway embankment.
22	Martin-sart.	Trenches (Front)	At 0445, IV Corps attacked on the Brigade's Right from Bray-sur-Somme northwards and captured Albert. A thick mist prevailed during the early morning and, under its cover, patrols from 2RWF were sent across the River Ancre to see whether Albert's capture had caused the Enemy to withdraw. A Company crossed the Ancre and established a bridgehead. *(The Brigade's War Diary states that it was a company from 17RWF that established a post across the river as 2RWF had been unable to cross due to the lack of crossing points on its front.)* During the day, the Brigade prepared for an attack to force the crossings of the river; but, it was then decided to abandon the project.
23	Martin-sart.	Trenches (Front)	A major British offensive commenced in the morning of 23, and, between 23 and 31 August, 38 (Welsh) Division advanced from the west side of the River Ancre to the outskirts of Morval. 2RWF's four companies crossed to the east of the river and assembled for an attack due east in the triangle. Zero 0130 on 24 August. The Brigade's War Diary provides the details of these crossings. At 0830, patrols from 2RWF crossed the river to find enemy machine guns still in position. Then, at 1000, platoons from 2RWF and 17RWF crossed the river and established touch with 113 Brigade on the right. By 1300, 2RWF had pushed two companies across the river and captured four prisoners. By the day's end, a further 11 prisoners and four machine guns had been captured.
24	River Ancre	Battlefield/ Advancing	2RWF re-assembled on the east bank of the river and spent the day there. The Battalion moved forward at 1600 to clear the "Triangle" and push forward with the rest of the Division. The move forward continued all night until 1600 on 25. Very successful attack. Over 200 prisoners and 17 machine guns taken. The Brigade's War Diary gives the wider context: In today's advance, 38 (Welsh) Division attacked the Objective Line: La Boiselle – Ovillers la Boiselles – Thièpval Ridge. 115 Brigade attacked with 17RWF in the front line with 2RWF to mop up in the area of Authville Wood and Nab Valley. By 0900, 2RWF

Appendix III: War Diaries (Extracts)

			had met with success in its mopping up and had captured 160 prisoners and 13 machine guns. Then, at 1600, 2RWF was ordered to move forward. By dusk, all battalions in the Brigade were on the move with orders to be in assembly positions by 0100 on 25 for further attacks on Mametz and Bazentin Woods.
25	Contal-maison	Battlefield/ Advancing	By 0200 all battalions were in position—with 2RWF on the Right. They met with little or no opposition and, by 0530, the crest of Mametz/Bazentin-le-Petit Woods had been reached and Pozieres and Contalmaison were taken. A position was established north-west of Mametz Wood. C Company then pushed forward towards Bazentin-le-petit and met with violent opposition and were forced back to the general line. C Company was attached to 113 Brigade and formed the Reserve battalion to that Brigade in an attack on Bazentin-le-Grand – Longueval. A and C Companies were in support; B and D Companies were the Right Flank guard to the Battalion. Much opposition on the ridge towards Bazentin-le-Grand especially machine-gun fire from the ridge above Montaban. By the day's end, lines were established just east of Bazentin-le-Grand.
26	Longue-val	Battlefield/ Advancing	2RWF was attached in reserve to 113 Brigade for its march on Longueval and Ginchy which commenced at 0400. *En route*, the Battalion was ordered to rejoin 115 Brigade. This done, by 1200 *(The Brigade's War Diary suggests it was not until 1400)*, the Battalion, along with the other battalions in the Brigade, took up defensive positions—in trenches—south of High Wood and was subjected to heavy shelling.
27	High Wood	Trenches	Battalion in the same position.
28	Lesb-oeufs	Battlefield/ Advancing/ Trenches	115 Brigade attacked eastwards moving on Morval and Lesboeufs. 10SWB and 17RWF in front with 2RWF in support and "finding" Left Flank posts. Zero 0545. Moving forward under a creeping barrage. No opposition met with as far as the objective (the Enemy had retired)—the railway line South West of Lesboeufs—which was reached at 0730. RWF took 20 prisoners. Much opposition met from Lesboeufs and Morval Ridge. 10SWB penetrated Lesboeufs but were held up there. Companies of the Battalion were disposed in support of 10 SWB and 17 RWF. At 1500, after the objectives had all been reached, the advance continued.

29	Lesboeufs	Trenches	2RWF in same disposition as at end of attack on 28 August. Battalion HQ established in the old German hospital near the railway—exposed to much shelling.
30	Lesboeufs	Trenches	Battalion still in front of Lesboeufs and subject to heavy shelling. Battalion HQ moved to trenches west of the hospital on account of shelling.
31	Lesboeufs	Trenches	Battalion established as on 30 August. No change in situation. The day passed fairly quietly with preparations being made for an attack on 1 September.
Sept			
1	Lesboeufs	Battlefield/ Advancing	The 38 (Welsh) Division attacked Morval and Sailly-Saillisel. The 114 Brigade attacked Morval. Zero hour was 0445. 115 Brigade attacked Sailly-Saillisel under a creeping barrage. 2RWF were Left Assaulting Battalion of 115 Brigade with 17RWF Right Assaulting Battalion and 10SWB were in support. 113 Brigade in support. The Battalion was formed up at 0330 for the attack with C and D Companies in the southern road just east of Lesboeufs and B and A Companies as support companies in the rear. From 0445, 114 Brigade attacked and captured Morval. At 0545, 115 Brigade advanced. 2RWF was lying under an Enemy Barrage. At 0630, the first objective, a road crossing the Morval – Bocquigny railway on a ridge, was reached and the leading companies were pushing down into the valley which had to be crossed before reaching the slopes leading up to Sailly-Saillisel. The Enemy, who were established in trenches in the valley and slopes leading to it, opened heavy machine gun and rifle fire along with trench mortars and rifle grenade fire. The Brigade noted severe fighting at 0915 and reported that a party from the 2RWF was overwhelmed in numbers and 'fought to the last man in a very heroic manner.' In the meantime, Le Transloy, which was reported to be in the hands of 19 Division, was found to be in enemy hands and the battalions of 17 Division, which was to operate on the Brigade's Left, was held up from commencement of the attack with the result that 2RWF's left flank was completely in the air. The enemy commenced to attack 2RWF's left flank at 0700. This attack developed first against the two front companies (C and D Companies), then against the two support companies and eventually from Le Transloy itself against advanced Battalion HQ, which was situated with the machine-gun Section attached to the Battalion. 115 Brigade were forced back on to the outskirts of Morval

			on a line facing north-east. Two companies from 10SWB were pushed out to form a defensive left flank. This operation was successful and prisoners were taken by them. Touch was established by the left company of these two flank defence companies with 17 Division about 800 yards south of Le Transloy. A gap of about 700 yards existed between 2RWF's left and the right of the defensive left company. This gap was filled by a post thrown out from Battalion HQ. At 1800, 113 Brigade attacked Sailly-Saillisel from Morval. This attack gained the main road running through the north of Sailly-Saillisel and enabled 115 Brigade to form on the light railway immediately to the west of Sailly-Saillisel. Regiments in the Brigade formed as follows in view of carrying out the attack the following day: --2RWF (organised in two Companies) on the right --10SWB on the left --17RWF in support. The machine-gun Section attached to the Battalion remained in front of Le Transloy guarding the left flank with troops of 10SWB still forming a defensive left flank.
2	Sailly-Saillisel	Battlefield/ Advancing	At 1700, the 115 Brigade was to attack lines at Mesnil-en-Arovaise and secure the trench line to a point 1200 yards south of the village. Order of battle for 115 Brigade: ■ 2RWF (organised as two Companies) on the Right, ■ 10SWB on the Left ■ 17RWF in support. A battalion of 113 Brigade was to make good Loon Copse on the left flank of the attack. The troops were to be formed up on the Eastern outskirts of Sailly-Saillisel ready to move forward at 1700 under a creeping barrage. The Enemy were found to be still in the village although it had been reported clear. The troops had therefore to fight their way through Sailly-Saillisel and met with heavy machine gun fire. This attack was carried on throughout the night 2/3 September and 2RWF reached a point 500 yards beyond the village. The battalion of 113 Brigade which was to operate on the left of 115 Brigade was similarly held up. During the night, the Enemy made an attack against the Left flank of 113 Brigade. Two companies of 114 Brigade, which was in support, were thrown out on this flank as a defensive left flank. At dawn on 3 September, the Enemy were found to have withdrawn.
3	Les Mesnil	Trenches	38 (Welsh) Division continued its advance. 115 Brigade to occupy the trench system from the Right of 113 Brigade into St. Martins Wood which the 115 Brigade was to join up with

| | | | 18 Division. 114 Brigade was, on completion of the above operation, to pass through and force the River Tortille and gain the heights overlooking it.

115 Brigade was disposed as follows:
--17RWF on the Right
--10SWB on the Left
--2RWF in Support. |
|---|---|---|---|
| 4 | Les Mesnil | Trenches | The Battalion was in the same position. It was formed into one company of four platoons—strength about 90 Other Ranks.

There was considerable hostile gas shelling during the night.

Meanwhile, 114 Brigade continued to advance. |
| 5 | Les Mesnil | Trenches | 2RWF was relieved by 21 Division 15 Durham Light Infantry taking over the Brigade area and marched back to huts and bivouacs south of Lesboeufs.

The Division was to have a short rest. |
| 6 | South of Lesb-oeufs | Bivouac | Very wet evening.

Baths for the men.

Clearing up, re-organisation and re-fitting. |
| 7 | South of Lesb-oeufs | Bivouac | Battalion in the same place re-organising and re-fitting.

The weather was fine—as it had been almost since 21 August. |
| 8 | South of Lesb-oeufs | Bivouac | Church services in the morning.

Lewis gun practice on the range.

Weather becoming unsettled. |
| 9 | South of Lesb-oeufs | Bivouac | Re-fitting and Lewis gun firing practice.

Concert given for 115 Brigade by a W. W. C. Party (the "Welsh Wails"). |
| 10 | East of Lech-elle | ? Bivouac | Battalion and transport moved in the afternoon to east of Lechelle.

Wet day. |
| 11 | East of Lech-elle | ? Bivouac | Officers reconnoitred line held by 50 Brigade near Gouzeaucourt.

2RWF moved forward and relieved 7 East Yorkshire in this Sector on the Right. Good relief. D Company Left Support. |
| 12 | Gouze-aucourt | Trenches (Front) | Front line heavily shelled. Some 20 casualties. |
| 13 | Gouze-aucourt | Trenches (Front) | Enemy attacked our front at 0920 after a heavy barrage on the Battalion's front and support lines. Beaten off by Lewis gun and rifle fire. A few Enemy penetrated into the trenches on the left and were driven out by Lewis gun fire leaving five killed in the trenches. Eight other dead were found later in |

Appendix III: War Diaries (Extracts)

			front of one of our posts.
			Hostile bombing aircraft were very active at night. One low flying enemy aircraft was hit by Lewis gun fired by B Company. Confirmed later by RAF.
			Inter-Company relief; D Company relieving B Company.
14	Gouzeaucourt	Trenches (Front)	Quiet day.
			Gas shelling around Battalion HQ.
15	Gouzeaucourt	Trenches (Front)	Quiet day.
			Weather drier and warmer.
			The Enemy was reported as carrying out an exceptional amount of bombing and fired much gas during the day.
16	Gouzeaucourt	Trenches (Front)	Fairly quiet day.
			2RWF was relieved by 10 Lancashires on night 16/17. Slow relief.
			Battalion marched to area around sunken road North of Equancourt.
17	North of Equancourt	Bivouac	Baths for the Battalion from 0800- 1100.
			Clearing up and re-fitting.
18	Fins Ridge	Trenches	2RWF relieved by 2 Argyll & Sutherland Highlanders and moved forward at 0615 to trenches at Fins Ridge. Brigade in V Corps Reserve during attack by Third and Fourth Armies: the Fourth Army on the Right and the Third Army on the Left.
			Moved at 2000 to trenches north-east of Dessart Wood.
19	Dessart Wood	Trenches	Brigade relieved 113 and 14 Brigades in line west of Gouzeaucourt. 2RWF relieved two companies of 13RWF and one company of 16RWF. Good relief.
			Battalion HQ together with 17RWF and 10SWB in south-east corner of Gouzeaucourt Wood.
			D Company—Left Support.
			Line subject to intermittent (the Brigade War Diary said constant) shelling and trench mortars which meant that the front posts were somewhat unsettled and, as a consequence, the relief presented some difficulties and was not completed until 0350.
20	Gouzeaucourt	Trenches	Fairly quiet day.
			Intermittent shelling. Heavy barrage on front and support 1900 – 2000.
			2RWF relieved by 12 Manchester Regiment. Slow relief. Hot

			meals provided half way out.
			Battalion quartered in huts in Lechelle.
21	Beaulen-court	Camp	Battalion and transport moved by route march to camp north of Beaulencourt.
22	Beaulen-court	Camp	Baths and re-fitting.
23	Beaulen-court	Camp	Re-fitting and re-organisation.
			Cinema entertainment started today under Divisional arrangements at Rocquigny.
			Probably, Cyril was on leave from 23 September – 6 October.
24	Beaulen-court	Camp	Lewis gun firing practice for all Companies on range. Classes for stretcher bearers.
			The Divisional Band played during the morning to entertain units.
25	Beaulen-court	Camp	As for 24 September.
			Two 2nd Lieuts. joined D Company.
26	Beaulen-court	Camp	As for 24 September.
			Parade.
27	Beaulen-court	Camp	Morning parade.
			Trench to trench practice attack.
			Classes in the afternoon. Officers in compass work under second-in-command. NCOs in map-reading.
28	Sorel-le-Grand	Huts and tents	2RWF moved by bus to Sorel-le-Grand into huts and tents.
29	Sorel-le-Grand	Huts and tents	Reconnoitring forward area. Brigade at one hour's notice to move to relieve an American Brigade.
30	Sorel-le-Grand	Huts and tents	Battalion still at Sorel-le-Grand. Lewis gun instruction.
			Messages passed from VI Corps that Bulgaria had surrendered unconditionally.
Oct			
1	Sorel-le-Grand	Huts and tents	Parade.
			Training and instruction in throwing German grenades.
2	Sorel-le-Grand	Huts and tents	Parade.
			Rugby match versus 10SWB in afternoon.
3	Sorel-le-Grand	Huts and tents	Order to move to trenches just out of Lempire.
4	Lempire	Trenches	2RWF moved to Bony; then to Hindenburg support east of Bony.
5	East of	Trenches	Still in the Hindenburg Line but left at 1545 for Le Catelet—in

Appendix III: War Diaries (Extracts)

	Bony		lines on the western outskirts of the village. Battalion in Brigade Support.
6	Le Catelet	Trenches	Moved to lines south of Basket Wood and due west of Pienne. *Cyril probably re-joined the Battalion on this date.*
7	West of Pienne	Trenches	Still as above. Orders received to co-operate in attack on Villers-Outréaux.
8	Villers-Outréaux	Attacking and billets in village	38 (Welsh) Division attacked during the morning with 115 Brigade on the right. Attack by 10SWB and 17RWF (Battalion in Support) held up but village of Villers-Outréaux (the objective) taken later in the day by B Company of 2RWF working around the east of the village. Tanks to mop up the village lines. 2RWF spent the night at Villers-Outréaux.
9	Villers-Outréaux	Billets	Replacement officers arrived. The day was spent in re-organising and resting.
10	Bertry	Billets	Battalion moved by route march to Bertry.
11	Bertry	Billets	Battalion still in billets in Bertry. All troops of 115 Brigade granted one day's rest.
12	Troisville	Billets	Brigade moved by route march to billets in Troisville.
13	Troisville	Billets	115 Brigade relieved 110 Brigade in line on Selle River. Battalion HQ at Rombourlieux Farm. D Company in Front Line.
14	Selle River	Trenches (Front)	Fairly quiet day but Battalion HQ shelled intermittently. Forward patrols. *Between 14 and 22 October, the Royal Engineers were involved in preparing for bridging the River Selle.*
15	Selle River	Trenches (Front)	Gas projectiles were fired and Heavy Artillery bombarded railway embankment and Posts east of the river. Forward patrols.
16	Selle River	Trenches (Front)	A and B Companies relieved C and D Companies at dusk. D Company to Support and C Company to Reserve on the Le Cateau road.
17	Selle River	Trenches (Front)	66 Division attacked on Right and captured 400 prisoners and Le Cateau station.
18	Selle River	Trenches (Front)	115 Brigade relieved by 114 Brigade. 7RWF relieved by 13 Welch Regiment. Battalion back to billets in Troisville.
19	Troisville	Billets	Baths allotted to 2RWF.
20	Troisville	In field and billets.	2RWF moved at 0506 to support 113 and 114 Brigades in attack on Amerval Ridge.

			Returned to billets.
21	Trois-ville	Billets	115 Brigade relieved 114 Brigade. 2RWF in Reserve. D Company lent to 17RWF on Left.
22	Trois-ville	In field and billets	A quiet day on the River Selle. 2RWF relieved by units of 33 Division and returned to Troisville
23	Trois-ville	Billets	115 Brigade in support of 33 Division in attack by V Corps in conjunction with Corps on Right and Left. 2RWF moved from Troisville at 0500 to assembly positions on Amerval Ridge, on Right. At Midday, 2RWF moved towards Richmont and occupied the second objective in the neighbourhood of Croix-Caluyau where the night spent.
24	Croix-Caluyau	Billets	2RWF called upon to fill possible gap between 33 and 18 Divisions. The companies being in houses along the main Forest – Englefontaine road.
25	Forest – Engelfo-ntaine	Billets	2RWF under orders to relieve 33 Division but relief postponed by 24 hours until 35 Division had completed the capture of Englefontaine.
26	Forest – Engelfo-ntaine	Billets	115 Brigade relieved 100 Brigade in line. 2RWF relieved the 2 Worcestershires and a company of the Highland Light Infantry. 2RWF held the Right half of the Division's front with the line through the eastern outskirts of Englefontaine. Battalion HQ at Brasserie.
27	Brasser-ie	Attacking/ in the Field	2RWF had the twofold role of consolidating a defensive line and acting as advance guard to push back in line from the main line of resistance. During the day, the Battalion attempted to establish posts east of the general line but, owing to heavy machine gun fire, were unable to do so. The Enemy raided the battalion on 2RWF's left at dawn but failed. The companies suffered several casualties from an Enemy barrage.
28	Brasser-ie	Attacking/ in the Field	The companies continued to push forward their line. Otherwise, a quiet day.
29	Brasser--ie	Attacking/ in the Field	Line advanced by C Company about 100 yards. Battalion on our left raided the enemy and were very successful. Poix and Englefontaine heavily shelled.

			In the evening, 115 Brigade relieved by 114 Brigade. 2RWF was relieved by 15 Welch. On relief, 2RWF returned to Croix-Caluyau.
30	Croix	Billets	Baths allotted to the Battalion. Clearing up. Weather fine.
31	Croix	Billets	Battalion in the same billets. Training and practice in close country fighting. Weather dry.
Nov			
1	Croix	Billets	38 Division held the Right Sector of V Corps front with 114 Brigade holding a line east of Englefontaine, 113 Brigade in Support and 115 Brigade in the Division's Reserve. The Division's artillery kept up its usual harassing fire during what was, otherwise, a fairly quiet day. 2RWF was in billets at Croix. Attack practice in Vendrecies Wood. Fine day.
2	Englefo-ntaine	Trenches	In the afternoon and evening, 115 Brigade relieved 114 Brigade in the front line taking over a three battalion front. 2RWF was on the Right. Battalion HQ in Englefontaine. Relief complete at 0530.
3	Englefo-ntaine	Billets	Quiet day. Preparations for attack the following day. The Division's GOC visited most battalions within the Division. The Division's Adjutant noted that Instructions had been issued that no more candidates for commissions to proceed to England and no further applications for commissions to be forwarded except for the Special Brigade and the Tank Corps.
4	Englefo-ntaine	Attacking/ in the Field/ Billets	*The Battalion's War Diary account for this day is the second longest description in its War Diary whilst Cyril was with the Battalion.* On the morning of 4 November, 114 Brigade attacked in an easterly direction to the Forêt de Mormal. Zero was at 0615. At this hour, the artillery opened, the infantry then advanced under the barrage. The tanks rendered valuable aid in silencing the enemy machine guns and clearing the way for the infantry to advance. The attack was a splendid success,

the enemy were completely overpowered, and retired in a disorderly manner, leaving in our hands many machine guns and prisoners. The Brigade reached its objective at 1015 and 113 Brigade then passed through to continue the advance. The day was a successful one for the Division.

The 38 (Welsh) Division attacked on the south-eastern outskirts of Englefontaine and the Forêt de Mormal. Its final objective was the rides in the forest running north-east and south-east from les Grandes Patures. The Division attacked on a one Brigade frontage with each brigade having an objective to capture and hold until the brigade in the rear leap-frogged through: 115 Brigade was to capture the first objective, 113 Brigade the second and 114 Brigade the third and final objective.

This attack was part of the resumed advance by the Third Army along with other British and French Armies. V Corps attacked, in a due east direction through the Forêt de Mormal with 38 Division on the Right and 17 Division on the Left. On 38 (Welsh) Division's Right, was 18 Division.

Zero hour was 0530 when the Division on the Left was to open the attack.

115 Brigade was to open its attack at Zero + 45 (i.e. 0615):
--2RWF on the Right
--10SWB in the Centre
--17RWF on the Left.
A tank was allotted to each battalion.

2RWF formed up by 0500 with its final objective (the first 38 (Welsh) Division objective) being the Blue Line—a Ride running roughly north and south 500 yards east of the western Edge of the Forêt de Mormal and in the wood a first Brigade objective had been given which was the Western Edge of the Forêt de Mormal, where the companies detailed to capture the Blue Line were to leap-frog through the companies leading the attack up the Western Edge of the Forêt de Mormal. 18 Division attacked at 0615.

The order of battle of 115 Brigade was as stated above and, at 0500, 2RWF formed up to go over in the following order:
- Right Front Company—C;
- Left Front Company—D;
- Right Support Company—B;
- Left Support Company—A.

The task allotted to 2RWF was not easy as two changes of directions had to be carried out and the front varied from 300 yards to 800 yards owing to the Right resting on a stream (ruisseau des Eclusettes) which twists a great deal in its course.

Appendix III: War Diaries (Extracts) 241

The front on the forming up of the line was about 500 yards and on the final objective about 1200 yards—the greater part of which was in a clearing. This meant that, on reaching the leap-frog, a third company had to push into the front line. The dispositions ordered therefore were, that on reaching the Leap-frog Line, B Company would become the Right Front Company, C Company the Centre Front Company, A Company leap-frogged through D Company and became the Left Front Company. D Company remained in the Leap-frog Line in reserve.

There were not sufficient troops within the {Corps} to completely mop up, and to have done it with troops of the Corps which became engaged in these houses would have unduly delayed the advance. 2RWF's Battalion HQ was made responsible for the final mopping-up of these houses.

2RWF moved to attack at 0615 behind a very heavy and accurate barrage put up by 38 (Welsh) Divisional Artillery. The morning was very misty and though it made keeping direction difficult, it hampered the Enemy's movements considerably and was very helpful to the Battalion in overcoming opposition which was particularly heavy in machine gun and trench mortar fire.

The tank allotted to 2RWF failed to appear, but one tank {?}NI, allotted to 18 Division, which had lost its way was intercepted and rendered valuable service to 2RWF during the Advance.

During the whole Advance there was a gap of about 400 yards between the Right of the Battalion and the Left of the Division on its Right and the Enemy enfiladed the Battalion heavily with machine gun fire and trench mortar fire from this flank. The tank gave considerable help in keeping down this fire. On the Final Objective being occupied, the Reserve Company, i.e. D Company, crossed the ruisseau des Eclusettes (the Battalion's Right boundary) and cleared the Enemy from just beyond the Right of the Final Objective and the ground in the rear as far back West as the village of Hecq. This Company dropped Posts during the manoeuvre and formed a defensive Right Flank to the Battalion.

The final objective was reached before 1700 and was subsequently consolidated before elements of the Division pushed forward with the result that the Division had reached beyond the line of the next day's first objective and was 5,000 yards[2] ahead of troops on either flank. The Division captured about 500 prisoners and 23 guns for casualties of about 600.

The 38 (Welsh) Divisional Adjutant recorded that the Division had attacked in the morning and captured a large

2. The Division's Field Ambulance war diary suggests just 4,000 yards.

			portion of the Forêt de Mormal and the village of Locquignol.
			The 38 (Welsh) Division's War Diary noted that the chief feature of the attack was that the manoeuvre forward took place in columns moving on small frontages and leaving considerable lateral gaps. The problem of keeping direction in the wood was thus solved and many of the enemy were captured from behind.
			The 38 (Welsh) Division's Field Ambulance Section had cars posted by 0530 and noted a very heavy barrage opening at 0615 and the first wounded arriving at 0655. It noted that the 38 (Welsh) Division's final objectives were reached at 1710.
			Battalion HQ, in the meantime, had moved into Reserve in the position formerly occupied by D Company, leaving our post on the Englefontaine – Hecq road where it crossed the ruisseau des Eclusettes.
			2RWF captured one Field Gun, six trench mortars and 28 machine guns (light and heavy).
			The casualties were 2nd Lieut. W. R. C. Keepfer, killed and 2nd Lieuts. G. P. Jones MM, C. H. Aslam, R. E. Griffiths and Ll. W. Llewelyn wounded. 10 Other Ranks killed and 65 Other Ranks wounded or missing.
			Enemy casualties: killed—about 40; prisoners—four Officers and approximately 120 Other Ranks.
			At 1600, 2RWF returned to billets vacated in the morning.
5	Englefo-ntaine	Billets	Battalion in the same place—day spent in clearing up and collecting captives.
			The 38 (Welsh) Divisional Adjutant listed 2/Lt W. R. C. Keepfer among the casualties of the previous day's battle. During November, 2RWF's casualties were: one Officer (i.e. Cyril) killed and four wounded; 11 Other Ranks killed and 84 wounded with one missing.
6	Forêt de Mormal	Bivouac	2RWF marched from billets to bivouac in the Forêt de Mormal.
			Very wet and cold.
7	Berlaim-ont	Billets	Battalion marched to Berlaimont where it stayed for four hours, afterwards proceeding to billets at Aulnoye.
8	Auln-oye	Billets	The Battalion moved up to Pot de Vin at 0530 and took up positions in the Field but returned to the same billets at noon.
9	Auln-oye	Billets	Day spent in clearing up.
10	Auln-oye	Billets	115 Brigade practice route march in the morning.
			Fine but cold.
11	Auln-	Billets	The day spent in clearing up and refitting.

	oye		HOSTILITIES ceased at 1100 hours.
			2RWF then stayed at Aulnoye in billets until 28 December 1918

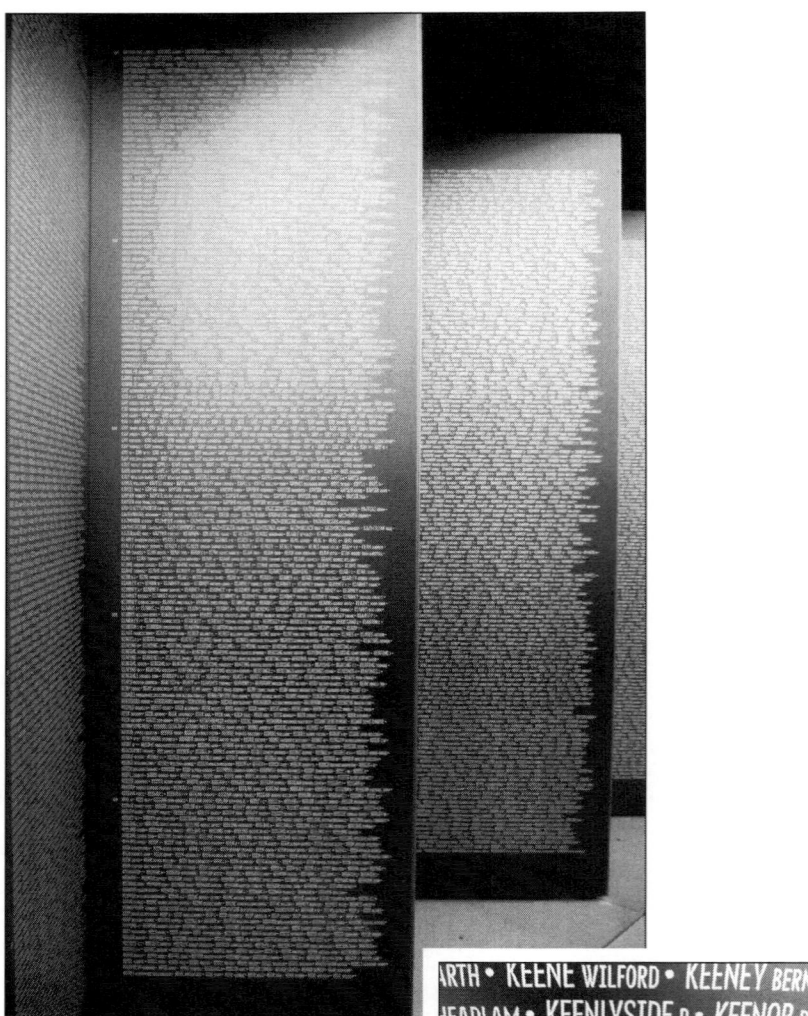

30 & 31. L'Anneau de la Mémoire. This is the metal panel (one of 500) on which Cyril's name is recorded −10 lines up from the bottom, just to the right of centre.

BIBLIOGRAPHY

Adams, Philip, *Not in OUR Name: War dissent in a Welsh Town* (Ludlow: Philip Adams, 2015).

Adams, Philip, *Daring to Defy: Port Talbot's War Resistance 1914–1918* (Ludlow: Philip Adams, 2016).

Anglesey, The Marquess of, *A History of the British Cavalry 1816–1919, Volume 7: The Curragh Incident and the Western Front, 1914* (London: Leo Cooper, 1996); *Volume 8: The Western Front, 1915–1918, Epilogue, 1919–1939* (London: Leo Cooper, 1997; reprinted Barnsley: Pen & Sword Books Ltd, 2012).

Badsey, Stephen, *Doctrine and Reform in the British Cavalry, 1880–1918* (Aldershot, Ashgate, 2008).

Barlow, Robin, *Wales and World War One* (Llandysul: Gomer Press, 2014).

Beckett, Ian, Bowman, Timothy and Connelly, Mark, *The British Army and the First World War* (Cambridge: Cambridge University Press, 2017).

Bickersteth, John Burgon, *History of the 6th Cavalry Brigade, 1914–1919* (London: The Baynard Press, 1920, reprinted and published by Nabu Public Domain Reprints).

Bird, John Clement, 'Control of Enemy Alien Civilians in Great Britain 1914–1918,' (PhD diss, University of London, 1981).

Clark, Christopher, *The Sleepwalkers: How Europe went to War in 1914* (London: Allen Lane, 2012).

Clayton, John Derek, 'The Battle of the Sambre, 4 November 1918' (PhD diss, University of Birmingham, 2015).

Depree, Maj. Gen. H. D., *A History of the 38th (Welsh) and 33rd Divisions in the last five weeks of the Great War* (originally published in the *Journal of the Royal Artillery* over five issues in 1931 and 1932 (Vol LVIII N$^{o.}$ 3 pages 332–74 and N$^{o.}$ 4 pages 448–95, and Vol LIX N$^{o.}$ 1 pages 46–69, N$^{o.}$ 2 pages 168–97, and N$^{o.}$ 3 pages 31–6; Reprinted as a single volume—Eastbourne: The Naval & Military Press Ltd., 2017)

Dunn, Capt. J. C., *The War The Infantry Knew 1914–1919* (London: Jane's Publishing Company Limited, 1987).

Edwards, Huw, *City Mission, The Story of London's Welsh Chapels* (Talybont: Y Lolfa, 2015).

Ellis, Capt. C., *The 4th (Denbighshire) Battalion Royal Welsh Fusiliers in the Great War* (Wrexham: Woodall, Minshall, Thomas and Co. Ltd., Principality Press, 1926).

Gilbert, Adrian, *Challenge of Battle: The Real Story of the British Army in 1914* (Oxford: Osprey Publishing, 2013).
Glover, Michael and Riley, Jonathon, *'That Astonishing Infantry': The History of the Royal Welch Fusiliers 1689–2006* (Barnsley: Pen & Sword Books Limited, 2008).
Glynn, Peter, *All That We Have We Gave: Denbigh Territorials in the 4th (Denbighshire) Battalion The Royal Welsh Fusiliers* (Denbigh: Gee and Sons Limited, 1999; updated and extended: Kindle Edition, 2017).
Graves, Robert, *Goodbye to All That* (London: The Folio Society, 1981).
Herwig, Holger H., *'Luxury' Fleet: The Imperial German Navy 1888–1918* (London: George Allen & Unwin, 1980).
Holt, H. P., *The History of the 3rd (Prince of Wales's) Dragoon Guards 1914–1918* (privately printed).
James, Edward Antrobus, *British Regiments 1914–1918* (Heathfield: Naval & Military Press Ltd., 1998).
Jones, Spencer, editor, *Courage without Glory: The British Army on the Western Front 1915* (Solihull: Helion & Company Limited, 2015).
Kearns, Cliff, *A Town at War – Denbigh and the Western Front* (Denbigh: Dol Awel Publishing, 2016).
Kenyon, David, *Horsemen in No Man's Land: British Cavalry & Trench Warfare 1914–1918* (Barnsley: Pen & Sword Military, 2011).
Kershaw, Ian, *To Hell and Back: Europe 1914–1949* (London: Penguin Random House UK, 2016).
Langley, David, *Duty Done: 2nd Battalion The Royal Welch Fusiliers in the Great War* (Caernarfon: The Trustees The Royal Welch Fusiliers Museum, 2001).
Lloyd, Nick, *Hundred Days: The End of the Great War* (London: Penguin Books, 2013).
Mallinson, Allan, *1914: Fight the Good Fight, Britain, the Army and the Coming of the First World War* (London: Bantam Press, 2013).
Mallinson, Allan, *Too Important for the Generals: Losing and Winning the First World War* (London: Bantam Press, 2016).
Messenger, Charles, *Call-to-Arms: The British Army 1914–18* (London: Cassell Military Paperbacks, 2006).
Morris, E.T., *Denbigh Diary: Notes From the Town* (Kindle edition, 2017).
Munby, Lieut. Col. J. E., *A History of the 38th (Welsh) Division by the G. S. O. Is of the Division* (London: Hugh Rees Ltd., 1920; reprinted: Uckfield, The Naval & Military Press Limited, 2003).
The Naval & Military Press Limited, *First World War and Army of Occupation: War Diary France, Belgium and Germany:*
- 3 Cavalry Division, 6 Cavalry Brigade, 3rd Dragoon Guards (Prince of Wales' Own), 30 October 1914–31 January 1919 (a facsimile copy of WO95/

1153/2);
- *38 Division 115 Infantry Brigade, Royal Welsh Fusiliers, 2nd Battalion, 1 February 1918–30 April 1919* (a facsimile copy of WO95/2561/1);
- *33 Division 19 Infantry Brigade, Royal Welsh Fusiliers, 2nd Battalion, Royal Fusiliers (City of London Regiment), 18th and 20th Battalion, Brigade Trench Mortar Battery and Brigade Machine Gun Company 1 November 1915–31 January 1918* (a facsilime copy of WO95/2423).

(Uckfield: The Naval & Military Press Limited, various dates).

Oatts, Lewis Balfour, *I Serve: Regimental History of the 3rd Carabiniers (Prince of Wales Dragoon Guards)* (Norwich: 1966).

Otte, T. G., *July Crisis: The World's Descent Into War, Summer 1914* (Cambridge: Cambridge University Press, 2014.

Owen, David, *The Hidden Perspective: The Military Conversations 1906–1914* (London: Haus Publishing, 2014).

Palmer, Alan, *The Salient: Ypres, 1914–1918* (London: Constable, 2016).

Parker, Paul, *Clockmaking in the Vale of Clwyd* (Published privately by the author, 1993).

Peate, Iorweth C., *Clock and Watch Makers in Wales* (Cardiff: National Museum of Wales, 1975).

Pritchard, W. H., *Dysg im edrych ... : Dathlu dauganmlwyddiant y Capel* (Ddinbych: Gwasg Gee, 1993).

Rawson, Andrew, *British Expeditionary Force: The 1915 Campaign* (Barnsley: Pen & Sword Books Ltd, 2015).

Richards, Frank, *Old Soldier Sahib* (Uckfield: Naval & Military Press Ltd., 2003).

Richards, Frank, *Old Soldiers Never Die* (Uckfield: The Naval & Military Press Ltd.)

Riley, Jonathon, 'Llewelyn Wyn Griffith and the London Welsh 1914 – 1918', in *Transactions of the Honourable Society of Cymmrodorion*, New series, Volume 21, 2015, editor Fulton, Helen.

Roberts, Andrew, *Elegy: The First Day on the Somme* (London: Head of Zeus Ltd., 2015).

Sassoon, Siegfried, *Memoirs of An Infantry Officer* (London: Faber and Faber Limited, 1997).

Sheffield, Gary and Todman, Dan editors, *Command and Control and the Western Front: The British Army's Experience 1914–18* (Stroud: Spellmount Limited, 2007).

Simkins, Peter, *Kitchener's Army: The Raising of the New Armies 1914–1916* (Manchester, Manchester University Press 1988; reprinted Barnsley: Pen & Sword Military, 2007).

Stevenson, David, *With Our Backs to the Wall: Victory and Defeat in 1918* (London: Penguin Books, 2011).

Stevenson, David, *1914–1918: The History of the First World War* (London: Penguin Books, 2012).

Stone, David, *The Kaiser's Army: The German Army in World War One* (London: Conway, 2015).

Stone, Norman, *World War One: A Short History* (London: Allen Lane, 2007).

Swan, Jonathan, 'Aliens (Restriction) Act 1914' in *Criminal Law & Justice Weekly*, Vol. 180, 13 August 2016.

Swan, Jonathan, *Law and War: Magistrates in The Great War* (Barnsley: Pen & Sword Military, 2017).

Ward, Dudley, *Regimental Records of the Royal Welch Fusiliers, Volume III: 1914–1918, France and Flanders* (Uckfield: The Naval & Military Press Limited, 2005).

Welsh Army Corps, *Executive Committee, Welsh Army Corps 1914–1919* (Cardiff: Western Mail Limited, 1921).

Westlake, Ray, *Tracing the Rifle Volunteers: A Guide for Military and Family Historians* (Barnsley: Pen & Sword Books Limited, 2010).

White, Jerry, *Zeppelin Nights: London in the First World War* (Vintage: London, 2015).

Winton, Graham, *Theirs Not To Reason Why: Horsing the British Army 1875–1925* (Solihull: Helion & Company, 2013).